DID YOU KNOW THAT . . .

* "Colonel" Tom Parker's real name is Andreas van Kuijk, and that he ran away from his native Holland and snuck into the U.S., where he claimed his new identity?

* Elvis never performed outside the U.S. because of Parker's fear of having his citizenless status discovered?

* Parker's early career included stints as carnival huckster, dogcatcher, and Santa Claus?

* Even after he made millions, he continued to hawk trinkets and souvenirs outside Elvis's concerts?

* He would lose as much as $75,000 a night at the Las Vegas gaming tables?

* He controlled the singer's life so completely that he chose the date, site, and guest list for Elvis and Priscilla's wedding?

. . . and much more, including a discography, a comprehensive listing of Elvis's live performances and **NEVER-BEFORE-PUBLISHED PHOTOS!**

ELVIS
AND THE
COLONEL

DIRK VELLENGA
WITH MICK FARREN

A DELL BOOK

Published by
Dell Publishing
a division of
Bantam Doubleday Dell Publishing Group, Inc.
666 Fifth Avenue
New York, New York 10103

ISBN: 0-440-20392-9

Reprinted by arrangement with Delacorte Press

Printed in the United States of America

Published simultaneously in Canada

August 1989

10 9 8 7 6 5 4 3 2 1

OPM

For Loes

"In matters of commerce, the fault of the Dutch is giving too little and asking too much."

(Old colonial wisdom)

Acknowledgments

The research for this book started the day after Elvis Presley died, in August 1977. I owe a lot to helpful people in Breda, New York, Tampa, Memphis, California, and Hawaii. This is a list of my main sources, people I interviewed and institutions:

In Holland: Joseph van Kuijk, Adriana van Gurp-van Kuijk, Toon van Gurp, Marie Gort-van Kuijk, Nel Dankers-van Kuijk, Jo van Kuijk, Marie Cornelisse-Ponsie, Karel Freijsen, Cees Frijters, Kees Fens, Leo Cantrijn, Piet Heijmans, W. H. Swijgman, Jan Buur, Leo Derksen, Harry Berende.

Gemeentearchief Breda, Streekarchivaat Oosterhout-Raamsdonk; Streekarchivaat Schouwen-Duiveland en St.-Philipsland; Raad van Arbeid Breda; Gemeentehuis Loon op Zand; Sociale Verzekeringsbank Amsterdam; Ministerie van Justitie; Dutch Elvis Presley Fan Club; Janssenauto's; Van

Gend en Loos in Utrecht; Gemeentearchief Rotterdam.

In America: Eddy Arnold, Hank Snow, Bitsy Mott, Sandra Polk-Ross, Jack Kaplan, Jean Aberbach, Lamar Fike, Albert Goldman, Blanchard Tual, Peter Herbert, Jerry Hopkins, Clyde Rinaldi, Albert Sweeney, Joe McKennon.

Department of Health and Rehabilitative Services in the State of Florida; County of Hillsborough, Tampa; Pensacola Historical Museum (Gordon N. Simons), City of Mobile (Musuem Department), Casemate Museum in Fort Monroe, Virginia; U.S. Army Military History Institute, U.S. Army Western Command at Fort Shafter, Hawaii (William Krantz); U.S. Army Museum, Hawaii, at Fort De Russy, Hawaii; Hillsborough Humane Society, Tampa; *Honolulu Star Bulletin; Honolulu Advertiser; Nashville Banner; Tampa Tribune;* Associated Press; William Morris Agency; Probate Court Shelby County in Memphis.

Special thanks to Gail Hochman, for her efforts to get this project off the ground; William Reiss at Jonathan Hawkins; Susan Moldow, Gary Luke, and Chuck Adams at Dell; Loeky and Arie Shickler for their hospitality in California; and photographer Johan van Gurp.

1

Palm Springs is a two-hour drive from Los Angeles. It lies in a bare valley between the San Bernardino National Forest and the Joshua Tree National Monument. It seems exhausted by the heat, lying, scarcely breathing, beside the dried-out Whitewater River. It's a place where you can't live without an air conditioner and pool. The first thing you notice is a notable lack of young people. Palm Springs is a place for the very rich and the very old. Like reptiles, they bask in the heat, trying to bake the chill of death out of their bones. Palm Springs has been called "God's Waiting Room."

The old man is sitting on his patio. He is wearing a loud Hawaiian shirt, shorts, and a baseball cap. He is bald and obese and he slumps in his chair like a half-inflated blimp. Nurses in white move in the room behind him. His wife is in a coma. Under normal circumstances she would be in a hospital. The old man pays six thousand a month so she can have intensive care at home. She is the closest thing the old man has to a companion.

The old man doesn't feel too well himself. He has a history of heart problems. His right shoulder is damaged and he has trouble using his right arm. A few years earlier he took a fall in an elevator in the RCA Building in Los Angeles. He was unable to get up, and the automatic door hit him over and over again, almost as though it were trying to beat him to death. In 1982 his health had been the subject of an affidavit read to a New York courtroom. "I am seventy-two years of age and suffer from a heart condition which would make it very difficult for me to travel to New York City in connection with this action. I spend much of my time in southern California in order to be near my wife, who is in a virtually comatose condition and is under continuous nursing care and medical supervision in Palm Springs, California. If I am forced to contest any part of this proceeding in New York, it will be a major hardship for me and I probably will be unable to attend the proceedings or assist my counsel in my defense." At the time, an attempt was being made to separate the old man from a multimillion-dollar empire. Ultimately the attempt would succeed and the old man would be left broken and bitter.

The phone is silent. There was a time when the phone rang all the time, and the adrenaline never stopped pumping. Now nobody calls. All that has gone, taken away by the courts. His former associates no longer bother to speak to him. He never went out of his way to be liked and few people ring to wish him well. He just sits and stares at a patch of snow off in the blue distance on one of the San Bernardino mountains. It is not clear whether the old man is dreaming of a cooler place or wondering about the chill of purgatory. He was raised a Catholic.

The old man's name is Tom Parker. He wasn't always called that, but that's the name he's used for half a century and it's the name by which most of the world knows him. Not just plain Tom Parker, though: *Colonel* Tom Parker. For more than thirty years he has enjoyed the vanity of the honorary rank. There was a time when the world talked about Colonel Tom Parker as living proof that the American Dream was attainable. He was a self-made millionaire, an earthy W. C. Fields figure who had grown up in the carnival, who had little formal education, and who had single-handedly changed the face of entertainment.

His creation was, of course, Elvis Presley. Elvis and the Colonel were inseparable through the twenty years that they were client and manager. They were a team, the heartthrob with the sideburns and the pudgy, jovial older man who looked on from somewhere in the background, directing the young man's destiny and building him into the biggest singing star of the twentieth century. He was there in pictures of Elvis. He was there in the pictures when Elvis was a wild, hip-swinging teen idol with greasy hair and cat clothes. He was there when Elvis went into the army and was waiting when he came out again. He was there in the pictures as Elvis bounced through the long series of indifferent movies in the sixties, and he was there in the seventies when Elvis was cramming himself into spangled jumpsuits and fighting the flab. Elvis 'n' the Colonel. It was a team. They went together in the mind of the public like Burns and Allen, Abbott and Costello, Roy Rogers and Trigger. In a lot of the pictures the Colonel's face was folded into a lazy, amused grin, as though he was enjoying some private joke known only to him.

Back in those days—the good days when the deals were always going down, the money rolled in, and the phone never stopped ringing—people said he was a natural genius, a shrewd, hardheaded kind of genius who was also a son of the soil, who liked to chow down on pork chops and gravy, who liked a good joke. Colonel Tom Parker was the rough-and-ready, down-home variety of genius. He was an *American* genius. People used to talk about him. They used to, but that was over.

The old man continued to stare bitterly at the tiny patch of snow on the distant mountain. Without switching his gaze, he reached down beside his patio lounger for a bottle of Mountain Valley water, bottled in Hot Springs, Arkansas. The old man doesn't trust tap water. He knows what's in it and he knows it'll kill him. He likes to keep a couple dozen cases of the water around the house. If the supplies start to run low, he calls one of the young men at RCA Records or the William Morris Agency—the young men who look after him. They are the only people who care about him anymore. RCA and William Morris handle his money and virtually everything else. After the courts took it all away, he had become what amounted to their ward, an elderly grandfather that nobody wanted.

Back in the days when they'd called him a genius, he'd had it all. Hell, there'd been times when he'd dropped seventy-five grand in a night at one of the casinos and thought nothing of it. There'd been so much money in those days, they'd pay money just to talk to him. He wasn't anybody's ward in those days. He was the one who took care of things; he was the supersalesman, the great promoter. It wasn't just Elvis Presley that he'd given to the world. He'd given them rock 'n' roll music, although if the truth was known, he never much liked that music and had always expected it to go away like some nine days' wonder. Of course, he wouldn't admit the truth. That was one of his maxims. Never admit you're wrong; it's a sign of weakness.

Something else the old man didn't ever admit was that there had been a madness around him and Elvis. There'd been just too much; it had become impossible to cope. Too much money, too much adoration, too many people, always smiling, nodding, and agreeing, too many people who wanted something. The old man shifted uncomfortably in his chair. Maybe he should go inside and watch TV. He got to watch a lot of TV lately. It sure beat remembering, particularly remembering the madness. It had pushed Elvis into drugs and orgies with Las Vegas showgirls while the old man dropped millions over the gambling tables.

More than the madness, he didn't want to think about the end either. Not so much the end of Elvis. That had pretty much been a foregone conclusion, and the Colonel had made adequate preparations for it. When he thought about the end, he meant the real end, when the judges and the smartass New York lawyers took it all away from him, when they took the Elvis empire, *his* empire, away from his control. They had no right to do that. He had built the empire, goddamn it, and he should have been allowed to run it until the day he died.

The old man started to get angry. They'd really stuck it to him, those judges and lawyers. Bit by bit, it had all come out. They'd made him sound like part buffoon and part cheap crook. They had used words like *self-interest* and *fraud.* They called him cheap just because he knew the value of a buck, and they called him vulgar because he gave the people what they wanted. The old man winced and let out a short gasp. The pain in his chest was back. He fought down his anger, and the pain subsided. The doctors were always warning him, he had to watch that sort of thing. He must not lose his temper. It could kill him.

The trouble was that it was so hard not to get angry. At the end, things had gone down so fast, it was like being on a runaway elevator. He'd twisted and squirmed and used every delaying tactic in the book until the other side—Priscilla Presley and the daughter, Lisa Marie, as the Elvis Presley estate—was forced by lack of money to come to a settlement that left him if not with his empire, at least with some of its money. What he couldn't prevent was one of the ultimate truths coming out. In a desperate delaying tactic he had been forced to reveal to the world what he'd concealed for half a century. He'd always told the world that he was born an American, born on the southern carny circuit sometime around 1909 or 1910. That turned out to be a lie. In fact he was an illegal immigrant without papers or passport. In fact he was a Dutchman called Andreas van Kuijk, not Colonel Tom Parker at all.

The old man's chest began to hurt again. He continued to stare at the patch of snow on the mountains, but he stopped thinking and remembering. Instead he let himself lapse into an unfocused bitterness. It was easier that way.

2

On Monday, June 28, 1909, Adam van Kuijk crossed
the cobblestoned marketplace in Breda, Holland. He
passed the wall of the towering gray cathedral domi-
nating the town and climbed the monumental steps of
the town hall. He was accompanied by two friends:
Hendrik Rogiers, a blacksmith, and Cornelis Roovers,
a shoemaker. Adam van Kuijk had come to the town
hall to register the birth of a child, a boy, who had
been born two days earlier. The two other men were
to act as his witnesses for the official notification. The
child was to be named Andreas Cornelis van Kuijk
(later the first name Andreas would be shortened to
the diminutive Dries). The registering of a new child
was nothing new to Adam van Kuijk. By the time
Andreas was born, he and his wife Maria had produced five children. In all they would have nine. The
oldest was Joseph—nicknamed Sjef—born in 1900.
After Joseph there were three girls: Adriana (1902),

Marie (1904), and Nel (1907). The birth of Andreas was followed by that of Engelina, also known as Lien, in 1910, Ad (1913), Johanna (1916), and Jan (1918). Two other children died soon after birth.

Even the most humble of men—and there is every indication that Adam van Kuijk considered humility a cardinal virtue—have dreams for their children. All parents, with few exceptions, hope the child will do as well, if not better, in life than they did. But there was no way Adam could have imagined that the two-day-old Andreas would half a century later be a millionaire who lived in America and called himself Colonel Thomas Andrew Parker—and that he would manage the most popular entertainer of the twentieth century.

There was little entertainment in the background of the van Kuijks. Order and duty, obedience and discipline—these were the primary family values. Adam was born in the town of Raamsdonk in 1866. His father, also called Andreas, is described in the surviving records as a "workingman." At age twenty-one, Adam was drafted into the Dutch army, as a private in the 3rd Regiment of the Field Artillery. Army life in nineteenth-century Holland was hardly arduous, and Adam was stationed at the Seelig Barracks in Breda, only twelve miles from his home. In those days, the artillery used horse-drawn gun carriages, and Adam discovered that he had a natural talent for tending animals.

Adam finally left the army in 1899, having signed on for a twelve-year hitch as a regular. His transition to civilian life was apparently easy, for he remained in Breda and got a job with Van Gend en Loos, a firm of freight handlers whose offices were on the prestigious Veemarkt, a main street with class and standing. Van Gend en Loos had hired Adam as a livery man and put him in charge of thirteen draft horses. And so, though out of the army, he still wore a uniform and still tended animals. Instead of barracks, however, he lived in an apartment over the stables at the back of the Van Gend en Loos building, on a much more modest street called Vlaszak.

Adam had started dating Maria Elisabeth Ponsie from Raamsdonksveer while he was still in the army. In a moment of passion—possibly greeting the twentieth century at Christmas 1899 or New Year's 1900— Maria became pregnant. By the spring it was obvious that they must marry, and so they exchanged vows on May 10. On September 19, their first son, Joseph, was born.

On the surface there would seem to be more in Maria Ponsie's heritage to explain the later showmanship of Colonel Tom Parker, than anything in Adam's background. Her parents, Johannes and Marie Ponsie, were floating peddlers who sailed the canals of the Low Countries, and the Zeeland Islands, up and down the rivers and estuaries of the Dutch delta and along the coastal fishing villages of Brabant. The Ponsies traveled from village fair to town market, year in and year out, setting up their booth and selling their wares. Sometimes they would sell earrings, cheap ornaments, and junk jewelry; at other times, homemade cups and dishes. When nothing else was at hand, the family would hawk puppets they'd made out of bits of wood and scraps of material. When they were hardpressed, they took old Bibles and hymnals that had been discarded by the church and restored them with fancy crepe paper covers, selling them as new.

It was a hard life, working the waterways in this manner, but there was also a sense of infinite variety and freedom. Johannes Ponsie never learned to read or write, but this lack of even the most basic education didn't appear to bother him. He was a strong, sturdy man who loved the wind and the water and the unfettered liberty to go where he pleased. Maria, the daughter, was born on September 2, 1876, the youngest of eight children. She grew up with her father's sense of freedom, and enjoyed the family routine amid the sound of yelling merchants, jugglers, and fortune-tellers, and the music of fiddles and accordions. Always there was the thick, penetrating smell of fish on the griddle, of fried potatoes with mayonnaise, of almond cakes and Dutch doughnuts. No matter how much she may have loved Adam van Kuijk when she was pressed to marry in haste in 1900, he was still ten years her senior, and possessed with an unbending military conformity. She could not have denied that she was trading a bright, if now and again precarious, freedom for a drab and respectable security.

It's also possible Adam may have harbored some regrets of his own at the precipitate marriage. He found himself not only with a wife and child, but also with a pair of dependent in-laws. Even before the wedding, Johannes Ponsie, who was sixty-nine by then, had decided it was time to quit his traveling ways and retire. As part of the marriage settlement, Johannes and his wife, Marie, would move in with the newlywed van Kuijks. The arrangement was a tight one, but just about workable. Adam's apartment above the stables of Van Gend en Loos had two living rooms. The Ponsies slept in one and the van Kuijks in the other. There was also a loft just large enough to act as a communal bedroom for the expanding family.

Even before he was born, some of the seeds that would eventually grow to form the complex personality of Colonel Tom Parker had already been sown. There was mother Maria, with her memories of her earlier easygoing, catch-as-catch-can life, and there was grandfather Johannes with a wealth of stories from a lifetime on the water. In total contrast, there was Adam, a stern father with a limited sense of humor. For him, nothing could transcend the concepts of discipline and obligation. The idea that children might be indulged was quite alien to him.

Like so many children in large families, the infant Dries, particularly during the first five years of his life, was raised by his three older sisters. Adriana, mostly called "Sjan" by the family, in particular acted as a second mother. For her little Dries was an animated doll who could be dressed up and paraded in a baby carriage through Breda's Valkenberg Park. The child responded to his sisters' games, cutting up and doing his baby best to make them laugh. Very early he proved himself a bright, quick-witted toddler who was inquisitive and fast to learn. Few things frightened him, and his curiosity appeared insatiable. There were times, however, when he actually scared his sisters. He slept with his eyes open. Even when he was in a deep sleep, his eyes stared blankly at the ceiling.

"You could pass him by, but he didn't see anything," Adriana recalls. "He slept on one side of the loft and the girls at the other. Sometimes he came downstairs still asleep, not noticing anybody. He went to the kitchen to drink a glass of water and then he went back to bed again. We had to lock the doors because sometimes at night he walked outside as if it was the most normal thing. Even when he was sleepwalking, he was able to unlock the front door. One of the neighbors, Mrs. Overbeek, once saw him standing in the street in the middle of the night."

By the time he was five, young Andreas had grown out of being a plaything for his sisters. He was no longer the little doll who could be taken for rides in the park. He had become independent, almost to the point of secrecy. He would vanish for hours on end to roam Breda's streets and alleys. His absence was hardly noticed in the large family. His sisters knew he was gone but didn't have a clue as to where he went and what he might be up to. He seemed perfectly able to take care of himself and, in a family where a new baby was almost an annual event, nobody worried too much about the little boy's wanderings. As the years passed, both these wanderings and the secrecy became ingrained parts of Dries's personality. Once his chores were done, he would simply vanish. For Andreas van Kuijk, the streets of the town were not only a playground but also a very practical place of learning where he would pick up the first lessons in freelance hustling. Even as a small boy, the future Tom Parker wasn't above picking up the odd guilder whenever and wherever he could. Indeed, he seemed to have a positive talent for happening across a piece of change. His friends were amazed that he could always come up with the price of a bag of candy for himself. The woman who ran his favorite candy store on the Kloosterstraat was frequently forced to comment on the regularity of his visits.

"You don't steal the money from your mother, do you?"

"No, I make it myself."

On the third Sunday in October, the carnival came to Breda. It took over the entire town as its tents and stalls spread through the Kasteelplein, across the marketplace—the "Grote Markt"—along the Halstraat and the Oude Vest all the way to the Kloosterplein, just around the corner from the Vlaszak, where the van Kuijks lived. Immediately after the mass in the cathedral, the normally dour town would temporarily become a place of music and laughter. In the bars there was raucous singing and, here and there, the robust wives of the town's workingmen would stake out the tavern entrances to prevent their husbands from going inside and drinking up the rent money. For a small boy—particularly a secretive, inquisitive one—the fair was an annual flash of noise and color in an otherwise drab and uniform world. As Andreas got older he discovered that the fair was not only fun but could also be very profitable. The odd coin, sticks of candy, and free tickets for the rides could be earned by an enterprising boy prepared to fetch, carry, or hold a bit of wood while the showman putting up his booth nailed it into place.

The whole town expected to get something out of the fair. Storekeepers would take their merchandise from the shop windows and rent the space to the sellers of nougat or the Dutch *zuurstokken*—acid sticks. Everyone seemed to profit from the fair, and Andreas van Kuijk didn't see why he should be any exception.

The center of attraction at the fair was the big top, the main theater tent on the Kasteelplein that was occupied by the Bouber family. In front of the city hall, the fire-eaters, the fat lady, the performing dogs, and the strong man all strutted their stuff. At the other end of the town's center, the more modest van Bever family circus occupied the Kloosterplein. It was simple stuff—a clown who played the trumpet, a dancing midget. There was also a wild donkey, and if you could stay on it for five minutes, you'd win five guilders. After a while the van Bevers started giving odd jobs to the kid who hung around. When he was older, he would work for them on a more definite basis. They would even have him ride around town on a tall, old-fashioned bicycle with a sandwich board strapped across his shoulders advertising the show.

It may have been that Dries was drawn to the van Bever operation because it was small and much more accessible to a curious boy. Maybe he was also taken by the way they worked with horses. His father worked with huge, solid, dependable workhorses. In comparison, the circus horses were a dashing, romantic spectacle. Where his father's horses were dull, the horses in the circus were romantic. As the years passed and the van Bevers prospered, the horses became a more and more important part of their act. Madam van Bever, the horse trainer of the family, would eventually be able to parade a string of Lipizzaner stallions.

Without a doubt, both Dries's ability to make money on odd jobs and his delight in the bustle of fairs and circuses was a direct legacy from the traveling Ponsies. Compared with their father's circumscribed view of life, the stories told by the resident grandparents must have had an aura of magic for the van Kuijk children. Unfortunately, only the elder ones knew grandmother Marie Ponsie, who died in 1907, two years before Dries was born. Adam van Kuijk, Dries's father, used the event to further ease the burden of relatives. When he was seventy-seven, grandfather Johannes Ponsie was moved into a Catholic *gasthuis*, a charity home for the aged. Dries's only direct contact with the footloose and freewheeling side of the family tradition were the regular visits to his grandfather, who would die just three days after the boy's eighth birthday. Dries van Kuijk may not have lived the way the Ponsies had, but there is little doubt he was influenced by their life of rambling huckstering.

Sadly for Dries, the circus that so fired his imagination was only in town a few days in the year. The rest of the time he endured the repetitive grind of a hardworking liveryman's son. To compensate for the drudgery, he started a collection of animals. There was a rabbit that lived in a hutch in the stables, and a crow that he trained to sit on his shoulder and to perch on the end of his bed while he slept. He attempted to catch sparrows with small traps hidden in the horse manure in the stable yard. Later on he would own a goat that he taught to do tricks, including climbing stairs. The goat would become the centerpiece of Dries's own mini-circus, which he put on for other kids—charging them two cents admission. Dries was undoubtedly devoted to his animals, but by an odd, paradoxical streak in his character, he impulsively sold the goat he had carefully and laboriously trained in order to treat his brothers and sisters to seats at the real circus. His father was less than pleased with his generosity and beat the boy for parting with the goat on what, in his eyes, was nothing but a whim.

There would be another beating when Dries's circus obsession got even more out of hand.

On Sunday afternoons, it was the habit of Adam van Kuijk—after he had brought his family back from church and had eaten a hearty Sunday lunch—to take himself to the unassuming Café van den Enden on a street known as the Beyerd. On these days Dries was left in charge of the stables while his father played cards. Dries eventually grew bored with spending his Sunday afternoons minding a stable that hardly needed minding at all, with nothing more to do than watch the horses nod and flick their tails as the flies flitted in and out of the shafts of sunshine that streamed through the big, half-open double doors. He knew there had to be something more exciting. Then Dries had an idea: Why not have his own circus, right at home?

For the next few weeks the other children were

excluded from the stables all through Sunday afternoon. Dries had warned them that everything would be spoiled if they came in before he was ready, and he could be extremely persuasive when he wanted to be. The other kids were also quite accustomed to both his secrecy and his surprises. If Dries was up to something, they knew it would probably be worth going along with him.

Finally the day came when he was ready to reveal himself. His brothers and sisters and a few friends were summoned. Dries, full of himself and very much in control of the situation, positioned the children around the stable walls. Quietly he moved in and out of the big, docile draft horses, untying them, letting them loose. The children felt a thrill of fear mixed with the excitement of a conspiracy. Had Dries gone quite mad? Surely his father would kill him if he knew that Dries was turning the horses loose. But since it would be Dries who got the beating, his brothers and sisters could just sit back and watch the fun. Dries next produced his father's long wagoner's whip. When he cracked it, the great horses began to prance around the stable at a slow trot. The kids watched speechless; it was just like the circus. Now they knew: Dries had spent all those Sunday afternoons training the horses.

Dries climbed up into a window niche from where he could preside over his handiwork. The horses trotted in circles as one, they turned and moved in the opposite direction. On command, they reared back on their hind legs. The children couldn't believe their eyes. They all knew that Dries was smart and always up to tricks, but this seemed scarcely possible. How had he learned to exert such total authority over the animals? All their lives his sisters would remember the spectacle of the boy performing with the huge draft horses.

A show like that was not easily kept a secret. The children quickly spread the word about Dries's circus all through the neighborhood. Sunday afternoons in Breda were not exactly thrill-packed and soon it seemed everyone was talking about what the van Kuijk boy had done with the horses belonging to his father's firm. It wasn't long before the story reached Adam as he played cards in the café. When he stormed into the stable, his face was dark and furious. It wasn't simply a matter of the boy's fooling around with the horses, he had been fooling around with the horses of the firm of Van Gend en Loos. Adam van Kuijk was responsible for taking care of these horses. By teaching the valuable animals a lot of stupid circus tricks, even putting them at risk, Dries had betrayed what Adam considered a sacred trust. His employers trusted him and his family to care for the animals as though they were their own, and now Dries had endangered the whole relationship with his antics. Adam rolled up his sleeves, took off his belt, and ordered his now equally grim-faced son to bend over a chair. It was high time he beat this circus nonsense out of him once and for all.

Dries and school did not get along. There was a free school in Breda for the children of the poor, but Maria van Kuijk didn't consider her family poor. No matter that money might be tight; she was the wife of a respectable workingman and she preferred to pay fifty cents per week per child so they could attend a "better" school, a place more in keeping with what she perceived as their status. The van Kuijks were also devout Catholics, and as a result, the better school that Maria selected was the Catholic boys' school on

Breda's Karrestraat, run by the brothers from
Huybergen, whose order was devoted to the care of
orphans and the education of the children of the
growing working class.

The brothers were easily as keen on obedience and
discipline as Adam van Kuijk was. They and their lay
teachers reinforced their beliefs with the strap and a
cruel, uniquely Dutch punishment that involved the
delinquent being forced to kneel with his knees thrust
into his wooden clogs, where he would remain until
the pain had taught him the error of his ways.

The error of his ways was something that seemed to
completely elude Dries the schoolboy. Playmates like
Karel Freijsen and Cees Frijters remember him as the
often-punished class joker whose only interest in
school seemed to be how soon the final bell would
ring. It appeared that he actually preferred to fill the
coal scuttle than pay attention to the teachings of
Brother Tarsicius or "Meester" Clarijs and that he was
positively delighted to have classes disrupted, as when
a cow escaped from the nearby slaughterhouse and
ran bellowing into the schoolyard.

The school was a stately building set back from the
Karrestraat at the end of a cobbled alley set between
two shops. The brothers operated what amounted to a
complete educational complex. As well as the boys'
elementary school, which Dries attended, there were
a high school, a monastery, a chapel, and, on the other
side of the yard, the girls' school, supervised by the
nuns and by far the most consistent attraction for boys
with wandering minds.

The final solution to school—the ultimate rebellion,
if you like—is simply not to go, to play hooky and give
up on the whole depressing institution. This was the
route Dries increasingly took. Some days he'd idle
away the afternoon watching the ships at the Prin-

senkade. Other days, he'd ride across town to the inland harbor of Oosterhout, where one of his mother's brothers kept his boat moored. When a circus or fair was in a nearby town or village, he simply disappeared without a word.

It started to seem as though Dries just didn't care. On one occasion he stole a delivery boy's bicycle and spent the day joyriding. The boy knew him and it was inevitable that he should go and tell Dries's father. Both at school and at home Dries was constantly in trouble and being punished for truancy and inattention. Nothing, however, seemed to change him. His attitude was that he'd do exactly what he wanted, and damn the consequences. If he hadn't started off, both physically and emotionally, with a hide like a rhinoceros, he certainly developed one through his school days. It would stay with him for the rest of his life. Later, when he was Colonel Tom Parker, it would enable him to ignore other people's advice and opinions and totally go his own way.

"We don't need tickets for the game."

"We don't?"

"Of course we don't."

Dries and his two close buddies, Karel Freijsen and Cees Frijters, were hanging out in back of the Breda soccer stadium. They were ten or eleven years old and the stadium had become a regular Sunday afternoon haunt. Unfortunately, all too often they found themselves hanging around outside the stadium, just listening to the roar of the crowd and trying to imagine the game. Even Dries lacked the ten cents for a ticket.

Cees drew in the dirt with his toe. "There's no way we can get in."

Dries grinned. "Sure there is. You're not thinking. What about your sister?"

Cees looked confused. "What about my sister?"

"She's going out with Toon Oomen, isn't she?"

Toon Oomen, the goalkeeper for NAC, the Breda team, was something of a hero to the small boys.

"He isn't going to give us any tickets."

"I'm telling you, we don't need tickets."

Dries outlined his plan. They should collect up some stuff, anything that might look as though they were taking it to Oomen inside the stadium.

"We tell the guy on the gate that Toon Oomen ordered us to help him carry his clothes and stuff. Once we're inside, we'll lose ourselves in the crowd and no one will be any the wiser."

Cees shook his head. "It'll never work."

"Sure it'll work."

All the way to the gate Cees kept telling himself that it wouldn't work. He only kept on going because Dries was leading the way and looked so completely confident. Cees was certain that when they reached the gate, they would be turned away even if they didn't get into any worse trouble. Then Dries was talking to the gatekeeper. There was a brief conversation that Cees couldn't hear and then, to his surprise, the man was waving them through.

Dries's next argument was that what will work once will work twice. At first Cees again had doubts, but he hardly bothered to voice them. Dries always got his way in the end, he was just so persuasive. For three Sundays they got away with the same deception. Finally, though, on the fourth week, when they were starting to think they might be able to pull the trick all through the season, something went wrong. Instead of waving Dries and his two companions through, the gatekeeper quickly grabbed Dries by the ear, cuffed him around the head a couple of times, and threw him out. Cees and Karel ran before the same could happen to them. Maybe Dries had become too confident or maybe someone had checked up on them and had asked Toon Oomen whether he really had a trio of kids running errands for him every match.

By the time Dries caught up with them, Cees was starting to wonder what kind of hell he'd catch when his sister got her hands on him. He was thinking about delaying going home as long as possible. To his surprise, Dries didn't seem in the least downcast. He told the others to wait and ran off in the direction of his house. Some minutes later he returned, clutching the family coal shovel and indicated that they should follow him to a point along the stadium fence as far from the gate and gatekeeper as they could get.

Dries looked quickly around to making sure no one was watching, then started digging away at the base of the wooden fence.

"One of you help me and the other keep watch!"

Karel scrabbled like a dog beside Dries while Cees was a nervous lookout. After some grunting and heaving there was a big enough space for them to wriggle through. Again they hid themselves in the crowd and settled down to watch the home team win the match.

It's not certain whether Dries van Kuijk actually finished all the grades in elementary school. According to the system, the pupils were separated into groups in the sixth grade. The achievers, group 6A, went on to high school, the "Mulo," and the rest either went into 6B, a preparation for the technical school, or quit school altogether. With Dries's attendance record it was highly unlikely that he ever made the A list. Karel Freijsen dropped out after the fifth grade and, as far as he remembers, Dries did the same.

Dries's sister Marie tells a different story. She thinks

that, possibly as a make-or-break attempt to teach the boy discipline, he was sent to Sainte Marie, a boarding school operated by the brothers from Huybergen. His name, however, does not appear on the school records. If he attended at all, his stay was a brief one. Conceivably even the brothers gave up on teaching the boy a sense of order. Whatever the truth of Dries's leaving school, it is fairly certain that before he was fourteen, he would have been back on the streets of Breda working at any job he could hold down.

Dries van Kuijk's employment record proved to be little better than the one in school. He worked for a grocer but after a few weeks was let go. The job was boring and he tended either to daydream or to vanish altogether. The next job was in a barbershop, but once again he tended to split whenever something interesting was going on in the street. At times he would do his disappearing act in the middle of giving a shave, leaving his customer lathered and helpless. His sisters still remember the incident when he took it into his head to shave just one side of a drunk's face and let him stumble out into the street with half a beard, much to the amusement of passersby.

Finally the family took a hand. His older brother, Sjef, had a steady job at the Preservenfabriek, the local jam factory, and it was decided that Dries would do the same. Once again, the idea seems to have been that the routine of factory work might finally get him to settle into something; once again, he totally resisted. After a few weeks he simply quit.

Each time Dries found himself out of work, he naturally gravitated back to helping his father, running errands and picking up what spare change he could by doing odd jobs around the streets. It seemed that this was the only life he truly enjoyed and that the only boss he could really endure was himself.

His father may have disapproved of Dries's feckless-ness, but by the time the boy was in his early teens, he was actually starting to need his son's help. Adam van Kuijk's health was failing. He was troubled by swollen feet and sometimes walking was almost impossible. Later a doctor diagnosed further trouble as rheuma-tism. In addition, his lungs were becoming progres-sively weaker. It wasn't only the duties Adam per-formed for Van Gend en Loos that became difficult. For a number of years he had been doing a consider-able amount of moonlighting, making deliveries on his own time. He filled in for other Van Gend en Loos drivers when they were sick. He moved furniture and even dealt in secondhand furniture and household goods. He hawked postcards to the soldiers in the various barracks in the town and polished the boots and belts of some of the town's policemen.

Adam could have made ends meet on his livery-man's salary, and the van Kuijk family, large as it was, could have managed without all his extra work. But Maria van Kuijk wanted to do a bit better than man-age, consumed by a desire to prove to the world that her family was a cut above plain working folks. Money had to be spent to send the children to a marginally better school, and she was proud that hers was the only family on the street with not only curtains at the windows but carpets on the floor. There was even a maid, a practially unheard-of extravagance for a woman of Maria's position. Her name was Limp Dinie and she cleaned the house for ten cents a day. There was other part-time help. Sjef, the oldest son, recalls, "She [Maria] didn't like working very much. She had somebody for every chore in the house. There were women to darn her stockings for her and she even found a man to whitewash the ceiling."

In order to pay for his wife's airs and graces, Adam

had to work impossible amounts of overtime. It is unlikely that the stiff, conservative former soldier took readily to the kind of small-time wheeling and dealing in which he was forced to become involved. More likely, he had this extracurricular business thrust upon him by his wife. It was the way the Ponsies had always behaved, the way both Maria's father and brothers had made their money, and she could see no valid reason why her husband shouldn't do exactly the same thing to give her the luxuries she felt that she had to have. Unfortunately, the work was gradually wearing him out.

It would be nice to think that the time they spent working together might have established some kind of rapport between the stern but ailing father and the rebellious, nonconforming son. Sadly, there may not have been enough time. Within two years of Dries's quitting school, Adam van Kuijk would be dead.

3

Adam van Kuijk died on July 6, 1925. He was fifty-nine years old and completely exhausted. He had spent time in Breda's Catholic hospital, the Ignatius-Ziekenhuis, but it seemed to have been of little help. The continuous hard work had simply worn him out. The firm of Van Gend en Loos wasted no time in getting rid of the grieving widow and her children. They wanted the apartment above the stable for the replacement liveryman and his family. Maria van Kuijk attempted to keep the children together, moving them to a small house on the Boschstraat. Unfortunately, it didn't work out. Without Adam, the family started to fragment and it became painfully clear that he had been its solid foundation.

Maria was quite incapable of accepting that she was a widow at the age of forty-eight. She simply folded up and, like her father and mother before her, handed all of her future to the care and protection of her children. She no longer took any responsibility for what might happen to her or how she would survive. For all their independence and initiative, the Ponsies, in their old age, were capable of an almost complete fatalism. Someone else could look after them. They no longer cared.

To be precise, the breakup of the family had started even before Adam's death. Two years previously, Dries's sister Marie had renounced the world and become a nun—a Franciscan sister. Within the confines of the narrow morality of small-town Dutch Catholicism, it was a way of escape. Dries was fourteen at the time of Marie's flight to the convent. He recognized the same feelings within himself. He continued to roam the city as always, but he found himself more and more drawn to two particular places. One was the abandoned World War I defenses along the Nonnenveld. The other was the train station. Once again, he could savor the bustle and urgency of people in motion, people who were going places and seeing the world—even if he wasn't one of them. On one occasion, when he was sixteen, he tried to ride for free on the passenger train to Rotterdam, but he was caught, brought back, and handed over to his father. Even as a first attempt at running away from home, it was rather inept. Later, Dries would perfect his technique.

During the time that Adam van Kuijk was hospitalized, Dries tried to leave again, but this time with his father's blessing. While he was visiting at the hospital, he said to Adam, "Please, Father, I want to go to Rotterdam and work on the harbor. I will stay at Uncle Jan's. Please let me go."

Later, he would visit his sister in the convent to tell her of his plans. "I am leaving. Father gave me his permission." He seemed to want to cut himself off from his family. When, in August 1925, Marie went through her formal admission ceremony at the convent, Dries was the only member of the family who didn't show up.

Jan Ponsie and his wife had had other of the van Kuijk children to visit at their home on Rotterdam's Spanjaardsstraat, but Dries was a little different. He determinedly moved in and made himself comfortable. He seemed to have little desire to return to Breda.

Jan's daughter, yet another Marie, remembers Dries as a quiet child, big for his age. "He was a dreamer. In a way, he saw me as his big sister. We played checkers and other games. He was quite content to be part of our family life. During the weekends, he stayed with us."

There was, in fact, a strange single-mindedness in the way he became a part of the Ponsie family. It wasn't simply that he'd moved to the big city; he was also, as far as possible, severing his ties with Breda in general and with his mother in particular. It was as though the move was an escape, and the break had to be as clean as possible. For a long time his only contact with his mother was to send her money.

At first Dries was perfectly content to relax in the bosom of the Ponsie family.

"He never had the urge to go anywhere in the evenings. He was happy to sit around the living room with the rest of us. Sometimes he sat down to read a little, but he was not much of a reader." Despite his almost withdrawn self-absorption, Marie had the feeling that there was more to the teenager than met the eye. "He never told me what he wanted out of life, but I knew he was busy making plans all the time. He wanted adventure."

Dries's stay with the Ponsie family began auspiciously. On January 17, 1926, the district judge in Breda appointed Jan Ponsie a legal guardian of Dries, as well as the other six minor children of Adam and Marie van Kuijk. The young man settled into his new home.

This phase of relative stability was not to prove long-lasting, however. Dries soon began to revert to his old ways. During the first year he seems to have been awed by Rotterdam, the proverbial small fish first encountering the big pond, and it took him a while to get used to the city. He didn't know the streets and, more importantly, didn't know the spots where he could pick up money in his old freewheeling manner. He tried a number of odd jobs, but eventually settled on working for a bargeman on one of the islands to the south of the city. The freedom in traveling the waterways on the barge was initially enough to keep Dries satisfied, but after a while the old boredom and restlessness returned. Every day he passed through the vast international port and saw the big oceangoing ships with their romantic names and exotic ports of origin. The sight of them filled him with an excitement he had experienced only once before, when he was around the circus. Further pricking his curiosity was the fact that on some of these ships he could see boys of his own age working on the decks. *They* were going around the world, while *he* was going around southern Holland on a barge.

Dries began disappearing again. At first he would be gone for merely a few hours, but then he began to stay away overnight. When his Uncle Jan questioned him, he claimed he'd had chores to do on the docks. The disappearances continued and Jan Ponsie ceased to accept the stories about chores and working overtime. Stern warnings were issued, but to little effect. Finally Dries vanished for a number of days.

When the boy eventually returned to face an angry uncle, his explanation was simple: "I'm working for the Holland-America Line." He packed his things and told the Ponsies, "I'm a sailor now. I have to go."

At this point in the story—as with many others in the life and career of Colonel Tom Parker—the facts become blurred. There is considerable doubt as to whether he really had a job with the Holland-America Line when he left the Ponsies' Spanjaardsstraat home. There is no sign of any Andreas van Kuijk in the company's records, although it is just possible he might have been hired on a temporary or probationary basis and his name wouldn't appear on any crew roster. It wasn't impossible for a young healthy teenager with a yen to see the world to sign on as deckhand and then jump ship at his desired destination. There was also the chance that he was lying when he told Jan Ponsie that he was working for Holland-America. He may have wanted to avoid being traced, or, more simply, he may have been indulging in a piece of self-aggrandizement—something not uncommon with the adult Parker—by claiming he was working for the prestigious shipping line when he'd actually signed on with a much more humble freighter or tramp vessel. Another possible, and infinitely more probable, explanation is that he stowed away.

Stowing away on an ocean liner, particularly back in the 1920s, wasn't especially difficult. The first stage for Dries would have been to hang out on the Wilhelminakade in Rotterdam, where the Holland-America liners docked. There he could watch for the unguarded moments when it might be possible to slip aboard one of the ships, or he could make friends with the sailors, sizing up which ones might be willing to take a bribe to smuggle him on board. If he made it onto one of the big boats, such as the *Rotterdam,* the

Volendam, the *Veendam,* or the *Nieuw Amsterdam,* it would be necessary for him to stay out of sight—and keep himself fed—for the eleven-day Atlantic crossing. Stowing away did require a certain amount of planning and scheming—skills at which Dries excelled.

The Holland-America ships stopped at Boulogne in northern France and then at Southampton in England before heading out into the Atlantic. The first western landfall was at Halifax, Nova Scotia, before the ship finally docked at Hoboken, New Jersey, at the pier at the bottom of Fifth Street. For a stowaway, the tricky part came next: One could hardly breeze through U.S. Customs and Immigration without a passport and some cash; but again, with the help of a couple of bribable sailors, it wasn't impossible.

Dries had broken the connection with the Ponsies even more completely than he had broken off relations with his mother. It seemed that each time he moved, he never expected to return, essentially burying the past. It was an odd instinct for a kid in his teens. For a number of months the family didn't know whether he was alive or dead; then a letter arrived. The Ponsies were amazed. "It was a letter from a Dutch family that lived in New Jersey. They wrote that Dries was with them and that he was such a nice boy," one member of the family recalls.

It wasn't Dries's choice to write. The family with whom he'd settled had urged him to tell his relatives that he was safe and well, but he absolutely refused, and it was only when they started pressuring him that he rather grudgingly gave them his family's address. From the first letter, a lively correspondence flowered between the two mothers of Dries's adopted families. The letters are long gone, but Marie Ponsie recalls some of the details: "They had a ten-year-old daughter, she was their only child. Dries must have been talking about me because the woman wrote, 'I hear you have a nice daughter; could she come to America too?' I guess the woman was homesick and missed Holland. That must have been why she let Dries in and invited me to come too. It was a well-to-do family. The woman wrote that she would love to come to Holland but she was too ill to travel."

In addition to a natural talent for covering his tracks, Dries was starting to reveal another innate ability. He was able to move in on people without their raising any of the usual objections. Somehow they didn't seem to mind having a large, taciturn Dutch boy sitting around in their living room. Dries was developing the lightest of touches—the mark of the instinctive parasite.

And then he was gone again. After months of acting the part of the dutiful son to a strange family in New Jersey, he disappeared more completely than ever before. The Ponsies received a letter telling them that Dries had vanished without a trace. He had said nothing, had left no note. The Dutch woman sounded distraught. *Her* boy was gone. Dries had clearly charmed her. "Have you heard anything?" she wrote. "All we can suppose is that he's trying to join the American army. He talked about it sometimes."

Andreas van Kuijk had not joined the U.S. Army— or the navy or the marines, for that matter—this time around. But what he *did* do is unknown. This is part of the past that Colonel Tom has been able to bury completely.

He resurfaced on September 2, 1927, now eighteen years old. Like a character in a Victorian melodrama, Dries showed up in Breda on his mother's birthday, knocking on the door at eight in the evening, exactly when the family was gathered to celebrate. He seemed to have decided to avoid the Ponsies altogether. He was back to square one, bearing gifts, grinning with sheepish contrition, and possessed with an absolute confidence that he would be forgiven. He was playing the returning prodigal in classic fashion. He may have been putting on a repentant face, but the one thing he wasn't about to do was explain to anyone what he'd been doing in the United States. Even when pressed he completely clammed up. His secrecy had become obsessive.

Dries appeared to have gone mad. He was standing on a table, arms outstretched in the full throes of a dramatic monologue.

> Ik ben een jongen van Jan de Wit,
> Eentje waar veel pit in zit.

He was reciting a rhyme about a boy who was bright and had a lot of talent, but who was also lazy and lacking in motivation. He refused to learn a trade and ended up working as a bellhop. By the standards of Breda, it was a big night in the old town. The occasion was the wedding of Dries's sister Adriana to a young man named Toon van Gurp. It was the first marriage in the van Kuijk family and the party at the house on Boschstraat was as big as the van Kuijks could afford. Dries had appointed himself the family clown and he was doing his best to keep everyone laughing and entertained. He had been back in Breda for exactly two weeks.

He was clearly reveling in the attention. Something had changed during his mysterious time in the United States. Nobody in the family could remember seeing him so spirited and outgoing—so theatrical—since the

Sunday afternoon when he'd turned the horses loose and made them perform for him.

He was now dancing an awkward one-legged comic jig. What he lacked in finesse he made up for in sheer energy. He continued with a slightly risqué tavern song. A few people glanced at the mother, wondering how she was responding to this behavior. Normally she would have disapproved, but she seemed so happy to have her boy home from God-knew-where that she was prepared to go along with all his nonsense.

After the party, Dries's clowning was the talk of the family. Some saw it as a hopeful sign. Maybe, after his restless wandering, he was starting to find his niche. Perhaps he might be discovering that his destiny was to be some sort of entertainer, maybe even an artist. It was both a surprise and a disappointment when they found that Adriana's wedding was the only time that he would spring into the limelight. They would never see the performance repeated.

In only a few months' time, Dries had started to dislike Breda once again. So many of the good things of his childhood had disappeared while he had been away. They'd torn down the bandstand and the pavillion in Valkenberg Park. The horse tram was gone. The place was growing and its quiet, country-town atmosphere was nearly a thing of the past. The place was neither homey nor, after New York, exciting. For a while he went back to his old ways of taking odd jobs when and where he found them.

During that fall of 1927, Dries had neglected to contact any of his old cronies from the streets. The return to Breda, despite his initial playacting, was neither a triumphal return nor even the repentance of a prodigal who had seen the error of his ways. It was a necessary, if unwanted, return to base, a period of taking stock and marking time before his next leap into the unknown. Emotionally, he had never come back. The clowning at Adriana's wedding had been a quirky final bow. From then on, his personality seemed to darken. His friends and relatives actually have trouble remembering him at all during this period. There are no longer any funny anecdotes. He was there in body, but his mind and his spirit were apparently somewhere else entirely.

The old casual life-style didn't seem to be working either. It may have been that a hustler can't have half his mind on the other side of the Atlantic, or simply that times were becoming a good deal more bleak. In Europe, during the late twenties, the postwar boom was long gone and the chill of the coming depression was already causing economies to shiver. The pickings on the streets were undoubtedly slimmer.

Dries took a job on the waterfront, loading and unloading market boats for a shipping firm called Huysers on the Prinsenkade. Huysers were regular customers of his father's old firm, Van Gend en Loos, and Dries may have employed a degree of low-level nepotism to land the job. In his case, however, pulling strings didn't take him very far. For his efforts he was badly paid, expected to show up for work at 6:00 A.M. and to spend his day carrying parcels and packing cases on and off river barges. It was the kind of job from which Dries would normally have walked away. In this instance he had a reason not to leave. He wanted to get back on the boats and back to Rotterdam. While he toted bales he was also looking out for a job on one of the canal boats.

The *Stad Breda* needed a deckhand and Dries grabbed the job. It was a single daily run between Rotterdam and Breda, but it was just the excuse he needed. Since his new ship spent as much time in Rotterdam as it did in Breda, there was no reason why he shouldn't live in Rotterdam. The *Stad Breda* was owned by Huysers and they operated a rough-and-ready hostel for their hands on the top floor of their main office in Rotterdam. It was here Dries installed his trunk and personal belongings.

Again he settled into a dreary routine. Piet Heymans, a skipper on one of the other Huysers boats, describes Dries's life: "The ships were sailing day and night. During the nights there were three men on board, the captain, the first mate, and the engineer. During the days there was a fourth man, the one we called the day hand. That was Dries's job. On the night trips the first mate took care of everything. They didn't need an extra hand then. Dries had to sort out parcels. He was a good lad. He acted normal and made no fuss." Pay on the Huysers boats was disgraceful and the hands weren't above a spot of petty pilfering to make ends meet. "Sometimes we took away a few cakes or a bag of flour," Heymans remembers.

During his time on the *Stad Breda,* Dries once again went into his withdrawal act. He rarely stayed in Breda and even more rarely visited either with his mother or any of the rest of the family. At the sailors' hostel he kept to himself and had a habit of taking long walks on his own. The other seamen who stayed at Huysers's top floor remember that he didn't drink, and nobody ever saw him with a girl. The latter was something that now and again caused comment. He was, after all, a healthy young man of almost twenty.

A rare exception to the general cutoff from the past was Dries's old school friend Cees Frijters, who sought out Dries when he came back to Breda one weekend. The two had lost track of each other after school. Cees had been drafted into the military, and, after he'd served his time, he figured on reenlisting and getting a transfer to the Dutch East Indies. He wanted to see his old school buddy once before he went away for good. (Dries had been exempted from the draft because he came from a fatherless family.) During the day they spent together, they had talked about the big plans that both had for the future, and the big adventures they were going to have. The two young men shared their dreams of faraway places, and both agreed that traveling the world was the ultimate adventure. All through this long and often animated conversation, Dries gave no hint to Cees that he had already crossed the Atlantic and spent months in America. It seems unbelievable that a young boy could be so closemouthed, but Cees Frijters never heard about the trip until years later. Dries seemed to be obsessed with secrecy.

His next disappearance was characteristically eccentric, coming, as before, with no warning. The first the family knew about his departure was when a trunk was delivered to his mother's house in Breda. It was Dries's trunk and all his belongings were in it—his three suits, his Bible, a rosary, and even a purse containing a few guilders. It also contained unopened birthday presents that the family had sent him two months earlier, indicating he must have disappeared in May 1929. The Huysers company had returned the trunk because they could no longer store it in their sailors' quarters. The family was convinced that Dries was out at sea.

After a long wait, a letter finally came. Toon van Gurp, Adriana's husband, remembers both the relief with which the message was received and the confusion and puzzlement it caused: "The letter was written in English. We found it very strange. Why should

Dries write in English? And he signed it Thomas Parker."

Somewhere on the other side of the Atlantic, Tom Parker had sprung fully grown from the head of Andreas van Kuijk.

Following this startling event, news came in dislocated shreds. Small black-and-white photographs of Dries arrived. "Never an address, only funny pictures. In one, Dries was standing next to a big American car, maybe a Buick, and it was taken in Honolulu. In another, Dries was sitting by a swimming pool. We figured that he was a chauffeur for a rich man."

Dries sent back just enough information to let his family know he was still alive. Beyond that there was a carefully constructed wall. He seemed to be making sure that the family would never be able to find him unless he absolutely wanted them to. The limit of his compassion was now and again to send money. His sister Jo kept bank receipts of these gifts, seventeen in all, and each for five dollars. They were sent from Washington, with no name of the sender, to the Frank Laurijssen Bank in Breda. The first check came in January 1930, the final one in February 1932. Apart from a dutiful and totally uncommunicative letter to his mother, also received in February 1932, these bank receipts would be the last the family would hear from him for well over a quarter of a century.

Strangely, Dries chose to maintain a correspondence with his old school chum Cees Frijters. He was in the Dutch army in Java now, and had an address for Dries in America. To him, Dries was Dries; there was no mention of this new Thomas Parker incarnation. "I had ten or twelve pictures he sent me in those days. Dries was in the U.S. Army; he was in Hawaii."

Dries's enlistment in the service was something not

even the family knew. He had arrived in America and gone for the security of his father's original calling. This turn of events at least explained the five bucks a month he sent his family. It wasn't done out of a sense of duty. In fact, enlisted men were expected to send part of their pay to their next of kin unless they had a valid reason not to.

Frijters still has Dries's pictures in an old photo album. They show a young man in overalls: in one he wears a uniform jacket; in another, a sweater and an army hat. He's clearly in a subtropical location such as Hawaii. In the most important of these pictures, Dries is shown sitting on a wooden construction with his hand on a bucket on which is painted FIRE and a code of letters. This code would provide one of the major clues that would later forge an unbreakable link between Andreas van Kuijk and the Colonel Tom Parker who would eventually manage Elvis Presley. Without that and a couple of other well-hidden pieces of evidence, Dries might have accomplished what he set out to achieve. He would have completely separated himself from his past and his roots and simply vanished into the darkness.

The Department of Defense in Washington has no record of the name van Kuijk in its files. However the *Army List and Directory* of July 1, 1930, does record one Captain Thomas R. Parker, a staff member of the Hawaiian Coast Artillery District stationed at Fort de Russy near Waikiki.

Alas, this wasn't Dries van Kuijk. Nevertheless, the coincidence of time, place, and name is astonishing. Furthermore, military records revealed that the 64th Regiment was part of the Hawaiian Coast Artillery. That would explain the "A-64" on the fire bucket in

Cees's photograph of Dries: "A" for *artillery,* "64th" for the regiment.

Here was a significant clue to the secret past of *Colonel* Tom Parker.

4

The hold of a freighter on the high seas must be one of the most miserable, wretched, and lonely places in all creation. The ominous metallic creaking of the hull plates and the constant throb of the engines mixes with the smell of hot oil and the residue of a thousand cargoes. Water streams down the walls and now and again a rat skitters by.

The constant pitch and roll of the ship as it rode the Atlantic swell kept Dries on the verge of nausea. All he could do was to huddle and wait for the awful journey to end. By the end of the second day, he knew with certainty there was nothing at all romantic about being a stowaway. Apart from the unavoidable discomfort, there was always the nagging fear that a hatch would open and the crew would discover him. It was not part of his plans to be dragged in front of the captain and handed over to the authorities when they reached port.

There was also the ever-present dull ache of hunger. The only food he had was brought on board in a rucksack. The best method to make the clandestine voyage even minimally tolerable was to try for as long as possible to lull oneself into a kind of numb half sleep. This also had its attendant problems. As the days passed the rats grew bolder. He had to sit with his rucksack clutched to his chest to keep them from getting into his food. Dries had no phobias about rats; there had been no shortage of them around the stables in Breda. He was well aware, however, of the animals' sharklike determination and the potential for a power struggle in the freighter's gloomy hold.

As well as the physical discomfort and the very tangible fear, there was also a strange psychological isolation. Dries had quite deliberately left his old identity in Europe, but it didn't stop him from feeling depressed and dislocated. He'd buried Andreas van Kuijk back somewhere between Breda and Rotterdam, but he had yet to fully develop a new identity. He wasn't Dries anymore, but who the hell was he? It was as though the eleven-day Atlantic crossing was the gestation period in the creation of this brand-new person, and the hold of the freighter was an uncomfortable iron womb. The young man sat cramped in darkness, waiting to be born.

The freighter's destination was Curaçao, in the Dutch West Indies. Slipping ashore while the boat was being unloaded proved to be no problem. Soon he was walking in the sunshine, smelling the island's tropical vegetation, and working the knots out of his cramped muscles. Many people might have thought that this Caribbean beauty spot, with its sea breezes and white colonial architecture, was about as close to paradise as they were going to get. Many a wanderer in the young man's position would have been quite content to submerge himself in the easy life of the West Indies. On Curaçao itself there were jobs at the oil refinery, or, if the young man preferred, there were plenty of boats to take him island-hopping.

The young man had more serious plans than just to live the bum's life in the Caribbean. For a start, he not only wanted out of Holland but wanted as well to be away from everything Dutch, and Curaçao, a Dutch colony where Dutch was the official language, was too Dutch for the young man. He really only had one goal: he wanted to get back to the United States. As far as he was concerned, it was the promised land, and he immediately set about getting himself there. Even for one with his totally illegal status, it seems to have been a remarkably easy task. Prohibition was still in force in the United States and running liquor to the ports along the Gulf was a thriving industry in Curaçao. It is possible to speculate that Parker traveled on a rum-runner. Nobody would give a damn about his lack of papers and wherever the liquor slipped past the authorities, the young man could slip right along with it.

Whatever his means of travel, Parker finally landed in Mobile, Alabama. Even though the tree-shaded streets of the old, French-style town were his initial goal, the young man was well aware that his troubles had only just started. Yes, he had arrived in the United States, but without papers and money, and with just the clothes he had on. All he had was a very simple plan. He would join the army. Military recruiters wouldn't ask too many questions about his background, and once he was accepted, he would have a certain legitimacy; he would virtually be an American. In addition, he knew from his father that the army was a place of order. Peacetime soldiers didn't

have to make too many decisions—an eas
could handle the work and the discipline.

He hitchhiked, rode trains, and walked u
reached Fort McPherson near Atlanta. Back in th
days the U.S. Army wasn't too particular about whom
it accepted, provided they didn't have TB or syphilis
and could manage a reasonable command of English.
For one last time he used the name Andreas van
Kuijk. Instead of shortening it to Dries, he began calling himself Andre.

Andre's enlistment coincided with a drive to get
volunteers to serve on army bases in Hawaii, at the
time an unpopular assignment with men who had
families on the mainland. In the days before cheap air
travel, it was just too difficult to get home on leave.
Dries—now Andre—of course, had no such problems.
Hawaii had an image of waving palms and maidens in
grass skirts strumming on ukuleles. Almost with a
shrug he signed on for Hawaii. Why not? From where
he stood, it looked about as far from Holland as he
could get. After basic training, he was shipped to Fort
de Russy near Waikiki and then on to Fort Shafter just
three miles northwest of Honolulu in the foothills of
the Koolau Mountains. Andre had been assigned to
the 64th Regiment—the antiaircraft section—of the
Coast Artillery. He was one of the thousand enlisted
men who manned the antiaircraft batteries, the three
searchlight batteries, and six machine-gun platoons
that were ranged along the southern shore of Oahu to
protect the naval base at Pearl Harbor from air attack.

When he arrived at Fort Shafter, he was interviewed by a forty-two-year-old captain from Nebraska
whose name was Thomas Parker. The interview was
something of an ordeal for Andre. His basic story was
that he'd been a sailor for years and that he was an
orphan with no living relatives. Beyond that he had

only filled in the sketchiest of details when he first enlisted in Georgia. He was afraid this officer might press him about his background and possibly catch him in some kind of lie. His only defense was to stick to a simple statement and if it went any further, take refuge in a poor grasp of English.

"No family, sir. No address."

Beyond that he could only look blank and behave like a dummy.

"Sorry, sir, I don't understand, sir."

Captain Parker explained it was army policy to deduct part of a soldier's pay and send it to his dependents. The captain clearly suspected some problem in the boy's past, such as having relatives from whom he was trying to disassociate himself. It was hardly uncommon; in fact, the army was full of men who wanted to bury their pasts. The captain's job was to pry the information out of the new recruit, but he was also a compassionate man who didn't like to see his men with family problems. He made a suggestion that allowed the boy to save face. If van Kuijk gave him the name and address of his next of kin, he'd write and explain what the payments were for and, at the same time, reassure them that the boy was all right and there was no cause to worry.

The private with poor English and the thick Dutch accent simply nodded. He couldn't do much else. It was obvious that if the officer didn't suspect the real truth, he wasn't far off. The only consolation was that even if his mother did get mail from him, she still wouldn't be able to find him if he didn't want her to, since his only return address was an army postal code.

From that point on, Andre seems to have been set on ingratiating himself with the captain in much the same way he'd ingratiated himself with the Ponsies and the family in New Jersey. He constantly offered himself for extra duties and volunteered for anything. According to some of his comrades, he barely stopped short of shameless fawning.

The defense of Hawaii in the early 1930s was hardly an arduous task. America was at peace, its mood was isolationist, and Hawaii was miles from anywhere. Still, any army likes to keep its men busy, and the 64th Coast Artillery was no exception. There were parades, inspections, and machine-gun and searchlight drills. Once a month they were put through an all-night march. For the most part, life in the 64th was one of dull army routine.

Even so, it was a routine that allowed plenty of time for the enjoyment of what Hawaii had to offer. In their free time Andre and his friends would lounge around Waikiki Beach, watching the girls or playing touch football on the hot sand in front of the Royal Hawaiian Hotel. On duty they had to behave like soldiers, but on their own time they could live like tourists. All in all, Andreas van Kuijk could feel justified in congratulating himself. His new life was sweet and easy.

Not only was Andre enjoying himself, he was also starting to loosen up a little. For the first time since he'd run away, he actually felt safe. He no longer considered his family as much of a threat, and saw no harm in sending them brief notes and the odd snapshot. However, he still signed his notes with the new name "Andre," or even, in one instance, "Thomas Parker." With his friend Cees he felt even freer to let himself go. He actually appeared to have a need to confide, and Cees was the ideal person. Both he and Andre were serving in the military, although on opposite sides of the world. To Cees, he was still the old Dries, and he used that name to sign his letters.

By the fall of 1931, Andre had all but completed his two years of overseas duty and was due to return to the mainland. At about the same time, the man whom to some degree he looked on as his mentor was also transferred from Hawaii to attend the Command and General Staff School outside Washington. (Thomas Parker would make major in 1935 and lieutenant colonel in 1940, but he was killed in an accident while on duty at Fort Hood, Texas, in 1945.)

Andre's own transfer was to Fort Barrancas, the Coast Artillery training center in Pensacola, Florida, only a few miles from Mobile, Alabama, where he'd first sneaked ashore. It was almost like completing a full circle. Fort Barrancas, a by-the-book military training establishment, was also quite a contrast to the reasonably easygoing routine of Honolulu. Andre began to have a few doubts. Did he really want to spend the rest of his life jumping every time an officer or a sergeant said jump? The rebel streak that had lain dormant during the two years in Hawaii was beginning to emerge again. By his own standards Andreas van Kuijk had given the U.S. Army his best shot. He'd never previously stayed at anything for two full years. Part of him wanted to move on, but there was still a major fear: Could he make it on his own outside the protective security of the army? The big world out there was beckoning, but, at the same time, it was a threatening and largely alien place.

The barrier dropped on the railroad crossing, the bell rang, and the lights flashed. The driver cursed under his breath and slowed the truck to a halt. Andre didn't care. He'd hitched a ride into town, but he wasn't in any particular hurry. He didn't have anyone to meet. The train was a while coming. Andre slid down in his seat and tilted his cap down over his eyes. If it was a really long freight train, they could even sit there for ten minutes. The driver could curse, but there wasn't a damn thing that they could do about it. That close to the depot, the trains were moving very slowly.

The locomotive rattled across the crossing. Andre hardly bothered to open his eyes. He'd seen plenty of trains. He barely raised one eyelid, but that was more than enough. He sat bolt upright.

"Will you look at that?"

Normally he didn't allow himself to show enthusiasm for anything. It never paid to let people know too much about what you liked, but in this instance it just slipped out. Rumbling slowly in front of him was a carnival train. Flatcars were stacked with folded canvas and dismantled equipment and rides; horse boxes and cages left the sharp smell of large animals in the heavy warm air behind the sluggish train. Sides of the cars were emblazoned with both the name of the carnival and the names of the individual attractions. One in particular caught van Kuijk's imagination: BUCHANAN'S ELEPHANTS. What more could a man want out of life than to actually own his own string of elephants, to have complete control over the big gray beasts, to have the power to make them bow and kneel, to walk around on their hind legs, to do anything that he told them?

A new passion stirred inside Andre, something deeper than the old rebellion that had driven him away from home and Holland. The smell of the animals conjured up so many images—the lights, the costumes, the girls with their long legs and spangles, and the prancing horses, the clowns, the characters and the freaks. The carnival felt like home. Admittedly it was a home he'd known for only brief periods, but even those few days in Breda had left him no doubt: more than anyplace else, the carnival was where he belonged.

All too quickly for Andre the train was past. He'd found his home again. He knew he couldn't play this military game for a moment longer; the first thing he had to do was get out of the damned army, and he wasn't concerned about how he accomplished the move. Van Kuijk knew that when the need for change became this strong, there was no point in resisting or making excuses. You simply followed your instincts. Andre glanced quickly at the driver as the truck lurched forward, bouncing across the tracks. There were times when he worried that people might be able to sense what he was thinking. The driver, however, was staring calmly through the windshield.

5

The Congress of Fat People, as its name indicates, was
a fat show. It was not just any fat show, however. The
Congress of Fat People aimed to be the best and biggest, the most awe-inspiring, mind-boggling fat show
on the entire carny circuit. There were no fewer than
four mountainous attractions: Baby Louis, Little
Emma, Big Boss Henry, and the Mountain of Flesh. In
addition to the blimps, there were any number of
featured freaks. The Two-Headed Baby competed
with the Royal Russian Midgets; Ernie De Fort, the
double-bodied boy, pitched alongside a whole series
of wild men from various remote jungles. Lower
down on the pecking order were the geeks who bit
the heads off live chickens, the bozos who abused the
crowd—who, in turn, pelted them with wooden balls
in hopes of dumping them into tanks of cold water—
and the worn-at-the-edges showgirls who made ends
meet by turning tricks on the side. When you traveled

with the carnival, the two things you didn't have to worry about were your identity and your status as a misfit. For the carnival was a community of misfits, a place where *anyone* could fit in, and where almost no questions were asked. So the fact that Tom Parker was an illegal immigrant with a false name and no papers amounted to no big deal here.

Life in the carnival was about as diametric a contrast to life in the army as Tom Parker could hope to find. In the army, particularly the peacetime army, everything had been done for him. He'd been told when to eat, when to get up, and when to go to sleep. The army even managed his money for him. In the carnival, he was once again on his own, forced to live by his wits. He quickly learned a lesson that would stay with him all his life: The only thing that stood between him and the sucker's money was the sucker himself.

Never giving the sucker an even break had become even more crucial and desperate in 1932, the year Parker hitched on with the Johnny J. Jones Exposition. The Depression had bottomed out and the New Deal was only a campaign promise. As the carnival wound its way up from its winter quarters in Florida through North Carolina, Virginia, Kentucky, Oklahoma, Nebraska, and all the way up to the Canadian border, it moved continually through a world of poverty. In the cities there were breadlines; in the country towns there were bank failures; outside both towns and cities all along the railroad tracks there were the shantytowns, the hobo jungles and Hoovervilles, where the destitute waited for a train to take them to something better. Even those who were working experienced their fair share of misery. Migrant workers, bulldozed off their land by bank foreclosures, were paid starvation wages. The newspapers were full of stories of bloody gangster slayings. John Dillinger in Chicago, Ma Barker and her family in Florida, Bonnie Parker and Clyde Barrow in Texas and Oklahoma, all took matters into their own hands. Bruno Hauptmann was charged with and later executed for the kidnapping and murder of the Lindbergh baby.

On a much more modest scale, the carnival, too, had to employ a good deal of larceny to survive the Depression. In the twenties the Johnny J. Jones Exposition was one of the biggest in the country. Then around Christmas 1930, its founder, Johnny Jenkins Jones, died after years of heavy drinking. The carnival was heavily in debt and the load fell on Jones's young widow, Hody Hurt. Barely thirty, she found herself in charge of a show that was losing thousands of dollars each season, and the middle of the Depression was no place to stage a comeback. Hody Hurt's first move was to start cutting back. Rides were dropped and men were laid off. Even much-needed maintenance was deferred and the carnival began to look decidedly shabby. By the beginning of the 1933 season, only twenty of its original sixty-four railroad cars were in use. The season started with weeks of torrential rain all across the southeast, the financially crucial first leg of the carnival's northward swing. It was a blow from which the show never recovered. October found The Mighty Monarch of the Tented World stranded in Norfolk, Virginia, with just one ride and no money to pay off the railroad company from whom they leased their wagons. One of the tents had been turned into a cookhouse where the few remaining hands could share scanty communal meals. Even back then, despite his poor English, Tom Parker must have had something going for him, if only that he was a fast learner, for he was able to hang on right to the end, one of the few who never quit or was let go.

And then a savior appeared. On November 11, Hody Hurt found a buyer for the show. E. Lawrence Phillips had one arm and a string of motion picture theaters around Washington. He'd been an old friend of Johnny J.'s and had always wanted to own a carnival. It was his chance not only to get his hands on one but also to bail out his old buddy's young and attractive widow. From the moment of the purchase, things began to look up. Phillips was both willing and able to invest in the carnival, enough to keep it on the road and even to restore some of its former glory.

From the outside, the carnival was a romantic place, with whirling lights, the carousel, the Ferris wheel, and the smell of crushed grass and of hamburgers cooking on an open grill. This was the province of legitimate operators, the men and women who ran the rides and the food concessions. Beyond them, however, was the darker side of the carnival, the land of a thousand scams. At one end of the scale was the supply of workaday vices. In the shadows beyond the lights of the midway, covert prostitution flourished with its attendant petty extortions. The most common were variations of the traditional badger game where the "irate husband" barges in either waving a pistol or threatening exposure. After a lot of talk the John agrees to pay for the hush-up and the fair moves on.

In the "key girl" operation the unfortunate sucker never even got to see the girl. While the cooch dancers were onstage, their pimps would sell keys to rooms at a nearby motel where, it was promised, the girls would later be waiting, ready and eager to party. In the course of a day the pimp might sell copies of the same key to a dozen or more men. When they arrived at the motel, they would, needless to say, find no girl, no pimp, and in some cases, even no motel. Again the carnival had moved on.

The other behind-the-scenes staple was gambling. From the rigged wheel of fortune through the shell game and three-card monte, to high-stakes poker games in guarded hotel rooms, games of chance, with the fix in to give the carny the edge, were the ideal methods of stripping suckers of their money. Pickings were particularly good in farming communities immediately after the harvest. With the crop just sold at market, the small-time farmer might be walking around with several thousand dollars—his cash income for an entire year—in his hip pocket. This was the kind of prize every dishonest carny dreamed about, the bankroll that meant that instead of scuffling through the winter, you could spend it in a fancy Florida apartment with an equally fancy broad.

Obviously, the citizens who found themselves on the receiving end of this multitiered system of short-changing—"turning the duke" in carny parlance—frequently took it badly. Gangs of townspeople might take the law into their own hands and arrive with bats or shotguns to take it out of the hides of those responsible. The police were forever turning up with their lights flashing in an effort to nail the gambling game or the girls turning tricks. The individual who took care of all this, the carnival's rough-and-ready public relations man, was formally known as the general manager, although the carnies simply called him "the patch." His job was to keep a goon squad on hand to deal with angry citizens and to bribe the police. One of the first lessons Parker learned was that corruption was virtually everywhere but you didn't talk about it openly. Town officials would take a bribe provided it was dressed up with a different name, such as a bond against damage, a courtesy gift, or a donation to a favorite charity. Money, jewelry, watches, sets of tires, cases of bourbon—all changed hands under an array of euphemisms.

If a carny did wind up in the local jail, the most important thing was to put up his bail. Carnies almost never showed up for court hearings. Post a bond and move on down the line. The sheriff or the police chief would probably keep the money. If you had to go back to that town again, all you had to do was keep a low profile or maybe grow a beard.

The combination of shared experience and the constant traveling welded a carnival into a closed society that felt set apart from the rest of the world. There were the hep and the squares, and the twain should never meet except in a transactional relationship in which the square came off worse. The carnies even had their own language, an out-of-the-side-of-the-mouth amalgam of Romany, Yiddish, pig latin, black slang, and jailhouse talk that made their society even more impenetrable. Their conversations would go like this: "Ix nix akken-cracken. There's a strange edd-weed in the asture-pasture."

Among carnies, "us" and "them" was absolute, and the suckers deserved all they got. The con or ripoff wasn't a crime since the suckers just begged to be robbed. Didn't they bring it on themselves? It was the will of whatever God looked out for whores, hustlers, and fairgrounds. One carnival veteran summed it up: "In the good old days, nobody believed that you could run an honest show—give the marks what they paid for, keep out the flatties and the con men—and still make money."

All this represented the lessons that Tom Parker was avidly absorbing and the philosophy that would stay with him all through his professional life. "He had a real sharp brain," recalls Jack Kaplan, a carnival colleague of Parker's. "He was quick on the talking, very quick. He always made the right moves."

The Ferris wheel moved very slowly. Only the white lights were turned on and a white spotlight played on the highest point on the wheel. There were just three people riding on it: a boy and a girl, dressed all in white, sat side by side in one car; an older man, dressed in a black robe, rode in the car immediately below them. Word had been spread around town during the week that on Saturday night there was going to be a special event at the carnival. Two kids—carny kids—were going to get married, right there at the top of the Ferris wheel. The women in the town were telling each other how romantic it was going to be, just like in the movies.

The wedding was scheduled for eight o'clock, and by seven-thirty it looked like half the town had turned out to see the show. They crowded around the base of the Ferris wheel, staring up into the night, waiting with anticipation. The young couple looked so cute, she in her wedding dress, he in his white shirt, white pants, and a white bow tie.

A tinny version of the wedding march blared from the public address speakers as the young couple reached the apex of the wheel. The wheel stopped and the music died away. The preacher stood up in his car and turned to face the couple. The car swayed slightly and the preacher grabbed quickly for a handhold.

"Do you, Thomas Parker, take this woman to be your lawful wedded wife?" he began. Some of the words were whisked away by the wind, but most of them drifted down to the crowd below.

At the end of the brief ceremony, the young man produced a large Bible on which he and his bride placed their hands. Then they embraced and kissed each other. There was a wild burst of applause. The spotlight faded and the wheel began to move again, lowering the minister and the couple to the ground. The crowd began to break up, drifting toward the other regular attractions, the rides or the hamburger stands, the wheel of fortune or the freak show. None of them was near enough to notice the smugly satisfied and less than pleasant smile on the face of the groom. They didn't know what he knew. They didn't know that the minister was one of the work crew who had helped assemble the Ferris wheel, that the "Bible" was a Sears catalogue wrapped in black paper, that the bride was one of the strippers from the Chez La Femme tent and that Lawrence Phillips, the carnival's owner, had been letting Tom Parker pull the same crowd-gathering stunt in every town since Charlotte, North Carolina. The suckers just loved a weird wedding.

Peazy Hoffman was a short, fat man with round glasses, an ever-present white hat, and an amiable but persistent attitude that rarely wavered. He also had a wife, Cleo, who had once been a high diver. After the carnival was taken over by Lawrence Phillips, he came in as the Johnny J. Jones Exposition's advance man. An advance man could make or break a carnival, and Peazy Hoffman was considered to be one of the best in the business. Before the Johnny J. Jones outfit, he had worked for famous names like the Lackman Expositions and Rubin and Cherry. If any one individual can be thought of as the guide and mentor of the man who evolved as Colonel Tom Parker, it must be Peazy Hoffman. When he saw stunts like the wedding on the Ferris wheel, Peazy recognized that the Parker boy had a natural flair for publicity. Conning suckers out of their money was the daily business of the midway, but the knack of being able to know what would pull in the rubes in the first place was, in Peazy's estimation, a God-given gift.

The logistics of taking a carnival through largely rural areas and making money were extremely complicated. The advance man normally hit town four days to a week before the show rolled in. He was responsible for bill posting, for the distribution of flyers; he had to buy space in local newspapers and arrange as much editorial coverage as he could possibly get. He might even have to grease the palms of a few local dignitaries to ensure there'd be no problems with permits and licenses. Increasingly he would have to deal with local radio stations, particularly in the South, where shows like the *Grand Ole Opry*, which started in 1925, had become a way of life. If the situation appeared to warrant it, he'd even hire local kids to run around the streets yelling, "Johnny's coming! Johnny's coming!" The advance man would do quite literally anything to make sure there was a crowd when the fair pulled into town.

At the same time, the advance man had to achieve all this at the lowest possible cost. It was his job to harass printers and to get drunk with the advertising managers of local newspapers until they dropped their prices and offered discounts. He hit up the local merchants and kept on talking until they either bought billboard space in and around the carnival or anted up merchandise for prizes and giveaways in return for some kind of promotional plug. The real talent in being a top-rank advance man was a capacity to cover all the angles and to maximize the dividends. Such was the lesson that Tom Parker learned while he assisted Peazy Hoffman and thumbtacked posters to telegraph poles, handed out flyers, and generally made the noise and distributed the paper. The key to success in anything was good promotion, and from Peazy's perspective—the same perspective that was rapidly becoming the young Parker's—a topflight, hustling promoter could take on the world and win.

It was while he was serving his apprenticeship under Peazy Hoffman that Tom Parker started to demonstrate that he was aware there was more to the world than the Johnny J. Jones Exposition. Just as he had done at regular intervals all through his life, Parker started to disappear. This time, though, when he returned, he had money. There was talk about how he was pulling scams in towns along the route and even doing stuff with other carnivals, but it was against the code to pry or look too closely.

Jack Kaplan was one of the ones who wondered but didn't ask. "He was in the show off and on, back and forth. He always wanted to go out and make a dollar. A hustler, that's what he was. Always on the go, seeing if he could get something going."

Parker was also growing a good deal more confident. He was still secretive, but now and again he would confide in Kaplan and others. "He wanted to be a big man in this country. He wanted to be a big promoter. That was his plan for the future. He was watching people, how they operated. He never missed a trick; he had good eyes; he could always see ahead, look into the future." There were even frustrated outbursts. More than once Parker asked Kaplan, "Them guys can do it, why can't I do it? I want to be the biggest promoter in the land."

Jack Kaplan was fourteen when he first met Parker. He knew that Tom was a lot older, but that was about all the information he had. "I had no idea where he came from; I never asked him," Kaplan says. "I knew he was a foreigner. He had broken English in those days. I thought he came from Pennsylvania, the Dutch country. He was talking like a Dutchman: 'Brassa brassa, was ist los, ja ja.' "

Every winter, in their annual migration, the carnival trains rolled slowly home to their winter quarters in and around Tampa, Florida. One by one they rattled over the Hillsborough River Bridge, past the state fairgrounds and the exotic Moorish structure that was Henry Plant's Tampa Bay Hotel. If the carnies of America had any kind of home, it was these winter quarters. Almost all the traveling fairs in the country wintered in and around the city. The Johnny J. Jones Exposition, although it played the Tampa State Fair every February, was one of the exceptions. It spent the winter farther east in De Land, situated between Orlando and Daytona Beach. Tampa, however, was the hub of the off-season action, and that was where Tom Parker headed at the first opportunity.

Parker viewed the winter with mixed feelings. Something inside him, perhaps a vestige of his Dutch upbringing, demanded that he spend time near water. There was a sense of relief and freedom when he breathed the salt air after months of seeing nothing but mountains and prairies. However, since winter was not a time for easy money, the style in which a carny spent the season depended almost totally on how much he had in his poke when the summer came to an end. Although it was highly unlikely that he was flat broke, each time he reached winter quarters, Parker went right on hustling. It seemed to be an absolute compulsion. It was also a chance to try out some of the tricks he'd learned while working through the year with men like Peazy Hoffman.

One of his earliest—and least successful—efforts was an attempt to sell a kid's pony ride attraction to what was in the early thirties the main shopping center in Tampa. When that failed, he went on to sell the owner of a major furniture store on the idea of having a "sleep endurance contest"—in other words, having a man or woman, probably broke and unemployed, lying in a made-up bed in one of the main display windows and promoting a special on mattresses. This rather tasteless novelty at least drew the required crowds, and Parker made his money. For all of his life, nobody was ever able to accuse Tom Parker of being a slave to unreasonable good taste. In another store promotion, he buried a man alive and let people look down into the casket through a peephole.

Christmas was a particular target for Parker's money-making schemes. Maas Brothers had opened their first department store on De Land's Franklin Street, and they hired Tom Parker to play Santa Claus as the centerpiece of their Christmas merchandising push. Parker operated as a pied piper on the streets around the store, luring children and their probably less than willing parents into the department store's "Toyland."

Again and again Parker came back to animals as the key ingredient in his stunts. In later years, when he was managing Elvis Presley and figured he was on top of the heap, he would frequently bore his underlings with the story of how he had once acquired an elephant. According to Parker—who was never noted for the accuracy of his reminiscences—he came across the owner of the elephant when he was too broke to feed the animal, so Parker took the elephant into town and made a deal with a local feed store. If they gave the animal a meal, the elephant would walk around while wearing a sign advertising the store. Next he drew up a similar deal for himself with a restaurant. Within a week he had done so well selling advertising on the elephant that he was not only supporting himself and the elephant, but he was also making a profit. There may not, of course, be a word of truth in this story as Parker told it, but it did become the basis of a collection of toy and model elephants that he exacted from friends and associates as a strange kind of tribute. Somewhere in Parker's psyche, the ownership and control of an elephant seems to have been the ultimate in showmanship.

Winter in Tampa wasn't merely a time for stunts and fooling with possibly imaginary elephants, it was also a time for moving around the carnival community in search of a better deal. In 1934 the Royal American Shows came, for the first time, to the state fairgrounds. It was something of a coup for the grounds' owner, P. T. Strieder, since the Royal American was debatably the best carnival on the circuit, and for some years had been taking dates from the Jones Exposition.

Carl Sedlmayer, the owner of the Royal American, was determined that the show would always live up to its boast that it had "the world's largest midway" and that it traveled on "the world's largest train." Carl Sedlmayer had bought a fifteen-car railroad show in 1921 and had built on it every year until, by 1935, there were sixty-five cars to carry twenty shows, fifty-two rides, more than a thousand people, plus portable carpenters' shops, neon-sign construction, a blacksmith shop, and enough electricity-generating equipment to light a city of forty thousand. Two former acrobats, brothers Elmer and Curtiss Velare, designed and built a double Ferris wheel and then added two more wheels to give a total of four running in combination. No other show had anything to compete with this monster ride. In addition to the wheels, there was a whole village of midgets, the Ripley Odditorium of Freaks, Raynell's Follies, and an illusion show featuring a headless girl. It wasn't surprising that the show was like a magnet to Tom Parker.

According to Jack Kaplan, Parker either was never quite able to land himself on the full-time payroll or he was starting to value his independant status. He had a number of situations going at once. "He worked for Ruby Velare, Elmer's wife, for a while. Ruby had a cotton candy stand and Tom helped her selling candy apples, apples on a stick, cotton candy, and popcorn." Later he moved on to other sections of the show, pitching sideshows, guarding railroad cars—whatever came up. During the summer of 1935 he took off with the Royal American, but he dropped out from time to time to do advertising work for Peazy Hoffman and the others at Johnny J. Jones.

It seems to have rankled Parker that the Royal American didn't immediately recognize his talent and elevate him to fame and fortune. In 1972, Elmer Velare, one of the brothers with the four-way Ferris wheel, was at a Showman's League convention in Las Vegas. Across the proverbial crowded room, he spotted Tom Parker. Velare hadn't seen Parker in more than thirty years, but there was no mistaking the Colonel's pudgy, almost baby face, with its pouting mouth and cold eyes. Parker had put on a bit of weight since their last encounter, but Velare supposed he must eat well now, since he was Elvis Presley's manager.

More to the point, Tom Parker had also spotted Elmer Velare. He stormed through the crowd with his flunkies hurrying to catch up with him. There was nothing particularly pleasant about either the smile or the triumphant glitter in the cold eyes. Nor was his greeting overly friendly: "Elmer, didn't I tell you I could be a promoter for you back in the thirties? Now

I'm a big promoter. I wanted to be a promoter but you wouldn't let me. Do you remember?"

Tom Parker was never too big to gloat.

There was one consolation derived from that period when he had achieved little success with the Royal American. It was during the time when he was free-lancing with the show that he met his wife.

The midway and sideshows of the Royal American were the centerpiece of the South Florida State Fair. As one of the major local industries, the Have-a-Tampa cigar company always had a stand at the fair. Tom Parker liked a cigar. It wasn't only the satisfaction of a good smoke; clenched between his teeth at a pugnacious angle, a jutting cigar compensated for his less than heroic jawline. He believed it gave him the air of grit and determination he was so anxious to cultivate. Thus it was obvious that he should amble by the Have-a-Tampa display stand. If nothing else, there was always the chance that they might be handing out free samples. On one occasion, however, in early 1935, he discovered something more appealing there than a possible free cigar—the girl behind the counter. Perhaps a year older than he, she was a handsome woman (although not so handsome that he'd feel out of his league) with flowing dark hair and the kind of ready smile that comes when you're constantly on display to the public. Tom Parker recognized a kindred spirit and turned on the charm.

Parker seems to have been something of a slow starter where women were concerned. While he was a teenager in Breda and even when he was in the army in Hawaii, there is no record of his obsessively chasing girls or even being particularly interested. (He didn't drink either; early experiments with beer turned him into a noisy, aggressive, and even violent drunk. It was no condition for a man without papers.)

Only when he joined the carnival did he finally seem to have started to appreciate the advantages of sex. Jack Kaplan tells of an affair in North Carolina with one of the revue girls whom Parker "married" in a phony ceremony on a Ferris wheel.

Charm was one of the tools of Tom Parker's trade, and he quickly had the young woman behind the cigar counter laughing at his jokes delivered with his still weird accent. He found out that her name was Marie Mott. When he met her later, he discovered that she'd been through a rough time with relationships and that she'd be more than susceptible to a smooth but understanding manner. Even with women, Parker never ceased to be the calculating operator.

Marie Mott was one of six children. Her father, a Spanish-American War veteran, attempted to make a go of blacksmithing in a number of small Florida towns and failed each time. In 1924, when she was nineteen, she met and married a photographer by the name of Robert Burl Ross. Ross was described as "something of a ladies' man" and, after a couple of years and the birth of Robert Burl, Jr., there was a divorce. After Ross, there was Willett Man Eagler Sayre, who married Marie on May 22, 1933. "He didn't do very much," said Bitsy Mott, her younger brother. "Marie had to go out working. He wanted to drive a truck or something but his jobs didn't last very long." This marriage didn't last long either, and by 1935, the year she met Parker, she was emotionally bruised and living with her folks and Bitsy. As a single woman with a ten-year-old son, her future looked a little bleak.

It's possible that Tom Parker's decision to marry Marie Mott was not wholly a matter of romance. It must have occurred to him that marriage to an American citizen might lend a certain legitimacy to his basically illegal situation. Marriage to an American citizen with a child, far from being a drawback, could only add to his sense of security. He could bury his past in a ready-made family.

The official story is the one that first surfaced in an Associated Press feature in 1956: "In 1932, while wintering with a carnival in Tampa, he met, wooed, and wed his wife Marie, who now helps him with the bookkeeping." There are three options as to how this version of events got published. Either AP got it wrong by accident, or Tom Parker got it wrong by accident, or by force of habit he deliberately rearranged the facts. Certainly the rest of the piece was a complete fabrication: "Parker was born forty-seven years ago in West Virginia, where his parents happened to be touring with a carnival. Mom and Dad died before Tom reached the fifth grade, so he wound up with his uncle's traveling show, the Great Parker Pony Circus. At seventeen, young Tom struck out on his own with a pony and monkey act."

A check of the Tampa courthouse records shows Marie Mott's two previous marriages, but there's no sign of any marriage between her and Tom Parker. This, of course, is not to say that the couple couldn't have been married anywhere along the carnival route. All Bitsy Mott is sure about is that there was no wedding party. "They probably went to a justice of the peace and that was all. A party was too much money." The other alternative could have been that Parker didn't feel he had enough documentation even for a country judge and that he and Marie Mott simply declared they were married and left it at that.

What is certain is that marriage began to ease Tom Parker away from the carnival and the traveling life. At first Marie would go out on the road with him. Each

November they would return to her parents' house on Platt Street, laden down with presents and souvenirs, and completely take over the household. Bitsy Mott remembers these occasions with a degree of bitterness: "When the tour was over, they would come to our house to stay. I was a little fellow at the time; I remember they used to move my Daddy and my Momma out of their bed and use the bed themselves. Daddy and Momma would sleep wherever they could. That would irritate me a little, I didn't understand." Apparently the bitterness didn't last. Bitsy Mott, once he was grown, went to work for the Colonel and remained one of the most faithful retainers in the Elvis Presley organization all through the fifties and sixties.

According to the official legend—the AP interview that recounts his birth in West Virginia—"Parker soon traded his pony for a typewriter and became a press agent for a series of carnivals, circuses, and showboats. He developed first-name friendships with Tom Mix and Wallace Beery, both carnival men before the movies found them." Once again the legend steers wide of the truth. It's more likely that Parker found that he was neither doing as well with the carnival nor rising as quickly through the carnival hierarchy as he would have liked. He wasn't becoming the big-time promoter that was his ambition and fantasy.

Part of the problem was that he was continually undercapitalized. Jack Kaplan remembers his methods clearly: "Parker came up the hard way. He promoted things without money. 'Yeah, pay you tomorrow. Pay you next week.'"

Clyde Rinaldi was a Tampa printer with a shop on Howard Avenue. He found himself on the receiving end of Parker's penniless promoting. Parker first approached him near the end of 1935, when he was trying and failing to run pony rides outside the big Franklin Street stores. Rinaldi had done the printing for the Royal American Shows and now Parker wanted some printing done for his own promotion. The snag was that he couldn't pay for the order up front and wanted to pay off the bill at a dollar a week. "I wouldn't say that he was broke, but he didn't have much money," Rinaldi remembers. He trusted the young man, however, and went along with the proposition. "It wasn't really a deal," he recalls. "It was more like a friendly relationship." Parker kept up the payments and everyone was happy. Two decades later, Rinaldi would be happier still when Parker rewarded the friendly relationship by placing enormous orders for Elvis Presley printing.

Before finally settling down, Parker took a final stab at making it with the Royal American. He bought a penny arcade on the midway and sold pictures of fighters, baseball stars, and pinups for one cent a shot. It made money and he enjoyed the work. (In later years he wouldn't be able to resist mingling with the crowds and hawking Elvis souvenirs outside Presley concerts.) Once again, though, there was the feeling that he wasn't getting anywhere. There was also the consideration that traveling with a wife and child was added trouble and expense. The temptation was becoming stronger and stronger to put down roots in Florida and to see what kind of business he could drum up by staying in one place.

When Tom Parker finally did leave the carnival, it amounted to a graduation. During his traveling and hustling days, he had received a unique education. He was now going to take that education and see what he could do with it on his own.

6

Gene Austin had really only one hit song. His recording of "My Blue Heaven" had been a smash all across the South, but by the time he ran into Tom Parker in 1939 and hired him as a booking agent, his glory days were over and he was reduced to playing small clubs and working as a side act in the carnival. This didn't deter Parker. The has-been tenor, his first human client, was certainly a step forward from ponies and elephants.

Tom Parker, the would-be promoter, was promoting a real live singer and he was determined to rise to the occasion. The tactics he employed were the only ones he knew, the methods he'd learned from people like Peazy Hoffman. He booked Austin all up and down the back roads of Florida and Louisiana. Parker would move into each town where Austin was scheduled to play a few days ahead of time and begin to plaster the streets with posters and high-pressure public relations, however unsophisticated. "Gene's coming." It was a direct rerun of the old "Johnny's coming" routine he'd run for the Johnny J. Jones Exposition.

At the level on which they were operating, Parker's methods proved reasonably successful. Gene Austin was pulling better crowds out on the rural circuit, which made him happy. Admittedly, he wasn't making hit records anymore. He wasn't making records period, but that wasn't why he'd hired the kid with the weird accent. When Parker had approached Austin after one of his shows and pitched himself as a deal-making promotion man who knew every road and every village in Dixie, the country singer realized he was looking at a shoestring operation. The young man was so energetic, though, it more than made up for his lack of capital or music business experience. Indeed, Austin was thankful for anything he could get, and, with Parker, at least he had someone working on his act.

Gene Austin took such a shine to the young man, and had so much confidence in him, that he started to have thoughts about easing back toward the big time. Maybe he could at least start playing in towns that had running water and paved sidewalks. Nashville was where it was happening and Austin proposed that they make the move to Tennessee. To his surprise, Parker hesitated. He wasn't sure; he had a wife and all that stuff, and he'd have to talk to her before they could make a major move like leaving Tampa. Austin was quite taken aback. What the hell was this? Was this the same guy who could go into a town and stick flyers to everything that didn't actually move? He had never seen the young man exhibit such worried indecision.

Eventually Parker would tell him no. He didn't feel

he was ready to uproot himself and leave Tampa. He made a lot of excuses. Austin could only shake his head. Parker had seemed like such a go-getter, he told all these stories about how he had sailed all over the world and yet here he was, balking about a simple move across two states.

It may have been that the idea of moving to Nashville brought out in Parker the caution of a man with no papers. Or it may have been a first symptom of the strange tunnel vision that dogged Parker all through his career. Parker could hustle a sucker without breaking stride, but when confronted with something that was good and legitimate, he more often than not totally failed to recognize its potential. He seemed to be so imbued with the carny ethos that he couldn't appreciate true value when he stumbled across it. Had he gone to Nashville, he might well have hit it big in the then expanding country music industry. For the time being, he elected to defer his dream of becoming a high-stakes promoter. As it was, and for whatever reason, Tom Parker decided to stay in Tampa and become a dogcatcher.

To be strictly accurate, he wasn't a dogcatcher. It was just another of his scams. Parker had decided that his traveling days were over and that he was no longer a carny. Of course, settling down in Tampa with his wife and her son didn't mean going straight and getting a job. He was going to continue to promote, but now his promotions would happen from a steady base in Florida. When he and Gene Austin decided that perhaps they weren't going to set the world on fire, his next target was—even for Parker—an odd one. Tom Parker was going to promote the Tampa Humane Society.

The Tampa Humane Society had a building on Armenia Avenue, a few miles out from the center of town. This animal shelter was built in 1929 by a pair of wealthy and well-meaning sisters, Allison and Helen Holland. For almost a decade the shelter had been administered by a field agent, H. C. Gordon. At the end of the thirties, however, H.C. was due for retirement and the Humane Society committee was looking for his successor. Parker's pitch to the committee was simple: He was not only good with animals, he also knew how to raise money. The committee absolutely bought his carny charm and smooth line. Maybe his accent was a little strange, but it didn't matter. The committee was sold. The logic was obvious: If he could snow the committee so deftly, he could also snow the public and have them digging deep for donations. Tom Parker was the new Humane Society field agent.

The job was as close as Parker would come to regular employment ever in his career, but at that moment the job was everything he wanted. He had a title and a desk. He had a certain degree of authority and the chance to bombard the public with pictures of puppies with big eyes and kittens in baskets. There were also fringe benefits. He got a free apartment, and when he converted his car into an animal ambulance by installing a cage in the back, he received free gasoline. Later, when the country entered World War II, there were even more benefits. With his semiofficial status he was allowed allocations of gas and tires that were denied other civilians. Yes, the Humane Society was a choice hustle.

Not that Parker didn't give value for money. He worked the hustle for all it was worth. He pushed the tearjerk quality of unwanted pets all the way to bathos. He gained the reputation of actually being able to cry on cue if the situation demanded. He constantly hit the local press with weepy stories and found a particularly warm reception from Paul Wilder, one of the editors of the Tampa *Tribune,* who used Parker's doggy and kitty stories on a regular basis in his "In Our Town" column. An example from February 13, 1941, clearly indicates the tone of these pieces.

"Puddles, the Humane Society cat-that-won't-go-away, has adopted a new sleeping place. She rests every day in a desk drawer, and is ever at the side of her mistress, Mrs. Tom Parker. Almost daily, someone tests Puddles for the fun of it, and tries to carry her away from the society. As soon as the door is open, she starts kicking and scratching so much that the carrier is obliged to turn her loose and she scampers back to her home."

On the strength of such deathless prose, Paul Wilder became one of the very few newspaper men whom Parker trusted and continued to trust when he hit the big time. Ultimately, Wilder would be rewarded with the very first exclusive Elvis Presley interview after the singer had gained superstardom.

Danny was less than optimistic. In fact, he was downright distressed. Sunday, December 21, 1941, was supposed to have been a red-letter day. If everything had gone according to plan, it would have been the day when he got his Christmas puppy. For an eight-year-old boy, this was a major event. His sister had been the one to tell him about it. She'd read to him from the newspaper, the Tampa *Tribune.* Santa Claus was going to be at the Humane Society animal shelter out on Armenia Avenue and was going to give away a hundred free puppies. With the single-minded determination of the very young, Danny had headed out on the bus. He was going to have one of those puppies for his very own.

Unfortunately, nothing was going according to

plan. When he arrived at the animal shelter, he discovered what looked like every other kid in town had turned up to claim one of the puppies. Later, on the radio, they would say that nearly a thousand people had come out in the hope of a puppy. Danny couldn't see how he could possibly be one of the lucky ones. His disappointment colored the rest of the afternoon. He could barely manage to laugh along with the other kids, even when Santa's goat started eating the Christmas tree. He didn't know that Santa Claus had a performing goat. He'd heard about reindeer, but never a goat. He was about ready to go home when Santa raised a hand and asked for complete silence.

"I want to know if there's anybody here that will take a dog that's homeless, dirty, and ugly."

At first, nobody moved. Nobody wanted to take home the worst dog of the whole bunch. Santa asked again. Still nobody wanted to accept the ugly puppy. Then Danny slowly raised his hand. At least he'd have a puppy for Christmas, even if it was the ugliest of the lot.

"I don't care if it's ugly."

Santa was silent for a moment, then motioned for Danny to come forward. Beside him was a box. Santa carefully opened it and lifted out a snow-white spitz puppy with a Christmas ribbon tied around its neck.

"I know if you're willing to take a bad dog, you will take good care of this one."

Danny couldn't believe what he was seeing. Santa held out the puppy, and Danny took it in his arms and hugged it to his chest. Even in this moment of joy, though, he couldn't help but notice there was something about Santa's eyes that didn't quite fit with the soft, gentle voice. The eyes were pale and cold. It was almost as though Santa had just played a huge and not very nice joke on the assembled crowd of children and was particularly pleased with himself.

For Tom Parker, the Humane Society was a jumping-off point for all kinds of schemes. Who could be so hardhearted as to refuse a man who dedicated his time to the protection of dumb animals? As well as seeking cash donations, he made the rounds of the stores to solicit gifts of merchandise. The obvious targets were stores that sold pet food. Cases of dog and cat food were an easy touch: Help feed the city's hungry strays. Parker always worked out some way by which the stores' generosity would be made known to the public. It was just a slight twist on the old carny routine in which stores "donated" merchandise as prizes in return for free advertising.

Parker didn't stop with merely promoting free pet food. Bitsy Mott, Parker's brother-in-law, remembered how "when they got overstocked, the Colonel went down to another store to trade it in for tuna fish or something that he and Marie could eat themselves." Unfortunately, the trading-off of the surplus pet food didn't stop with just a few cases of tuna. On one occasion when the committee of the Humane Society was conducting an inspection of the shelter, they were surprised and not a little perplexed to find the cold storage crammed with the best-quality hamburger and even boxes of prime sirloin. It was clear that Parker's wheeling and dealing far exceeded the society's needs. They demanded to know if he really intended to feed all this top-grade meat to the animals or if he was merely lining his own larder. Parker cried right on cue. He described the heartbreaking condition of some of the dogs and cats when he found them. In certain cases the only thing they could digest was good lean meat. It was unlikely that any of the committee actually believed Parker, but they let it go. In all likelihood they realized that such a shameless con artist had to be an asset to the society and that it was worth their turning a blind eye to his side deals. Parker had made the Humane Society self-sufficient for the first time since its foundation, and they weren't about to let him go.

Parker must have seen this confrontation as the green light. The Humane Society had given him the nod to declare open season on suckers. The deals became more and more outrageous until they finally culminated in the Humane Society pet cemetery. It started as a fairly modest operation, just a plot in back of the animal shelter, where people could bury their deceased pets. Tom Parker, however, never one to ignore human grief, knew many people became as emotional over a pet's death as they might over that of a relative or a close friend. His first idea, gravestones, was Parker at his flamboyant sleaziest. He contacted a Tampa stonemason who would make miniature tombstones for fifteen bucks a pop. In turn, Parker sold them to the bereaved for fifty. One of the first pets to be immortalized was Little Sonny, the pet of R. C. Jackson. Little Sonny was followed by Mickey, Peggie, Fifi, Gypsy, Girlie Bon Ton, all the way to Mrs. L. Patterson's Spotty Boy: "My Dear Little Pal, Gone to Rest, March 16, 1943." With the headstones moving briskly, Parker widened his net, working out a similar deal for little doggy and kitty coffins.

A new low was reached when Parker got around to the floral tributes. He'd make his pitch just after the funeral, asking the pet's owner how long he or she would like him to maintain fresh flowers on the loved one's grave. If Parker got lucky, the pet owner would ask for the supply of flowers to be kept up until his or her own death, and be charged accordingly. As Gabe

Tucker recorded in his book, "The source for the flowers was a florist he'd talked into giving him the wilted flowers left over at the end of the day. 'They're yours for free,' the florist said, 'in exchange for hauling them away.' When the owner saw the sagging flowers on the grave of a beloved dog, Parker used to say, 'I wish you could have seen them yesterday when we placed them. They're a bit wilted now but they looked sensational then.'"

Tom Parker's pet cemetery is still there in back of the Humane Society shelter on Armenia Avenue. The little gravestones are still there, not only in remembrance of the interred animals but also as mute testimony to the transcendental greed of Colonel Tom Parker.

Apart from taking care of the animals and raising money to support them and fatten his own bankroll, Tom Parker had one other responsibility: He was expected to place the strays in good homes. To Parker, this was really nothing more than an extension of the PR campaign that made the money for both him and the Humane Society. Each time Paul Wilder ran one of his animal sob stories in the Tampa *Tribune*, the shelter was besieged with calls and callers wanting to adopt pets. Each time he ran one of his public promotions, such as the Christmas puppy giveaway, the same thing happened. The placing of pets went as efficiently as anything else to which Parker applied himself. But something deep inside that convoluted psyche seemed to resent giving the public something for nothing. He seemed to have a need, whenever he got the chance, to somehow shortchange the people who turned up to claim pets.

One of his favorite tricks was to palm off a puppy that would grow to be a truly enormous dog, on someone who told him in advance they could only manage the smallest breeds. The story is told about a wealthy widow who was assured by Parker that the puppy she was taking wouldn't grow any bigger than a toy poodle. In a matter of months the dog had grown to the size of a small pony. The widow came back to the shelter yelling bloody murder about being cheated, but Parker didn't seem fazed. He simply took the huge dog's leash and started to haul it back toward the pens. He dragged the dog in such a way that it immediately resisted and, in a fortuitous dramatic effect, actually began to howl. Parker shook his head. The widow was right, the dog was too big; nobody else would take it. It was sad it would have to be put down just because it was so big. The dog continued to howl and by this time the widow was close to tears. She took the leash back from Parker. How could she let this poor animal die when it wanted to be with her so much?

In later years Parker would tell his cronies tales about all the people he'd conned with cute little puppies that grew into giant dogs. As time passed the tales became increasingly wild and he claimed clearly impossible TV stars and politicians among his victims. He took a positive, if twisted, pride in the number of people on whom he'd foisted completely unsuitable pets.

Two weeks before the day Tom Parker dressed in a Santa suit and gave puppies to little Danny and a hundred or so other kids, the Japanese had attacked Pearl Harbor. At first Parker was hardly touched by the war unless he managed to profit from it in some way. Then, on January 8, 1942, (coincidentally Elvis Presley's seventh birthday) the draft board came knocking. Even though the thought of inquisitive authority must have turned Parker's stomach to ice, he responded immediately. On the initial draft form he stated he was married, with one dependent child. He listed his employer not as the Humane Society but, for some inexplicable reason—unless from the very start he'd decided to throw up a smoke screen—as "Gene Austin from Hollywood." He was born on June 26, 1909, in Huntington, West Virginia. He made no mention of his previous service experience. It was Andreas van Kuijk who'd been in the army, not Tom Parker.

The draft board accepted him for exactly what he claimed he was and no check was made. He was classified 3A—"registrant with child or children"—and given a deferment. Tom Parker remained deferred until after the invasion of Europe; but in the latter half of 1944, there was a second letter. Parker had been reclassified 1A—"available for military service." Most sources agree that at this point Parker began to move heaven and earth to keep himself out of the army. Two months later, at the medical examination, he got his own way. The man who previously had been fit as a fiddle and strong as an ox managed to convince doctors that he was unfit. In this way the Colonel managed to avoid his only available war.

Not only the military shook up Tom Parker's ideas during these war years. Through the winter of 1943 an MGM film crew was shooting in and around Tampa. It was a war movie, *A Guy Named Joe,* starring Spencer Tracy as an angel and Van Johnson as a lonely GI, and directed by Victor Fleming. It was an infinitely forgettable piece of schmaltz—forgettable to everyone except Tom Parker, and he only remembered it because it had started his blood racing and his feet itching all over again. The unit manager, a man named Jay Marchant, had needed a number of animals in the production and had gone to the local Humane Society. There he'd encountered a smiling Tom Parker, who assured him he could fill all his needs.

Hanging around the movie location with his animals, Parker once again caught the show-biz bug. He wanted to be on the move again. He wanted to be a part of it all. He knew there was a hell of a lot more to life than clowning around Tampa, Florida, as the local dogcatcher.

7

World War II produced all kinds of changes in the way that show business brought entertainment to the public. In England, the big swing bands, spearheaded by the Glenn Miller Orchestra, played to fields full of GIs —in virtual khaki Woodstocks—while they waited for the buildup to D day. In bomb-shattered London, Danny Kaye and Bing Crosby rocked the Palladium. Back at home, Hollywood was running full bore, pumping out propaganda and escapism. Radio had never been so important in people's lives, particularly in the rural South, where country music shows like the *Grand Ole Opry* had become local institutions. In fact, country music was spreading across most of the country. The migrations of the Depression and the mass movements during the war years had made the population highly mobile and much less insular. More and more people were being exposed to honky-tonk ballads and western laments. Even Tom Parker was doing his best to promote the sound of fiddle, guitar, and high nasal harmonies. In 1941, in addition to his duties as Humane Society administrator, he was also promoting country and western concerts at the National Guard armory in Tampa.

One of his regular presentations at the Fort Homer Hestorly Armory was the *Grand Ole Opry* road show. The show's two big stars were singers Roy Acuff and Bill Monroe. Country comedienne Minnie Pearl was also on the bill, and she remembers that Parker was something of a standout among local promoters. "We went down there and he tied our show in with some chain [of stores] like Kroger."

Once again, Parker was working the local merchants. His deal was that they include a coupon in their local press advertising. If a customer brought in the coupon, he or she could get a discount on tickets to the armory show with each purchase. Parker got free advertising and the store—theoretically—got increased business. "It was a smart promotion because it filled the house several times. The man was thinking even then."

These National Guard armory shows gave Parker his first taste of big-time country music—at least, as big-time as it got in the early 1940s—and he liked what he saw. He began edging toward this new music, becoming more and more involved in the Tampa country promotions. In fact he became so involved that people began to take notice. Roy Acuff, influential not only as an entertainer but also as a businessman with his Acuff-Rose song-publishing empire, asked Parker to quit messing around with two-bit promotions in Tampa and come to Nashville and work full-time for the *Grand Ole Opry*. "I presume I was the first one ever to invite Tom to Nashville. He had helped me sell a flour company I had behind me then, helping to advertise it in the state of Florida." Acuff didn't know that Gene Austin had made exactly the same offer a few years earlier. Once again, and equally inexplicably, Parker turned it down. He still wasn't ready to leave Tampa. Roy Acuff offers only a partial explanation. "He wanted to have complete control. That's his style and he's been very successful with it."

Once again we run up against the paradox in Tom Parker's character. On one hand there is the restlessness and ambition, but on the other there is a conservatism, a fear of the unknown, that made it hard for him to take risks. Parker seems to have been obsessed by his being a man with no papers and, as such, constantly at risk of exposure. Such roots as the character Tom Parker had, had been put down in Tampa and he was reluctant to leave them. Fortunately, it wouldn't be too long before something came along that spared him having to make a blind jump into the next stage of his career and allowed him to ease into it bit by bit.

As the war in Europe and in the Pacific ground on, it started to have a direct effect on life at home. Gasoline and tires were in extremely short supply and a lot of people, particularly country people, were no longer able to drive into the city to go to shows of the kind Tom Parker was promoting at the armory. Country music was particularly hard hit, and its leading lights began to cast around for an answer. The obvious one was, if the people couldn't come to the shows, then take the shows to the people.

The old-fashioned concept of the tent show was given a new lease on life. A circus tent, a half-dozen acts, and the buses and trucks to carry them brought the shows to back-road towns and the numerous army camps dotted all over the South. The *Grand Ole Opry* itself was sponsored by radio station WSM in Nashville; the first bill was headed by blackface act Jam-up and Honey, and also included Minnie Pearl and a singer named Eddy Arnold, who had previously played lead guitar in Pee Wee King's Golden West Cowboys. In addition to the musicians, there was a need for experienced men, road-smart roustabouts with experience in the carnival or the circus. Minnie Pearl writes in her autobiography, "These were a group of working men who traveled with us to put up and take down the tent. They had come from circus backgrounds. They had a lingo all their own, which we copied."

When the tent show came to Florida, Tom Parker was right there. He hired on as the *Grand Ole Opry*'s advance man, and used all his carny experience as he slapped up the posters and hit the newspapers and radio stations. He hadn't uprooted himself from his comfortable base in Tampa, but at least he was back on the road again.

As he worked he also watched. On the surface, there was nothing too impressive about Tom Parker. Gabe Tucker, who by then was playing fiddle in Eddy Arnold's band, describes how he "moved in a sloth-like, lumbering way, still dressing in military boots, preferring a worn shirt and trousers and a wrinkled windbreaker." As he shambled through the tent show, laying a pall of cigar smoke behind him, his brain was always working, always figuring angles and probing for the weak spot that might enable him to carve out a piece of the action.

One of the first things Parker noticed was that these hillbilly entertainers didn't have personal managers. Most of the artists who played on the *Opry* were booked out by WSM's artists service department. If a manager could offer a complete service to his client and at the same time break the monopoly the radio stations held over the exploitation of country music, there might be one hell of a lot of money to be made. Parker also focused on the artist who might be the first candidate for his brand of personal management.

Eddy Arnold had only just quit being a sideman and was wondering whether he could really make it as a solo attraction. At that point he was part of the Joe Frank stable. Joe Frank, after Harry Stone, the general manager of WSM, was reckoned to be the most powerful man in Nashville and was even called the "Flo Ziegfeld of country music." Just as during his carny days Parker had admired and modeled himself on the old-time promoter Peazy Hoffman, Joe Frank was everything Parker wanted to be in country music. Born in Alabama in 1900, Frank had moved to Chicago in the twenties and become involved in artist management. In the thirties he met Gene Autry and handled him through a highly successful career of western movies and hit records. He was the man who first put Roy Acuff on the stage of the *Opry* and nursed the legendary Ernest Tubb to his massive 1942 hit, "Walking the Floor Over You."

Parker not only wanted to be Joe Frank, he also wanted to beat Joe Frank at his own game. Though a total outsider, Parker began to make a few moves on Arnold. Eddy Arnold, basically a friendly twenty-six-year-old farmer's son from Henderson, Tennessee, started to buy the central idea behind all Parker's arguments. It was possible for him to get a lot more money than the radio stations were giving him. "When I came along, I started selling a lot of records, but the country boys were not making a lot of money, relative to the way they do now." The radio stations and the major promoters were completely in each other's pockets, and it was into these pockets that most of the money disappeared. Tom Parker promised he'd change all that if Arnold would let him handle his affairs. "Let me handle the business, you do the yodeling."

The Tom Parker business setup was hardly slick. He'd hired his long-suffering brother-in-law Bitsy Mott and also his gofer from the animal shelter, Bevo Bevis, who was willing but far from smart. On the road, he worked out of a beat-up Studebaker and a trailer with the legend EDDY ARNOLD THE TENNESSEE PLOWBOY emblazoned across the back and sides in foot-high letters. Bitsy Mott doesn't disguise just how funky those early days were. "We had a rough start. We used to play in little towns in Texas. You didn't have big auditoriums, we had to play in barns, and sometimes you had to kick the debris out of the way before you could let people come in. Cows had been in there. We nailed posters on the posts, we went to theaters, made deals at newspaper offices. In the early days we had to do all these things ourselves."

Where publicity was concerned, there was no trick so low that Parker wouldn't stoop to it. On one particular day he was driving down Howard Avenue in Tampa when he spotted a hillbilly band doing a live broadcast outside a newly opened grocery store. He braked the Studebaker to a screeching halt, climbed out, and waddled toward the band. To everyone's total amazement he grabbed the open mike and asked the band if they knew Eddy Arnold's new song, "Mama, Please Stay Home with Me." The band and onlookers were stunned, but Tom just went on talking about how marvelous Arnold was. Before anybody could pull him away from the mike, he'd invited the band, the crowd, and the listening audience to come down and see Eddy Arnold at the state fair. Parker had quite simply and barefacedly stolen minutes of airtime on someone else's show.

It was during these early barnstorming days in

country music that the first Parker legends were born. Prime among them was the tale of Colonel Parker's dancing chickens, which first met the printed page in Jerry Hopkins's book *Elvis*. "As the Colonel tells the story, he sent his assistant to the nearest general store to buy a two-dollar hot plate and an extension cord, which he placed in the chicken cage and covered with straw. The hot plate was plugged in, Bob Wills and the Texas Playboys went into 'Turkey in the Straw,' the curtain went up, and a bewildered audience saw two chickens high-stepping around the cage trying to keep from burning their feet."

The whole production was staged to avoid paying a twenty-dollar entertainment tax. With the chickens, the *Eddy Arnold Show* could be reclassified as an agricultural event and not be liable for the tax. Maybe the strangest thing about the Colonel and his chickens was not so much that he did it in the first place but that, years after, he continued to boast about it.

Parker slowly opened the envelope. Everyone in the room was grinning from ear to ear. He pulled out the imposing document and read it over.

"An honorary Louisiana commission?"

Bob Greer nodded.

"Signed by Governor Jimmy Davis."

Parker ran his hand over the signature.

"So it is."

"When I was in the carnival, Jimmy Davis was a hillbilly singer. He don't forget his old friends."

"This makes me a colonel?"

"Signed and sealed and entered into the State's business of the day."

"A colonel?"

Gabe Tucker laughed. "Suits you perfectly. With all the smoke you blow, you need a title."

Parker stared at Tucker with mock solemnity.

"Thank you, Mr. Tucker, for this title. See to it from now on that everyone addresses me as the Colonel."

"When Tom's your manager, he's all yours. He lives and breathes his artist. I once said to him when he was managing me, 'Tom, why don't you get yourself a hobby—play golf, go boating or something.' He looked me straight in the eye and said, 'You're my hobby.'"

The Colonel's energy was starting to pay off. In 1946, Eddy Arnold had a hit with "That's How Much I Love You." In 1947 he had seven number-one hits in the country charts, followed by eight more the next year, the biggest being "Bouquet of Roses." (He actually released only four records that year, but both sides of each became hits.) Arnold and the Colonel, even in the barnstorming days, had been determined to smooth off some of the act's rural edges, in the hope of going for a national market. Arnold didn't actually abandon the cowboy hat and string tie, but he was aiming at the image of the smooth country crooner. The idea of polishing for the mass market would be tried again on Elvis Presley, with truly disastrous results. The craving for a kind of respectability, however, didn't deter the Colonel from indulging his taste for carny-style gross-out promotion. Instead of the Studebaker and the trailer, Eddy Arnold had a rented plane. The name on the side was now in letters two feet high.

It was also the moment to leave Tampa. The Colonel couldn't pretend any longer that he could do business anywhere but Nashville. The move was conducted in what was emerging as the typical Parker style. He simply moved in on Eddy Arnold and his wife, Sally, at their pleasant four-bedroom house in

Madison, a quiet northern suburb of Nashville. Tom and Marie Parker arrived and proceeded to abuse Arnold's hospitality for months at a stretch. The Colonel moved in his flunkies and set up an office right in the family living room. He conducted business in the loud, boisterous chaos that had also become part of the Parker style. He yelled, he bullied, he demanded to be amply fed three times a day. It may have all been a part of the Colonel "living and breathing his artist," but Eddy knew his marriage wouldn't survive the Colonel's doing his living and breathing right here in his own home. What could he tell Sally about Tom Parker that would calm her down? Parker never told him anything personal. "I had no idea he ever lived in Holland," Arnold says. "I had no idea about his past, about his service in the armed forces. I had no idea how much education he had."

Eddy Arnold knew the only way to get Tom Parker out of his house was to find him an office. The answer was obvious. Eddy owned a second house in Madison on Gallatin Road, which he turned over to the Colonel in 1948. The Colonel settled in and made it his first permanent home. Somewhere along the line, ownership seems to have been transferred to the Colonel. It's unclear whether Parker actually bought the house or simply bullied it out of Arnold, though the latter would have been very much in character.

As Parker became more successful his stinginess surpassed all reasonable bounds. He was a cheapskate who treated his employees abominably. He bordered on being vicious, stating that his policy was to pay the people around him "just enough to keep them in the fold but not enough to make them feel sufficiently secure to strike out on their own." Gabe Tucker's story about Parker's meanness is a typical example. Gabe was broke when Tom Parker demanded that he accompany him on a trip to New York. Tucker protested that he barely had the money to eat.

"Tell you what I'll do. Let's make a deal. You go with me to New York and I'll pay expenses and pay you five dollars a day. We'll call it a companion fee."

They drove to New York and then through Florida, Tennessee, Louisiana, and Texas, all the way to California. Most of the time Gabe Tucker got promises instead of cash, but after a couple of grueling weeks on the road he was finally paid. As Parker handed over the cash he fixed Gabe Tucker with a cold fish stare.

"You plan to take the old man to dinner, don't you, now that you've gotten paid?"

Tucker knew that one way or another he'd be made to pay dearly if he didn't agree. It was quite likely Parker would start working on Eddy Arnold to get him fired out of the band.

"Yes, sir, Tommy. I certainly do. I'd like you to be my guest tonight for an elaborate dinner."

The Colonel bled Tucker each payday. He had to spend almost all his pay buying meals for Parker, and he came back from the trip as broke as he started. This, too, was part of the Parker style.

"Tom Parker announced one day that he and the William Morris Agency had gotten me a movie contract. Me? A movie contract? My mind boggled, but I knew Tom Parker and I swallowed hard and said, 'Fine. I'll do a movie.'

" 'Two movies,' said Tom.

" 'Two?'

" 'Yep, two. It will take you about three months and make you and the producers a lot of money. Everybody in America will have a chance to see the Tennessee Plowboy in a size bigger than life.'

" 'Three months to make two movies?' It didn't seem possible.

" 'Well, they'll be a little lean on quality and budget, but they'll be acceptable pictures.'

" 'Okay,' I said, 'two movies it is. Three, four, or five months. I don't care. I'll be lovable in all of them, but if Hollywood will gamble on me, I'll gamble on Hollywood. By the way, what am I supposed to do in movies? Dive off cliffs?'

" 'Just sing and play your guitar,' said Tom."

There's little point in trying to track down *Feudin' Rhythm* or *Hoedown.* The two films Eddy Arnold made for Columbia Pictures were dumped into the vaults in double-quick time. All Eddy Arnold could do was shrug.

"They were not great masterpieces. I just thought at the time that I just had to make a movie."

Twenty years later cruel tongues would claim Elvis Presley's run of truly awful movies was Parker's revenge on Hollywood for the failure of Eddy Arnold's film career.

This stab at Hollywood may have gone down the tubes, but Parker was making major advances in the music industry. He wasn't particularly loved—his reputation was that of a rude, conniving bumpkin who made unreasonable demands and trusted nobody— but he did have a number of powerful friends who would stand him in good stead in the future. The cornerstones of the Parker/Eddy Arnold operation were the contracts with RCA Records, and Hill & Range, the music publishers. Steven Sholes headed RCA's country music division and Parker went out of his way to cultivate the friendship. The links he forged with Sholes were sufficiently strong that when the Colonel was first looking for a record deal for Elvis, Steve Sholes was the obvious choice. The links with Jean and Julian Aberbach, who owned Hill & Range, were equally strong. They also had first offer on Elvis Presley's music publishing when the Colonel started shopping for a deal.

The Aberbach brothers were Austrian Jews who, anticipating the rise of the Nazis, had moved their family music publishing business from Berlin to New York. In the 1940s they discovered the rapidly expanding field of country music and became one of the first major song publishers involved with the Nashville crowd. Both Steve Sholes and the Aberbachs were actually working with Eddy Arnold before Parker came into the picture. Indeed, in some respects the train was well in motion when the Colonel climbed aboard. In those early days Parker wasn't strictly a "manager" in today's terms. Basically he was plying his old trade as a promoter and advance man. He really didn't start to handle the higher-level wheeling and dealing until he'd had time to familiarize himself with the workings of the music business. Even then he didn't bother to modify his coarse carny manner.

With Tom Parker at his side, however, Arnold was for the first time in his career properly paid for his personal appearances and his radio shows. The Colonel—who always collected the money—frequently got half of it before the performer even set foot on stage.

It could be said that Tom Parker's success with Eddy Arnold was more a matter of luck and fortunate timing than any innate skill on his part. Eddy Arnold was already on his way up and country music was rapidly expanding. All Colonel Tom Parker did was catch the wave and ride with it.

Parker's major contribution to Eddy Arnold's career was introducing both himself and the singer to the William Morris Agency. The agency was founded in 1898 during the heyday of vaudeville and had rapidly grown into a show business legend. William Morris himself, in 1929, had brought the Marx Brothers from Broadway to Paramount studios. The client list, taken year by year, ranges from Al Jolson to Katharine Hepburn and reads like a stage and screen hall of fame. Despite his rude country ways, Parker was able to strike up a healthy working relationship with Harry Kalcheim in the New York office. Parker, above all, felt comfortable in William Morris. At the top, it was structured so the most senior executives were able to operate almost independently. This meant that Parker could feel he was dealing with an individual rather than a faceless corporation, and this seems to have meant a lot to him. Of all the relationships that the Colonel formed at this time, the one with William Morris was by far the most important. They would look out for him all through the rise and fall of Elvis Presley. At the end, when Parker had been broken by lawsuits, William Morris took care of his affairs and gave him financial support.

In these men and organizations that had come together to manage the affairs of Eddy Arnold, the Colonel had not only a trusted team but also a winning team. It was the team that would deal with the phenomenon of Elvis.

In 1953, Eddy Arnold sent Tom Parker a telegram. "Your services are no longer required. From receipt of this wire consider yourself dismissed." The Colonel had been fired. The reasons for this abrupt severance are hazy, but the fact that Arnold could terminate the relationship with so little fuss and muss says a good deal about the contract between them. If there was any document at all, it was less than sophisticated.

The whole relationship was based on a simple handshake. According to Eddy Arnold, "We did not have a written contract. We agreed and shook hands." What is much more interesting than the nature of the agreement are the reasons it ceased to exist.

One of the great unsolved mysteries in the Colonel Tom Parker story is that people with whom he's done business will never talk about him. Even individuals who've been quite obviously victimized by Parker refuse to tell their stories. They may be clearly enraged at the mention of his name, but still they won't reveal anything but the sketchiest of details. It's as though Parker had the capacity to force a vow of silence.

There's no suggestion that he defrauded Eddy Arnold, but the parting of the ways came so suddenly, it deserves more comment than Eddy Arnold's minimal explanation: "Tom and I had conflicting personalities. Tom is a very flamboyant man and I'm a very conservative man."

The most likely reason behind the breakup is that the Colonel simply got on Eddy Arnold's nerves. Colonel Tom Parker was a loudmouthed blowhard, "a noisy man, telling stories, wearing that old battered five-gallon hat of his." Eddy Arnold describes himself as a conservative, and others depict him as a well-mannered quiet man who sought a dignified life. Parker would always be there hectoring, bullying, and bawling his opinions about everything under the sun. After a while the stress of dealing with the Colonel on a day-to-day basis just got too much to handle and Eddy Arnold baled out. Bitsy Mott suggests that the final straw with Arnold may have been Parker's more bizarre promotional tricks. "He called *Variety* in Vegas and he got a half-page ad that said: *Eddy Arnold Sold Out for a Year.* I can't remember the exact year, but after that people started calling in. This Eddy Arnold must be great. I must see if I can get him in. The Colonel answered: Yes, we just happen to have a cancellation. So he filled the rest of the year up. When you're sold out, everybody wants you."

Oscar Davis, who was managing Hank Williams at the time of Williams's death and later went on to be yet another of Parker's business buddies, pictures it even more strongly. He describes how one day Parker was laying out a two-page newspaper advertisement when Eddy walked in unexpectedly. Parker tried to conceal the layout and Arnold was furious, not only because he hated the crude, shoddy promotions but also because the Colonel was always pulling them behind his back and, as far as Arnold was concerned, tampering with his name and reputation without consent. Adding to his growing irritation was Arnold's realization that in most instances he could take care of his affairs without Parker's assistance.

Whatever the real reason for Arnold's dumping his manager, the result was that Tom Parker became that most wretched of creatures, the manager without a client. It was around this time that he palled up with Oscar Davis who was in much the same boat. His client had dropped dead on him. On the way to a show in Canton, Ohio, on New Year's Day, 1953, country genius Hank Williams had died of a combination of vodka, morphine, and chloral hydrate. The two out-of-work managers made a daily practice of hanging out in the lobby of the WSM radio building in Nashville that was the nerve center of the *Grand Ole Opry* business operation and, as a result, the nerve center of country music. If asked why, they'd probably have said they were just showing the flag, reminding the radio people and the country music wheeler-dealers who constantly passed through that they were still alive. There was also a second, sleazier reason. A number of down-at-heel hustlers, including Parker and Davis, would cluster there like scavengers, using the lobby phones and trying to create the illusion that they actually had offices in the prestigious building.

Bill Williams, who did PR for the *Opry*, had the unenviable task of driving this crew of undesirables out of the lobby. Parker was by far the most difficult to get rid of. When the free phone in the lobby was disconnected, Parker tried to weasel his way into empty studios to use the phones there. Williams may not have liked Tom Parker, but he had a grudging respect for his persistence. "He had that knack, grabbing up acts that others had passed by. He was noted, even then, as a man who had a remarkable ability to recognize talent."

Parker was back in the situation where he'd do just about anything to make a buck. In one of his best shots he worked as a publicity man for Frank C. Clement, the governor of Tennessee. He helped Clement in his campaign in 1953 and they remained good friends. The governor so appreciated Tom's support that he gave him a second honorary title: Tom Parker was now a double colonel. He also had an open door to a powerful politician; and although he instinctively knew that his future was in music and that if he stayed in politics he could never be anything more than a peripheral figure, it was still something of a comfort to know he had important friends to whom he might turn in times of trouble.

Politics might have briefly smiled, but Parker was running into stormy weather in the music business. Nothing he tried seemed to take. His best idea was to attempt to start an artists management bureau for the *Louisiana Hayride*. The *Hayride*, the main rival to the *Opry*, was less hidebound by tradition and more prepared to experiment. Where Hank Williams was too wild and drunk for the *Opry*, the *Hayride* welcomed him with open arms. Much the same would happen to Elvis Presley (although in Elvis's case, he didn't have to be drunk to be wild). Parker reasoned that a close tie-in with the *Hayride* would give him a solid base from which to fight what he saw as the *Opry*'s monopoly. Unfortunately, the marriage was never quite consummated and the Colonel had to cast around for other ideas.

Joe Frank had died on May 4, 1952, and Parker was hot to pick up the stable of acts he had represented. Joe Frank had one of the most respected artist rosters in Nashville, including Ernest Tubb, Cowboy Copas, and Red Foley. None of Frank's former clients, however, seemed anxious to replace him with Colonel Parker, so once again it was back to the drawing board.

Hank Snow was a controlled, coldly arrogant little man. Some people would call him God-fearing, others, a chilly prude. He was something of an outsider in Nashville. He was born in Nova Scotia in 1914, and just the fact of his being Canadian was enough for Nashville: He was a damn foreigner. Snow also didn't help himself. Standing barely five feet four inches tall, the singer drastically overcompensated for his diminutive size with a stiff, abrasive self-confidence and clipped, curt style of speech that actually concealed a mass of insecurities.

"I was very skeptical of myself and I didn't really have a lot of confidence because I was competing with too many of the established artists at the time."

Pushing forty, he was also a good deal older than most artists working Nashville in the early fifties. Back then, it was much more of a young man's town than it is now, and Snow's age just added to his generally unapproachable aura. Ernest Tubb was about his only friend and mentor. In 1948, Snow had relinquished a perfectly healthy career in Canada and come south to hook up with Tubb and seek his fortune in the United States. Tubb had put Snow on at the *Opry* in 1950, but the reception was scarcely more than lukewarm. Despite hits like "I'm Moving On" and "I Don't Hurt Anymore," the fortune was slow in coming. Hank Snow had claimed a lucrative niche for himself, but that was about all. Major stardom continued to elude him.

The last thing Hank Snow needed was the kind of all-enveloping management service that the Colonel offered. Snow efficiently took care of his own business, even to the point of promoting large tours, which he headlined. What he did need, however, was someone who could work with him on bookings and act as advance man on these tours. It was a tempting offer for Parker, even if it wasn't the kind of complete control he had dreamed about. At least he would be working regularly. In 1954, the Colonel became "General Manager of Hank Snow Attractions."

The relationship between Tom Parker and Hank Snow was very different from the old one with Eddy Arnold. Both were experienced businessmen and the only possible way for them to work together was in a clearly defined partnership. They created Jamboree Attractions, which at first booked out the Hank Snow road tours, but Parker, contractually free to work with other talent, kept on building the operation until, in just over a year, they represented the Carter Family, Faron Young, Slim Whitman, Ferlin Husky, Onie Wheeler and Snow's son, Jimmy Rodgers Snow. Jamboree was rapidly becoming one of the biggest independent booking agencies in the South.

A lot of people considered Oscar Davis a good deal smarter than Tom Parker. Unfortunately, they'd also tell you that he was unstable, that he didn't have the discipline and couldn't hold on to his money. Somehow it always got away from him, and he'd be forced to do promotion or advance work for Jamboree or some other outfit. During one of these stints working for Parker, he came into the office raving about a young singer he'd just seen. The kid's name was Elvis Presley and the word Davis kept repeating over and over was *sensational*. For Hank Snow, the name Elvis Presley should have had a ring of doom attached to it. Elvis Presley would be the reason why Tom Parker turned on him and bilked him out of a potential fortune of millions.

The phone was ringing as the Colonel walked into the Jamboree office, but Hank Snow was too nervous to answer it.

"Well, Colonel, I hear we've signed the kid."

The Colonel shook his head.

"Uh . . . no, that isn't exactly the way it happened."

Hank Snow's face was tight.

"What?"

"That isn't just exactly the way it happened."

"Have we signed the damn kid or not?"

"No, we haven't. I have signed him."

Snow got slowly to his feet. For an instant it looked as though he was going to punch the Colonel.

"What the hell are you talking about?"

There was something a little ludicrous about the two men facing each other. The diminutive Hank Snow, with his implausible toupee and protruding ears, was quivering like an angry bantam rooster. Parker, the complete opposite, slouched like a complacent blimp with a string tie, fish eyes, and that sour rosebud of a mouth. The Colonel made a slow, contemptuous gesture of dismissal.

"You didn't seem to want any part of this deal from the beginning. I have signed him. You don't figure in it at all."

Snow was absolutely speechless. He couldn't believe what he was hearing.

"That's a strange way to treat your partner after I went to Memphis and helped set up the deal with his mother and daddy."

Even as he spoke Snow saw how Parker had suckered him. Parker, God damn him, had set it up so Hank Snow had cut himself out of the Elvis Presley deal. He remembered the phone call some months earlier when the Colonel had put forward a crazy proposition.

"Hank," he'd said, "tell you what we'll do. You put in everything you make and I'll put in everything I make and we'll buy this boy's contract and we'll manage him. I'll get him signed some way and we'll make millions." Then the Colonel had suggested that Snow also throw in his RCA royalties. He clearly recalled how furious he'd been. Nobody messed with his record royalties. They were the heart of his income, his lifeblood. Record royalties were what kept you in your old age. Right then he'd told Parker there was nothing he wanted badly enough to risk his record royalties. Later, on tour, when Elvis Presley was constantly being booked for his road shows, Snow had made a number of disparaging remarks about the kid. What in hell was he supposed to do? What was he *supposed* to think about this greasy punk with his raucous bawling and obscene gyrations? His goddamn fans disrupted the rest of the show. In addition, they shared absolutely nothing in common, unless it was a taste for Cadillacs. It didn't mean, though, that he didn't think the kid might make a million bucks. And now Tom Parker had aced him out of it. Ideas of revenge raced through Snow's mind; then he realized it was all pointless. He just wanted to get as far from Tom Parker as possible. His voice was quiet and calm. He wasn't going to give the fat man the satisfaction of seeing him get mad.

"Let's just me and you call it all off."

The Colonel nodded. It was impossible to read what he was thinking.

"Fine. We'll just divide up our holdings in Jamboree Attractions and I'll write you a check for my part. That will be the end of it."

"Suits me. The sooner the better."

When it came down to it, the assets of Jamboree amounted to nothing more than a couple of boxes of printed stationery. Parker whipped out his checkbook and wrote Snow a check for half. Snow stormed out. Parker sat behind his desk for a few minutes, quietly smiling. Then he stood up and dumped all of the Jamboree stationery into the wastebasket. He sat down again and started to doodle on a pad. He was thinking about his new logo. Maybe a covered wagon. He'd call the new company All Star Shows.

8

The campaign the Colonel mounted to become Elvis Presley's manager had been more like a big-game hunt than a business deal. Tom Parker quite literally had stalked Elvis as though he was skittish prey. Indeed, as far as Parker was concerned, Elvis was exactly that. Somewhere deep inside, Tom Parker knew that Elvis was the biggest game in the jungle.

At first he had played it offhand. He'd let Oscar Davis do all the running. He knew Oscar's great nose for talent and let him go with it. For a few weeks Davis couldn't talk about anything else. *Elvis Presley, Elvis Presley.* Oscar wanted Parker to see Presley, he wanted him to meet with Presley. If anyone was around to notice, Parker would just grunt.

"What kind of name is Elvis Presley?"

In the end he'd let Davis bully him into getting together with the kid. This historic meeting took place in Memphis, in an unprepossessing coffee shop across the street from an auditorium. Elvis was sitting in a booth with his musicians Bill Black and Scotty Moore, as well as Judd Phillips, the brother of Sam Phillips who owned Sun Records and was releasing Elvis's first singles. Oscar Davis steered Parker over and sat him down next to Elvis. Parker's first question was blunt and to the point.

"You got a manager, son?"

Elvis explained that Scotty, the guitar player, was taking care of business, but it was really only a temporary arrangement. The kid was greasy, dressed like some Beale Street pimp, and with sideburns like a truck driver's. He also looked as though he was nervous as all hell, and his fingernails were bitten down to the quick. Parker hoped he wasn't on pills or anything. All the trouble Oscar Davis had had with Hank Williams was still too fresh in the Colonel's memory. While Parker's cold fish stare weighed up the young man, Elvis went on talking in what stopped just short of being a terrified babble. He had just given up his day job driving a truck for the Crown Electric Company and he was trying to make it full-time as a singer, but dates were hard to come by. The Colonel grunted.

"Get out of those Monday night schoolhouse dates and up where the big money is."

"Yes, sir."

Presley plainly didn't have a clue as to what the older man was talking about. The Colonel muttered something about maybe putting him on the bill of one of his promotions and began to ease his bulk out of the booth. When he was directly opposite Judd Phillips, he glanced back at Elvis.

"You know something, son, Sun Records isn't the right company for you."

Elvis looked uneasily at Judd.

"They've been real good to me, sir."

The Colonel shook his head. He knew best.

"You need a big company. Better possibilities for a guy like you on a big label."

Nobody in the booth knew whether Parker was giving advice or just taking the opportunity to be obnoxious about Sun Records in front of Sam Phillips's kin. Elvis, Bill, and Scotty watched him waddle away. They were convinced they'd been given the brush-off by the big-shot booking agent, which did nothing for their already low spirits.

After this unspectacular first meeting the Colonel had withdrawn into the shadows. He still maintained the fiction that he had no interest in Elvis. Covertly, though, he started sending out his spies. The split with Hank Snow was a long way in the future and the Colonel saw no reason why he shouldn't use all their mutual resources. Hank's son Jimmy, himself an aspiring singer, was the youngster in the Parker/Snow camp, the closest to Elvis Presley and the fans who were reportedly going crazy about him. Accordingly, Jimmy was dispatched to bring back a report to the Colonel. What was this kid with the weird name and the acne all about?

Lubbock, Texas, was a rock 'n' roll town on the New Mexico border. Buddy Holly was born there and on one occasion when Elvis played a concert there, angry youths attempted unsuccessfully to cream him for the way he got their women in an uproar. When Jimmy Snow noticed on the Elvis Presley date sheet that Elvis was playing at the Lubbock Cotton Club, he decided it was a venue at which to see Elvis at his best. At showtime, Jimmy Snow was absolutely sold.

" 'Elvis the Pelvis,' as he was already being called, sauntered onstage in black pants with pink stripes down the legs, topped off by a black jacket and pink shirt with the collar turned up to catch the ends of his hair. He grinned seductively at the girls in the front rows. Hips grinding and shaking, legs jerking and snapping, arm flailing the guitar to a fast drumbeat, he drove the women into hysterics."

Jimmy Snow seems to have been awed. He wrote, "I cannot go back."

The Colonel didn't visibly share his enthusiasm. He continued to monitor Elvis's progress and was pleased to note that, despite the kid's obvious popularity, things were not going quite according to plan. To coincide with the release of his second Sun single, "Good Rockin' Tonight," Sam Phillips had booked Elvis into his first date on the *Opry* on September 25, 1954. Elvis didn't cut it on the *Opry*. He was too wild, too "black," and altogether too unusual for the staid, straitlaced country institution. The audience looked embarrassed and Jim Denny, the manager of the *Opry*, suggested that Elvis should go back to driving a truck.

At first the rejection was a severe blow to the morale of Elvis and his sidemen, although their spirits recovered somewhat when less than a month later, they got a shot at the *Louisiana Hayride*. The *Hayride* was much more able to cope with Elvis; its listening audience was more prepared for his frenetic new sound, and *Hayride* boss Frank Page offered him a one-year contract.

Once again the Elvis bandwagon seemed to be back on the road with no help from the Colonel. Bob Neal, a well-known Memphis DJ, had taken over the management from Scotty Moore, and having negotiated the *Hayride* deal, he seemed set to ensure that Elvis fulfilled his potential. Neal proved, however, that when the chips were down, he had no potential of his own. He simply didn't have the contacts. All he could do was book Elvis onto the schoolhouse circuit. He even needed Tom Parker's help to fix a date for Elvis in Carlsbad, New Mexico, in February 1955. His final desperate throw was to put up the expense of flying Elvis, Bill, and Scotty all the way to New York to audition for Arthur Godfrey's pioneer TV hit, *Talent Scouts*. It was a long shot that didn't pay off. Arthur Godfrey turned Elvis down flat and Elvis's always fragile confidence was seriously undermined. The Colonel decided it was time to close the net.

There was a Jamboree Attractions tour going out in early 1955. It started in New Orleans and then looped around through Louisiana, Alabama, Georgia, Virginia, Tennessee, and then down to Florida. It was a huge package show that included Faron Young, the Wilburn Brothers, Slim Whitman, Martha Carson, the Davis Sisters, the Carter Sisters, Onie Wheeler, and Jimmy Snow. Hank Snow topped the bill. The Colonel decided this would be an ideal moment to debut Elvis in one of his promotions and at the same time demonstrate to the kid just how Jamboree Attractions went about doing things. Elvis Presley was booked into the tour.

Bearing in mind that Parker was always more than happy to kill two birds with one stone, it's highly likely that he had more than one motive for putting Elvis on this particular tour. Elvis was already getting a reputation for disrupting package shows. He brought in his own fans, who didn't give a damn about acts like Faron Young or the Davis Sisters. Before Elvis came on, they screamed and hollered for him, and while he was on they went so crazy that there was no way that a fiddle, guitar, and accordion band could follow him. Parker must have been aware that placing Elvis in the middle of this tour would goose up the other performers and prove a personal affront to both Hank Snow's ego and his Holy Joe conservatism. Not only was

Parker closing in on Elvis, but into the bargain he was getting to play one of his merciless practical jokes on a whole tour *and* pushing Hank Snow into a number of public displays of anger at, and disapproval of, Elvis, his fans, his music, and his act. As far as owning a piece of Elvis was concerned, Hank Snow was unwittingly cutting the ground out from under his own feet. With the Colonel, deviousness came straight from his not inconsiderable gut.

By April 1955, the time was ripe for a second meeting with Elvis Presley. This time, however, Parker allowed Elvis to come to him. Elvis had heard that the Colonel had booked him into the tour and wanted to thank him personally.

"I've heard a lot about you, Colonel, and I want you to know that it's very nice of you to have me on this show. Me and my band appreciate the work. You just tell us what you want us to do, and we'll sure do it. Just the way you want it."

The hook was in; the Colonel put on his blandest smile and complimented Elvis on his black outfit with lavender trim. Elvis looked relieved and then blurted out exactly what the Colonel wanted to hear: "Colonel, I sure wish my mama and daddy were here to meet you."

"Well, son, maybe we can arrange that this tour. I sure do want to meet your folks. I hear they are wonderful, God-fearing folks."

The Colonel's background research had shown him that Elvis was the only child of a doting mother and a somewhat shiftless father. Since the kid was still legally a minor, the parents' approval would be crucial in any deal. He didn't see that the father would be any trouble, but the mother might need a bit of softening up before she was won over.

In the spring of 1955 the Colonel paid a courtesy

call at the Presley home on Getwell Street in Memphis. As was his habit, Parker stretched the short visit into an all-day stay as he talked and talked. Over and over, like a dog worrying at a bone, he told the Presleys how much he admired their son and his million-dollar talent, and over and over he projected how that talent could be turned into a million dollars in hard cash. As he'd expected, the father was no trouble. The dollar signs lit up in his eyes and never went out. The mother, Gladys, wasn't convinced. She looked so much like her son, yet where he was soft and malleable, she was hard and distrustful. It was a hardness Parker had seen many times before, a hardness born of hard times and depression.

The couple seemed uncomfortable with the bulky, balding man who never stopped talking. The mother was protective of the kid in the first place, and she didn't like him playing this rhythm and blues stuff. He was working too hard and doing too much traveling. He was pale and he looked tired all the time. Gladys knew that her boy wasn't eating or sleeping enough. The Colonel immediately turned this to his advantage. Without directly criticizing Bob Neal, he gave the impression that if Elvis was in his care, he certainly wouldn't be working him so hard.

Gladys still wasn't convinced, and Parker knew he would have to bring up the big guns. Hank Snow, believing that he was cut in on the Parker deal, was sent over to give Gladys the treatment. Hank Snow wasn't a fat wheeler-dealer with weird eyes and a baggy suit. Hank Snow was a big star, almost a household word. He was so clean, he squeaked when he walked. Between his own God-fearing image, his rhinestone suit, and the custom Cadillac in which he arrived, he all but convinced Gladys that he and the

Colonel, as Jamboree Attractions, would be the ideal team to take care of her son's future.

It seemed it wasn't possible for Colonel Tom Parker to do any kind of major deal without somehow introducing an element of the bizarre. In the matter of signing Elvis Presley, Parker used another crony—the country comedian Whitey Ford, who worked as the "Duke of Paducah"—to administer the coup de grace to Gladys Presley. Even Elvis was brought into the con game, which the Colonel outlined as if it were a military exercise. Elvis was playing in Little Rock, Arkansas, and since it was a relatively short drive from Memphis, Gladys and Vernon had been invited to the show. The Duke of Paducah was to stick close to Gladys and apply overkill soft soap.

"When we get to Little Rock, I'm going to stay out of sight. You will have the dressing room with Elvis. Elvis is gonna bring his mother and father in there, then Elvis is gonna say, 'Now Mama, the Duke here has been with Parker for a long time. He knows him from A to Z. He'll tell you anything you want to know about him.' That's your cue to soft-soap the old lady."

The Colonel busied himself elsewhere in the theater, while in the dressing room it was smooth to the point of being greasy. In the thick rural accent he used on the *Grand Ole Opry,* the Duke explained what a Christian gentleman the Colonel was, how he was going to make Elvis a star, and how Elvis would make so much money, he'd never be able to spend it. Gladys, not as dumb as they took her to be, asked a couple of pointed questions. She wanted to know to what church the Christian gentleman belonged, and most important of all, how could Elvis possibly sign with this Colonel when he'd "already signed with Mr. Neal and Mr. Phillips and the radio station down there in Shreveport." The Duke burst out with a from-the-belly rolling chuckle. "Time the Colonel gets through with all these people, not only will Elvis be free but them folk will be bragging because they once worked for Elvis Presley." Right on cue, Elvis came through the door and introduced the Colonel. At that point Gladys must have known she was outflanked. Elvis wanted to go with the Colonel, Vernon wanted Elvis to go with the Colonel, and then all these people kept coming around and talking at her, people she'd only previously heard talking on the radio. It was all too much. She didn't trust the Colonel, but she couldn't fight the whole world.

Parker knew that once Gladys had caved in, there was really only the mopping up left to do. Manager Bob Neal was the last obstacle, and Parker leveled with him as much as his psychological makeup would allow him to. He explained that RCA and Hill & Range were moving toward putting up major money to buy Elvis's recording and publishing contracts. Neal had no control over any of this and if he fought it, he would eventually be aced out. If he cooperated, the Colonel would cut him in for a slice of his commission. Bob Neal was smart enough to know that a slice was better than nothing. He knew in his heart that he didn't have what it took to manage someone with Elvis's potential. He went back to his radio show and record store probably quite relieved that he'd come out of the encounter so painlessly.

The field was now clear for the Colonel to present Elvis with a most extraordinary contract.

Special Agreement between ELVIS PRESLEY, known as artist, his guardians, Mr. and/or Mrs. Presley, and his manager, MR. BOB NEAL, of Memphis, Tennessee, hereinafter referred to as the Party of the First Part, and COL. THOMAS A PARKER and/or

HANK SNOW ATTRACTIONS of Madison, Tennessee, hereinafter known as the Party of the Second Part, this date, August 15, 1955.

COL. PARKER is to act as a special adviser to ELVIS PRESLEY and BOB NEAL, for the period of one year and two one-year options for the sum of two thousand five hundred dollars per year, payable in five payments of five hundred dollars each, to negotiate and assist in any way possible the buildup of ELVIS PRESLEY as an artist. Col. Parker will be reimbursed for any out-of-pocket expenses for traveling, promotion, advertising as approved by ELVIS PRESLEY and his manager.

As a special concession to Col. Parker, ELVIS PRESLEY is to play 100 personal appearances within one year for the special sum of two hundred dollars, including his musicians.

In the event that negotiations come to complete standstill and ELVIS PRESLEY and his manager and associates decide to free-lance, it is understood that Col. Parker will be reimbursed for the time and expenses involved in trying to negotiate the association of these parties and that he will have first call on a number of cities, as follows, at the special rate of one hundred seventy-five dollars per day for the first appearance, and two hundred fifty dollars for the second appearance and three hundred fifty dollars for the third appearance: San Antonio, El Paso, Phoenix, Tucson, Albuquerque, Oklahoma City, Denver, Wichita Falls, Wichita, New Orleans, Mobile, Jacksonville, Pensacola, Tampa, Miami, Orlando, Charleston, Greenville, Spartanburg, Asheville, Knoxville, Roanoke, Richmond, Norfolk, Washington D.C., Philadelphia, Newark, New York, Pittsburgh, Chicago, Omaha, Milwaukee, Minneapolis, St. Paul, Des Moines, Los Angeles, Amarillo,

Lubbock, Houston, Galveston, Corpus Christi, Las Vegas, Reno, Cleveland, Dayton, Akron, and Columbus.

Col. Parker is to negotiate all renewals on existing contracts.

Even as an interim measure that could only anticipate the departure of Bob Neal, the contract was a lulu. Although Parker was ostensibly hiring on with Elvis Presley and Bob Neal as a consultant, there isn't a single word in the contract regarding what Parker would do for Presley and Neal except the ultimately nebulous "to negotiate and assist in the buildup of Elvis Presley as an artist." As soon as he signed the contract, Elvis found himself owing Parker twenty-five hundred dollars and, worse still, was in hock for a hundred cut-price gigs. Even if the buildup of Elvis Presley as an artist was relatively modest during the first year, the asking price could be anything up to ten times more than the two hundred bucks Parker would be paying him. The kicker was in the final paragraph. If the Colonel was going to negotiate all renewals on all existing contracts, he had complete control. The agreement was virtually open-ended, and he could take it in any direction he wanted. There was even a fast sideswipe that would enable him to take out Hank Snow anytime he wanted: "Col. Thomas A. Parker *and/or* Hank Snow Attractions" meant that it could become *just* Col. Thomas A. Parker whenever Col. Tom Parker decided that Hank Snow was redundant.

In many respects the contract was a microcosm of Parker's overall view of the world. Don't let the sucker ask what the Colonel was going to do for him, just make it clear what the sucker was going to do for the Colonel. The inescapable conclusion has to be drawn that the Colonel, although fully expecting to make millions on Elvis Presley's talent, looked on Elvis as a sucker from the very start.

Parker had one more task for Hank Snow before he dropped the bomb on him. Snow had sold healthy numbers of records for RCA and had a good deal of influence with Steve Sholes, the director of country music. Despite his personal distaste for Elvis's performances, Snow agreed to talk up Presley to Sholes and to lay the foundations for a possible future deal. Although Parker fully intended to cut Snow out of the Presley management arrangement, the Colonel had no qualms about exploiting Snow and his contacts up to the very last.

Parker was homing in on RCA because it was the major label he already knew through Eddy Arnold and Hank Snow. When Sam Phillips finally realized he had neither the capital nor the organization to press and ship the quantities of records that Elvis would undoubtedly sell in the future, he decided to sell out his interests in the young performer. Now the Colonel was in the driver's seat, and he wanted to go in just one direction. His best idea was to re-create the business setup that had existed around Eddy Arnold. RCA would be the record company and the Aberbach brothers with Hill & Range would handle the music publishing.

There were other offers. Decca came up with just five thousand dollars while Dot went as high as seventy-five hundred. Even Ahmet Ertegun and his partner, Jerry Wexler, with their fledgling Atlantic label, expressed an interest. It's possible that if Parker had listened to them, history might have been changed. Ertegun and Wexler were founding a music industry dynasty with black acts like Ray Charles, Joe Turner, and the Drifters. Part of their strength was that they let their artists go their own creative ways without attempting to dilute their work for the mainstream pop audience. If they'd been handling Elvis's recording, the world might have been spared such atrocities as "Daddy Big Boots" or "Do the Clam." Unfortunately, Atlantic and all other possible contenders were scared off by Parker's first asking price of fifty thousand dollars.

Steve Sholes wasn't too crazy about the fifty-grand price himself. The best that RCA could come up with was half that figure, and even for this twenty-five thousand, Sholes had to put his own neck on the rails. He had to guarantee personally that the advance would be recouped within the first year of the contract. In addition to the RCA offer, the Aberbach brothers would come in with a further fifteen thousand for Elvis's song publishing. This maneuver actually tied Elvis to Hill & Range *for the rest of his life,* but it didn't overly concern the Colonel. At the time, he was only interested in raising enough money to secure total control of Elvis Presley.

With offers of forty thousand in place, it was now time for a few days of sleight-of-hand. Parker went to Sam Phillips and wrote him a personal check for five thousand dollars, telling him that if he wasn't "back with the cash Tuesday noon, you've got a gift of five thousand dollars." This was the advance payment of an agreed-upon thirty-five thousand dollars. A further five thousand would go to Elvis himself. For this, the Colonel would own Elvis's Sun contract and would be able to turn around and sell it—keeping his own tight strings on the deal—to RCA and Hill & Range.

When the papers were signed, Colonel Tom Parker as good as owned Elvis Presley. When Elvis was twenty-one, on January 8, 1956, Parker came up with a new contract for Elvis to sign as an adult. It ratified all previous contracts and agreed that Elvis would pay the Colonel twenty-five percent of his earnings plus reimburse him for all expenses. In return, Parker would be his "sole and exclusive adviser, personal representative, and manager."

There was nothing else to do apart from cut out Hank Snow, which Parker ruthlessly accomplished. The one puzzle in the whole dubious business was why Hank Snow accepted Parker's double-dealing with so little fuss. Why didn't he sue? A good lawyer could almost certainly have broken Parker's first, homemade contract. As time passed it must have been abundantly clear that Snow had been cheated out of millions. Didn't he want to exact some kind of revenge on his former partner? All accounts describe him as an angry man but, paradoxically, a man who seemed afraid to speak out. After Eddy Arnold, Snow is the second of the Colonel's former clients who refuses to talk—the second clam-up. On occasions, he has hinted he has the goods on Parker, but he has always stopped short of telling the whole story. Today, Hank Snow is still an angry man who hasn't found the right weapon to attack Parker, even after thirty years. But he has sold his story to a national magazine. "I had the lawyers read the story and we made an agreement with the magazine. They take the full liability. Now my hands are tied. I don't want to be disloyal to the agreement."

It can only be supposed that when the Colonel contracted with a client, he liked to have something on him. The ideal situation would be to be able to control him with the threat of disgrace, scandal, or prosecution. It wouldn't have been beyond the Colonel's devious nature to ensure his own security by knowing where the bodies, if any, were buried.

9

Nineteen fifty-six was the year of Elvis Presley. He was suddenly thrust into the living rooms of America, and America responded by going into various kinds of shock. He was adored by teenagers, denounced by evangelists, and lampooned by *Mad*. Most important of all, he was on television. In a single year he had worked his way through the Dorsey Brothers' *Stage Show*, *The Milton Berle Show*, and *The Steve Allen Show*, appearing finally on what was then the pinnacle of entertainment—*The Ed Sullivan Show*. In fact, the reception was so great that Sullivan brought Elvis back for two additional outings. It was an ironic development, since the older showman's first reaction had been to swear that he wouldn't touch Elvis with a ten-foot pole. Whether they loved or hated him, the coast-to-coast TV audience couldn't ignore Elvis Presley. He was talked about, written about—a true phenomenon. No working comedian could afford to leave a crack about Presley out of his act.

Tom Parker, too, had hit a pinnacle. As far as he could see, he'd finally built the better mousetrap. He had the hottest star in show business, so didn't that make him the hottest manager, the hottest hustler, on the nation's midway? Elvis's records seemed to have taken up permanent residence at the top of the charts. His live appearances were causing riots and Hollywood was beating a path to his door. There was nothing to do but cut deals and watch the money roll in. Even if he did make a slip in this new jungle of the big time, he had the men from the William Morris Agency to watch his back. As with Eddy Arnold, Parker had taken Elvis directly to William Morris and they remained his agents, booking his concerts, until the day he died. RCA, Hill & Range, and William Morris—Parker had his heavyweight wagons drawn into a circle.

One of the sweetest deals was with Harry Saperstein to build a gigantic souvenir industry. Within a matter of weeks the Presley likeness was on lunch boxes, trading cards, pencil cases, and record players. There was an Elvis stuffed doll, an Elvis four-string plastic guitar with the automatic Hold-A-Chord—"strum immediately." According to Parker's philosophy, merchandising was about as good as it got. It was being given money for doing absolutely nothing and nothing appealed more absolutely to the old carny in Parker.

Indeed, you could maybe get the Colonel out of the carny, but no way could you get the carny out of the Colonel. On some levels his carny background manifested itself in simple idiosyncratic quirks that were cute and made good copy. Good ole Tom was just a sucker for the smell of the crowd. He couldn't resist strapping on a change apron and hawking souvenirs or pictures to the lines outside a Presley concert. If an open-air show was threatened by rain, he could spend all day fussing over the possibilities of the umbrella concession. He also liked to bring his old carny buddies into the operation when and where he could. One of these was his old traveling partner, Jack Kaplan: "Me and Parker used to sell seats, programs, and pictures. All the people came in, but nobody knew who we were."

Other manifestations of his carny spirit were a lot less quaint. The mean streak in Parker saw kids who were idolizing his client as a multitude of marks who only deserved to be shortchanged and humiliated. Evidence of this bent was the disgraceful support acts on the Elvis Presley stage shows. Parker had hired another old pal, Chicago promoter Al Dvorin, whose assignment was to maintain a steady supply of weird-through-dreadful bargain basement acts—straight from the classifieds in *Variety*—to open for Presley. There were acrobats, jugglers, tired nightclub comedians, and broken-down country singers. There was even Frankie Connors, an old-time Irish tenor Parker had known in Tampa. The crowds simply howled for Elvis through all these unfortunates' attempts at putting on a show, and then went berserk when Elvis finally hit the stage.

During a stint in Chicago, this technique of Parker's achieved complete tastelessness. He sent Jack Kaplan to the Morrison Hotel, a well-known carny hangout, to round up all the midgets and dwarfs he could find. They were paraded for photographers, presented with Elvis souvenirs and a set of official documents, and formally designated the Elvis Presley Midget Fan Club.

The cynical claimed Parker employed the freak

show to open for Elvis because it ultimately made Elvis look good. According to this theory, Parker was petrified of inadvertently giving exposure to a new and possibly greater talent. A second and maybe more plausible explanation was that initially Parker was simply being cheap, but when he saw the results of his cheapness, he also found to his delight that he was putting one over on the hysterical teens in the audience, and this that motivated him to greater and greater excesses of bad taste.

Paul Wilder, the small-town reporter who used to write the lost-doggy stories for the Tampa *Tribune,* was another old-timer whom Parker trusted always to be on his side. When *TV Guide* was agitating for an Elvis interview, Parker announced it could only be conducted by Wilder. It would be held in Lakeland, Florida, in August 1956. As the negotiations continued, the interview concept expanded. In addition to the printed interview—"The Plain Truth About Elvis Presley"—there would also be a limited edition giveaway record of edited highlights, as well as a direct message from Elvis to his fans, which would be broadcast over selected radio stations, with local DJs reading Paul Wilder's questions from a printed sheet. (Only five hundred of these special 45's were pressed. Today they change hands for around five thousand dollars each.)

When the appointed day arrived, the Colonel appeared to have the whole interview under tight control, even answering a few questions himself. He seemed to be going all out for the picture of modesty: "Presley was a star from the first day he ever started going into show business." All the Colonel had to do was to hold out for his price. "I lost some deals and gained others by waiting." When Paul Wilder asked him what his greatest value to Elvis was, his answer was a simple two words: "My experience."

As to anything connected with Parker's origins, the tape is not particularly revealing. His accent is a little strange. He has a certain amount of trouble with his *th*'s and *r*'s and words like *exploit.* Nobody, however, seemed to have cause to doubt that Parker was anything other than what he'd always claimed to be, least of all Elvis Presley himself: "Colonel Parker is the kind of person I've been raised with."

Parker had good reason to want to control the media. Already a number of unfortunate stories were surfacing about the Colonel's hustling past. The favorite concerned his involvement with the distribution of a patent medicine called Hadacol. The supreme irony was that of all the tales that could have been told about Parker, this particular one seems to lack any foundation in fact.

Certainly Hadacol existed. It had been invented and brewed by a Louisiana state senator by the name of Dudley J. LeBlanc, known affectionately as "Uncle Dud." Uncle Dud had mounted a massive advertising campaign to build the sales of his patent tonic into a multimillion-dollar concern. His claims were as outrageous as his image. Hadacol would cure coughs, sniffles, rheumatism, and the common cold. It would even "make old people feel young." The campaign culminated in a lavish Hadacol road show that toured the country and starred such topflight acts as Mickey Rooney, Minnie Pearl, Connie Boswell, Ernest Tubb, and even heavyweight champ Jack Dempsey. In addition, there was a chorus of bathing beauties, a Dixieland band and a twenty-piece orchestra. To get in to see the show, all you had to do was to produce a Hadacol box top. Ultimately, however, a number of states banned the tonic because its ingredients fluctuated from batch to batch, and Uncle Dud was forced out of the business.

On the surface, it would seem that the promotion of Hadacol was exactly the kind of grandiose piece of trickery with which Parker might have been involved. He might even have boasted about it, and indeed a number of people, including the arch gossip columnist Louella Parsons, made exactly that connection. During the time that Uncle Dud was in court, Elvis Presley's manager found himself being referred to as "Colonel Tom (Hadacol) Parker." It was something that infuriated Parker and if anyone wanted to be permanently banished from the Colonel's good graces, they only had to mention the name. Under other circumstances it might have been possible to assume that the Colonel's sensitivity about Hadacol was the product of a guilty conscience. In this instance, however, in the late forties and early fifties, Parker simply doesn't appear to have had time to become involved in the Hadacol scam except in the most peripheral way—for instance, booking Minnie Pearl or Ernest Tubb into the Hadacol road show. If he had, it seems highly likely that Gabe Tucker, Bitsy Mott, or Jack Kaplan would have known about it.

It was like something out of a nightmare. The strings of Freddy Martin's orchestra sawed in and out of the arrangement. The drummer, playing with brushes, had trouble finding a backbeat. The piano player could honky-tonk through, but he and Bill and Scotty weren't enough to hold the whole mess together. Elvis, his nerves kicking in, didn't know what to do except work harder. He shook and yelled and sweated and the middle-aged gamblers who'd rather have been watching Patti Page or, better still, a stripper, were leaving in droves. The agony was finally over and the last song staggered to an end. Elvis was too upset to remember Freddy Martin's name when it was time to introduce him. Martin, the longtime Vegas pro, put a show-biz face on it that was little more than a thinly disguised sneer.

"Ladies and gentlemen, you'll have to excuse Mr. Presley for not remembering my name. I'm new in the business."

When he came off stage, Elvis was white with fury. He couldn't bring himself to speak to the Colonel. The Colonel was responsible for the disaster: Playing the New Frontier Hotel in Las Vegas in the spring of 1956 had been the Colonel's idea. Elvis hadn't wanted to do it, his instincts told him that he shouldn't get away from his loyal teenage audience. Most of his crowd was too young even to be allowed inside a Las Vegas casino. He'd let the Colonel sell it to him. The Colonel had explained how T. W. Richardson, the president of the New Frontier, had been badgering him for weeks to let him be the first to present Elvis Presley in Vegas, how Las Vegas was where it was at, Vegas was prestige and a run in a major lounge would make important people sit up and take notice. The final and most persuasive argument was that Las Vegas was the gravy train.

"Wait until you hear the deal I made with Richardson."

"What's the deal, Admiral?"

"He's giving us $17,500 a week."

Elvis was stunned.

"Good Lord."

There was really no more to say.

The next day the newspapers reported the extent of the damage. "Elvis Presley wound up his first nightclub date, a two-week stand at the New Frontier Hotel. Elvis was somewhat like a jug of corn liquor at a champagne party. He hollered songs like 'Blue Suede Shoes' and 'Tutti Frutti' and his body movements were embarrassingly direct. Most of the high rollers breathed a sigh of relief when his set ended." After two weeks, Parker tore up the contract and they left Las Vegas with their tails between their legs.

According to *Time,* Parker attempted a final piece of hick bravura before he departed. He refused to accept a check from the New Frontier. "No check is good. Some are pretty good but they got an atom bomb testing place out there in the desert. What if some feller pressed the wrong button?"

It was one of the first times that Parker demonstrated his inability to improvise. He couldn't adapt to new situations and new methods. Over and over he would make it plain that he felt he'd done all of his learning. He'd received an education on the streets of Breda, in the U.S. Army, and in the carnival. That was all a man needed. In taking Elvis to Las Vegas, Parker had shown that he could perceive no real difference between Elvis Presley and the cowboy crooners with whom he'd previously dealt. He imagined he could handle Elvis Presley in exactly the same way as he had Eddy Arnold. He couldn't see the first hairline cracks of the generation gap. His best plan was to ease the boy away from this wild-man music that Parker didn't trust, felt threatened by, and almost certainly wished would go away. Every chance he got, he nudged Elvis in the direction of the safe and the conventional. It always proved to be a retrograde move.

In 1956, though, Elvis wasn't quite as agreeable to being nudged as he would be in later life. Parker didn't have him under complete control, and Elvis was capable of getting mad as hell and refusing to take it. Still smarting from what had been his first public humiliation since he'd been hailed as a star, Elvis was dispatched on an extensive and grueling road tour. After a while the strain began to show. The gilded twenty-one-year-old rock prince blamed it all on his paunchy, middle-aged manager. In turn, Parker threw a fit and took to his bed. It was an almost maternal show of guilt-inducing ill health that Parker would repeat many times in the future, and it clearly worked on the mom-obsessed Presley.

Bitsy Mott recounts: "It was so bad, we had to put him in bed for a while in the hotel and call a doctor. He was upset with the situation about Elvis because Elvis was getting a little belligerent. He didn't want to show up on time. The Colonel wouldn't go to the hospital; he stayed in bed for two or three days." Parker seems to have played this first deathbed scene to the hilt. He confided to Marie: "I feel I only have a short time to live." At one point he even attempted to dump Elvis. Bitsy Mott continues: "As a matter of fact, he offered him for sale. He told Oscar Davis, who was our advance man at the time, that he could have Elvis for one hundred thousand dollars. It was quite a bit of money for a young entertainer. Oscar couldn't raise the money and the word had gotten out on Elvis being a little hard to handle."

As the days passed, Parker's resolve seemed to stiffen. His strength returned. Says Mott, "They gave him some medication. He was fine after that. He took it easy for a while." While taking it easy, though, Parker was also laying his long-term plans. If he was to avoid having to have further heart attacks, he would be forced to place Elvis on a much shorter leash. He didn't want his moneymaker snapping at him each time he got pissed off. As far as Parker was concerned, control was a matter of two factors—surveillance and isolation. The first thing Parker needed was a spy in the Elvis entourage, the now clearly definable Memphis Mafia. He wanted to know what Elvis was doing and thinking the moment that he did or thought it. The second thing was an ongoing process: Elvis was already pretty isolated by the fan hysteria he created. What the Colonel wanted was to distance him farther from anyone who might introduce subversive ideas or, above all, anyone who might criticize Parker and his methods. This scheming on the Colonel's part undoubtedly sowed the early seeds of a nightmare that would grow and grow until it destroyed both star and manager.

One set of companions was particularly threatening to Parker. When Elvis first visited Hollywood for any protracted stay, he naturally gravitated toward the brat pack of the time. In the mid-fifties it was the clique of "rebel" actors and actresses—Nick Adams, Natalie Wood, Russ Tamblyn, Dennis Hopper, and Sal Mineo—who had recently lost their leading light with the auto-wreck death of James Dean. Apart from being budding stars and frequent names in the fan magazines, they were also young professionals with managers and agents of their own, and this scared the hell out of Parker. All they had to do was to sit around comparing notes with Elvis and he'd quickly discover that the twenty-five percent of his income that he gave to Parker plus the ten percent he gave to William Morris on all his movie and concert earnings was far in excess of the norm. It wouldn't take too much of this kind of conversation before Elvis took a long, hard look at his friend and manager and their whole business relationship. The next thing you'd know, Elvis would be on the phone to some interfering Beverly Hills lawyer and the fat would definitely be in the fire. At home, on the road, and particularly in Hollywood, Elvis had to be kept away from outsiders who might expose him to dangerous ideas.

On the home front, Colonel Tom's first move was to recruit the loyal and infinitely long-suffering brother-in-law, Bitsy Mott. He could take care of the home front. Parker called him in for a meeting. "Bitsy, I need someone to stay with Elvis all the time. Instead of selling pictures and programs, would you like to take over as security man? Be with Elvis? Your job is Elvis. You go everywhere with him." The message is implicit: The security Parker was talking about was his own. Mott's assignment was to report on Elvis, to guard him from interlopers and keep him on the straight and narrow as defined by Tom Parker. In Hollywood, the Colonel looked for the weakest link. Nick Adams was a perfectly adequate young actor, but he constantly hung on to someone else's coattails. First it was James Dean, and when Dean was gone he looked in the direction of becoming Elvis's shadow. Tom Parker instinctively recognized that Adams's insecurity was the kind with which he could do business. Parker initially flattered and befriended Adams and when the time was right, covertly hired him as his eyes and ears in the Hollywood entourage. Adams was to report back to the Colonel and steer Elvis away from the possible subversives.

Within a year the Colonel appeared to have achieved most of his objectives. He had Elvis so solidly sandbagged that he could get away with forbidding him even to have private conversations with the people who wrote his songs. Mike Stoller, of the Leiber and Stoller song team who'd given Elvis "Jailhouse Rock," "Loving You," and literally dozens of other classics, once knocked on the door of Elvis's Los Angeles hotel suite. Elvis greeted him with nervous embarrassment, explaining that the Colonel would never approve a one-on-one meeting.

The Colonel's psychological stick came with a considerable material carrot: The Colonel was going to put his boy in the movies. He'd attempted the same thing with Eddy Arnold and it had been an all but abject failure. This time around, he was going to see that nothing went wrong.

Hal Wallis was ten years older than Tom Parker. He'd been in the movie business since 1922, when he'd moved from Chicago to Los Angeles and become the manager of the Garrick movie theater. In 1928 he was made chief production executive of Warner Bros., and fourteen years later he left Warners to form his own independent Hal B. Wallis Productions. By the time he came to Parker's attention in 1956, he had close to four hundred films to his credit, including *Little Caesar, Casablanca, The Maltese Falcon,* and even *Kings Row,* with Ronald Reagan. Wallis's hit of the moment was Anna Magnani in the screen adaptation of Tennessee Williams's *Rose Tattoo.* Hal Wallis was, however, nothing if not catholic in his tastes. Early in 1956 he had noticed Elvis Presley on the Dorsey Brothers' show. "Early the next morning, I telephoned Tom Parker in New York and told him that I wanted to sign Elvis to a film contract. The Colonel was aware of me and my work and listened. Clearly counting the dollars in advance, he cautiously revealed that Elvis would 'probably' be out on the Coast soon and would 'consider the possibility of a meeting.' "

Colonel Tom may have been counting the dollars in advance, but he wasn't about to fall for the first overture. In fact, when Hal Wallis called, Parker couldn't fall for any overture. It was February 1956, and Parker had yet to get Elvis's signature on a contract. Technically, he wasn't his manager. As usual, he went through a series of maneuvers he considered the epitome of shrewdness. Hal Wallis's productions were distributed on an exclusive basis by Paramount. Parker had Elvis play a series of Paramount-controlled theaters through Florida and up the East Coast. While keeping Wallis at arm's length, the Colonel organized the mailing of thousands of letters from fans begging to see their idol on the screen. He even did some checking on Wallis's credentials. In Los Angeles supervising Elvis's spot on *The Milton Berle Show,* Parker asked Berle if "this Hal Wallis" was any good as a producer. Berle reassured him that Wallis was one of the most seasoned, respected, and successful producers in the world. But still Parker continued to stall. The tactics may have been gauche, but ironically they had exactly the right effect on Wallis.

"I telephoned, telegraphed, and harassed Colonel Parker until he finally brought Elvis to Hollywood for a meeting and a screen test." Elvis arrived at Paramount studios on April 1. The test thoroughly satisfied Wallis, and in the next weeks a contract was drawn up and signed. Elvis would make three pictures for $100,000, $150,000, and $200,000, respectively. Hal Wallis wasn't, however, the only game in town. Parker had also inked a similar two-picture deal with David Weisbart at 20th Century-Fox. The combination of the two studios meant Elvis would have four movies in front of the public before the end of 1958—*Love Me Tender, Loving You, Jailhouse Rock,* and *King Creole* —and at the end of that time, Wallis would still have one picture in hand on his contract.

Although, in style and taste, miles ahead of the fun 'n' sun quickies that Elvis ground out in the sixties, the first four Presley pictures were by no means masterpieces. They were put together with speed and economy. Elvis still had time in 1957 to do two major concert tours, one in the Northeast in the spring and the second through the Pacific Northwest in September. The public didn't know it at the time but this swing through Vancouver, Spokane, Tacoma, Seattle, and Portland would be Elvis's last major tour for well over a decade. The Colonel's plans for his boy didn't include playing rock 'n' roll shows in ballparks.

One sorry footnote to Parker's scheme to wean Elvis away from rock 'n' roll was his alienating Elvis's original musicians, Scotty Moore and Bill Black. The guitarist and the bass player had been with Elvis from the very start. They had auditioned with him at Sun Records, had driven thousands of miles on back-road tours, and had been in no small way responsible for the sound of the initial hits. Yet, with Parker in charge of the purse strings, when the gravy started to flow they saw none of it. At the height of Presleymania they were being paid a flat two hundred dollars a week and were expected to pay their own touring expenses. They received no record royalties and no shares in the increasingly enormous profits, even though Scotty Moore had been Elvis's first manager. By the end of the Northwest trip they'd have had more than enough of Parker's methods and the constant money problems they created. Both men quit. Parker most probably didn't give a damn. If Elvis wasn't going to tour, why should he need musicians? Parker was not only saving the operation four hundred a week, he was also silencing two more voices from the pre-Parker past. His control over Elvis tightened one more notch. It almost certainly never occurred to Parker that in separating Presley from Black and Moore, he was breaking up one of the most powerfully creative trios in the history of popular music. Trio-schmio! As far as Parker was concerned, rock 'n' roll was just another freak show. The sooner it ran its course, the better.

The big mystery in the relationship between Parker and Presley was how a seemingly cheap, petty individual like Colonel Tom could exert almost total control over a man who for years was the world's most powerful male sex symbol. (Indeed, a research project in the early seventies discovered that Elvis Presley was the second most recognized person on the planet. The only individual recognized by more people, worldwide, on all continents, was Mao Tse-tung.)

The easiest and most often quoted explanation was that if Presley ever complained, Parker had an unassailable answer. Hadn't he made Elvis the foremost entertainer in the world? Hadn't he made him a multimillionaire? So what was there to complain about? Trust the Colonel, the Colonel knows best. Unfortunately, on closer examination this argument proves so facile that it defies logic. Elvis may have been no Einstein, but he was certainly smart enough to notice Parker's obvious blunders and his steadfast refusal ever to leave the United States except for brief excursions into Canada and Mexico. Another explanation, which almost deserves a place in the *National Enquirer*, is that Parker had Elvis hypnotized. There is plenty of evidence that the Colonel was a competent carny hypnotist, but even Svengali would have had a hard time maintaining mind control for more than twenty years. To find something closer to the truth we have to examine the personalities of both men and the way they'd automatically interreact.

According to the Colonel's scale of values, Elvis was not only the layer of golden eggs, he was also the ultimate mark. Parker knew the traditional hustler psychology for dealing with marks. You found their weakness and you went after it with a hammer. In the carny, the weakness was usually something as simple as lust or greed. In the case of Elvis Presley, it was much more complicated. There was no time like the first couple of years of stardom to observe Elvis's very basic schizophrenia. Onstage he was a shimmying fiend, sexual anger in pink-and-black cat clothes. Out of the spotlight he was the complete reverse, a greasy, painfully shy kid with bad acne scars. He was obsessed with his mother and close to obsequious with his elders. There were even moments onstage when the weak, vulnerable side surfaced for a moment. Watching video tapes of the Dorsey Brothers' show (where he's not cut off from the waist down), it's possible to see an instant of bemused bewilderment after a particularly violent bump and grind. Did *I* really do *that*?

Confronted with such an obvious emotional mess—in this context, the sexual limitations that Albert Goldman delineates in his biography *Elvis* start to make a little more sense; maybe Elvis's full sexuality only came out onstage—the Colonel knew exactly what to do. He separated the two halves. It was simple divide-and-rule. The embarrassed, vulnerable side could be easily intimidated. The indomitable Gladys Presley had already set the patterns of domination; all Parker had to do was to gradually transfer the near servile loyalty and dependence from mom to manager. The wild boy in the spotlight was a bit more of a problem. As far as Parker was concerned, this one had to be tamed.

In his desire to tone down the public Elvis, Parker admirably demonstrated his complete lack of perception. It wasn't a matter of morality that motivated him to push his client in the direction of conservatism. Parker had seen too much sleaze to be outraged by Elvis and his pelvis. The problem was, he didn't believe in him. He didn't understand that the sexual anger the young Presley poured out was something exactly in tune with the rest of his generation. Parker had probably never seen a James Dean movie. He thought Presley was merely a gimmick, another freak like the midgets, whores, bearded ladies, and cooch dancers Parker had run in the carnival. Parker distrusted gimmicks: they were short-term propositions; they could even blow up in your face. He was at an age when he wanted something sound. He wanted to turn Elvis into the complete lounge act—and in a strangely warped way, that was exactly what he did.

Taming Elvis Presley was a fairly formidable task and Parker was aware that, on his own, he might not be able to put a bridle on all that raw energy. He did, however, have a formidable ally in the form of the U.S. Army.

It was no secret that, before the fifties were out, Elvis would have to contend with the draft. Every young male in the country was faced with the same problem. In Elvis Presley's case there were essentially three options. The first was that Elvis could get out on some sort of medical disability as Frank Sinatra had done. The second was the Glenn Miller route. He could go in on a Special Services deal and, although technically a soldier, he could still play music. The third was the hard way. He could go in just like any other draftee grunt. It was this one that Parker favored. The U.S. Army had provided Parker with his first secure adult home and he thought Elvis would benefit from a dose of the same. Boot-camp discipline would knock some of the starch out of Elvis's breeches and might also help create the new clean, all-American image for his boy that Parker considered the more durable product.

There was also another, more serious, reason to play it as patriotic as apple pie: The Colonel feared that if he took any major steps to keep Elvis out of the army, someone might come nosing around his own service record.

The idea of Elvis disappearing into the army was not without its attendant dangers. The greatest worry was that Elvis would never really reappear again, that he would come out to a world that had moved on and forgotten him. If this scared anyone more than Parker, it was RCA Records. Seventy-five percent of their million sellers were Elvis Presley records. He was currently responsible for some twenty-five percent of the company's profits. Parker was shrewd enough to realize that if Elvis only did a minimal amount of recording during his army stretch, he could quite literally have RCA on its knees for each new title. He could come down with each new tune like Moses from the mountain. If there were two things the Colonel liked, they were power and attention. He warmed to a twofold strategy. On the one hand, he would have to use everything he knew about promotion to keep Elvis's name in front of the public. On the other, he would severely curtail the flow of new product. Both RCA and the public had to be hungry as hell for something new from Elvis when he came marching home. Parker was going to turn the screws until everyone would be aching for the return of the King.

Patriotism or no patriotism, it wasn't possible for someone with the commitments of Elvis Presley simply to drop everything and pick up a rifle. When the first draft date came around, it was necessary to arrange a sixty-day deferment so he could finish the movie *King Creole*. It was almost like a swan song of the wild young rock prince. His sideburns had already gone and, both publicly and privately, he faced an uncertain future. For Parker it was the calm before the storm. The Colonel spent his time playing blackjack with costar Walter Matthau. At one point

Matthau, losing heavily, ran out of money and wanted to play cards on credit. Bodyguard Red West was watching the game and recalls Parker smiling the childish but dead-eyed smile: "No, you want to play, you play with cash."

Finally the movie was wrapped and the deferment had run out. The strategy may have been that Elvis should go into the army like any other inductee, but nobody said he would have to go quietly. The Colonel knew this was his last chance to orchestrate a media event with Elvis in the flesh. He was well aware that it might have to hold the faithful for a whole two years. The final train trip from Los Angeles to Memphis was converted into something close to a religious procession. The rock prince was going back home one last time before he entered into a completely alien future, a future that couldn't help but change him. Elvis himself had been told that nobody knew about his presence on the train. He would be able to have the rest and privacy that he needed before jumping into the organized chaos of the induction process and the horrors of basic training.

Parker unfortunately was lying to his client; he had alerted radio stations all along the route. He'd whispered conspiratorially to each individual DJ: "I have a little secret. Elvis's private train will be pulling into your station. Elvis would feel so welcome if you and some of your listeners would go down to the station when the train stops there. He'd like to shake your hand."

Elvis shook no hands. In fact, he never emerged from the train, but it hardly matters. There was instant hysteria. All day the radio stations played Elvis records and constantly repeated the train's arrival time at every station, even at every railroad crossing. Kids drove hundreds of miles in hopes of catching a

fleeting glimpse of Elvis. All along the route, the fans
waited and watched. As the train rumbled past they
cheered and waved. They knew Elvis wouldn't come
back exactly the same as he had left them. Parker
acted as though the whole thing was news to him, but
inside he was jubilant. It was all the confirmation he
needed. There was no doubt that the idol worship was
there; all he had to do was keep it on the boil while the
idol was in the hands of Uncle Sam.

Elvis Presley's first day in the army would prove to
be a total circus, with Colonel Tom acting as absolute
ringmaster. He was seemingly able, at least for the
day, even to upstage the military. The rationalization
was that the press should be given one last crack at
Elvis before he vanished into the anonymous life of a
buck private. Once he was in, there would positively
be no more press conferences, no TV interviews, and
no photo opportunities. Accordingly, the press went
berserk and, egged on by Parker, acted like animals.
   More than two hundred media people showed up at
the Memphis draft center and trailed Elvis through
the initial examination procedures. Parker arranged
for the increasingly uncomfortable Presley to stand in
front of the cameras and read a telegram from Tennessee Governor Frank Clement—Parker's old
buddy. "You have shown that you are an American
citizen first, a Tennessee volunteer and a young man
willing to serve his country when called upon to do
so."
   As he moved through the military process and the
media scramble, Elvis finally lost his temper with his
manager and snapped: "It's me that's going in and
what happens will be to me, not you." Parker went on
blandly smiling and pouring out quotable one-liners
for the microphones and steno pads. "I consider it my

patriotic duty to keep Elvis in the ninety-percent tax bracket."

Elvis and the other draftees were bused to Fort Chaffee across the Mississippi bridge in Arkansas. The media followed. At Chaffee the circus would escalate to its triumphal climax. Elvis would lose his hair to the army. The almost unhealthy fascination that surrounded this event would seem to indicate that more than one reporter, and maybe even Parker himself, was seeing it as if not actually a symbolic castration, at least a form of degradation, a public humiliation that would start the taming process. It was a humbling that clearly must have appealed to the streak of bully in Parker. In all the photographs he's standing just behind the army barber, a battered black hat pushed back on his head, a shiny, single-breasted suit hanging from his bulk like a tent, and his polka-dot bow tie only half knotted. He's about as close to gloating as any man can be who knows that the world's press is watching him.

At the start it was almost as though Elvis had never gone away. The movie and sound-track records of *King Creole* would maintain a fair semblance of a normal release schedule. This wasn't quite good enough, though, for RCA, who was looking to the future with the somewhat desperate knowledge that they had next to nothing in the can. They wanted product to put in the stores, and all they were getting from Colonel Parker was the suggestion that they repackage the old material. As usual the Colonel had a simple argument. The earlier 45's should be reissued as second-time-around compilation albums. Wouldn't the fans buy any "new" Elvis package even if it was old stuff? They were that crazy. Hell, hadn't one fan told the press she'd buy a record of Elvis sawing wood? ("How would you know it was Elvis?" she was asked. "They'd put a picture of him doing it on the cover," she replied.)

Besides, the Colonel continued, what would happen to the myth of Elvis's being the ordinary soldier if every time RCA wanted some new tracks, Elvis simply ducked into a convenient recording studio? Somewhere along the line a compromise had to be reached. Parker, despite his devious and stubborn nature, had to come to realize that he couldn't simply leave RCA with no material for two full years. On a weekend pass for June 11 and 12, 1958, Elvis was rushed to RCA's Nashville studios, where he cut five sides. The first to see the light of day was the country standard "A Fool Such as I."

RCA was not quite satisfied. Unless they started recycling B sides—a move that ought to have been too blatantly cheap even for the Elvis industry—they still only had two and a half singles to fill up more than eighteen months. Again they complained and again the Colonel tossed them the most meager of bones. In October 1958, Elvis was to be transferred to Germany. Parker proposed that on the day he left the country, he should give a major press conference. RCA could record that and issue it as an EP. The Colonel was now sailing perilously close to unreality, putting out records of Elvis Presley sawing wood, but at no point does he seem to have had any qualms in this regard. Quality control was never one of Colonel Tom's overriding considerations. When the army agreed to just one more circus, RCA had little choice but to go along with the deal.

A neatly uniformed Elvis gave his press conference, flanked by the Colonel; RCA's Steve Sholes; and a trio from Hill & Range, his music publishers, Jean and Julian Aberbach and Freddy Bienstock. It was strictly by the book. Elvis even included the standard disclaimer to the fans: He wasn't about to marry. "I thought I was in love once but my first hit record saved my neck." He even invoked his mother. "She would always try to slow me up if ever I thought I wanted to get married. She was right. It helped my career not to be married." The reference to his mother must have been particularly painful. She had died just two months earlier, on August 14. It was a loss that had devastated Elvis, perhaps permanently. All the Colonel knew, though, was that his wonderful new product was maturing exactly according to plan; he interlaced his pudgy fingers and smiled that cold, smooth-as-a-baby smile.

Of course, not everything in the Colonel's garden was totally rosy. There was one cloud on his horizon. In Germany, his boy was quite beyond his reach. It was possible to go on isolating him; army regulations could be bent so Elvis could live in his own off-base apartment. Selected members of the Memphis Mafia could be shipped over to keep him amused as well as under constant surveillance. Jean Aberbach could even be shuttled across the Atlantic as a surrogate manager. The one thing the Colonel couldn't do was go over there in person. He couldn't cross the frontiers involved. "In Paris I had to represent him for two weeks, when Elvis liked to spend some time there," says Aberbach, who had no idea why the Colonel refused to make the trip to Europe. "He said he didn't speak the language. It made sense to me. I always thought that he was from Wisconsin. There was something with his accent, but it was not European to me. He never talked about Europe. He only mentioned the dog cemetery and the elephant he had when his parents died."

There was one enormous consolation for the Colonel, which arose from his inability to leave the country. With Elvis out of the way, he was the center of attention. Back in the States he didn't let the grass grow under his feet. Simultaneous with Presley's arrival in Germany, the Colonel threw his own press conference in Nashville to report on the healthy state of the Elvis Presley balance sheet and the success of *King Creole*. The Colonel declared happily how, although in the army, Elvis would net some two million bucks by the end of 1958 and 1959 would be a whole lot better. The press dutifully responded by calling him a "genius" and a "magician." Parker's not inconsiderable vanity sat up and took notice.

The Parker rumor mill was also cranked into action. Elvis would give a welcome-home concert that would be transmitted by closed-circuit TV to a hundred auditoriums across the country. It was pure fantasy, but a fantasy surprisingly ahead of its time.

Movie mogul Harold Mirisch had offered Elvis the lead in his production of *West Side Story*. Elvis had demanded Natalie Wood as a leading lady, but even when he was given her, he still turned down the role —a story Mirisch neither confirmed nor denied. If it is true, it's certainly one more blunder on the part of Parker the manager.

In May 1959, Tom Diskin, who had become Parker's virtual head of disinformation, called a Nashville newspaper and, aware that the story would be picked up by the wire services, told how Elvis had signed a deal for a series of annual ABC-TV spectaculars. His salary would start at a hundred thousand dollars for the first show. The story was a complete fabrication, but it made headlines and that was all that counted.

By the middle of 1959 the facts were a good deal less healthy than the rumors. June had seen the release of the last piece of original material—the single

"Big Hunk o' Love"—and from then on there would be nothing but reissues until March 1960. The public would have to be content with packages like *A Date with Elvis*, an LP containing ten reissues hidden inside a gatefold sleeve lavishly illustrated with pictures of Private Presley, a "personal" telegram to the fans, and a calendar on the back on which they could tick off the days until the King's return. Even though these reruns of old tunes sold far, far better than they deserved, by October 1959, Elvis had no records at all in the top hundred, something that hadn't happened in four years. Parker, however, wasn't going to compromise again and rush Elvis back into the studio on another weekend pass. There was nothing RCA could do but hunker down and wait for the Presley discharge, hatching plans to press a straight million of whatever tunes first became available.

For the very first time, through that winter, the Presley empire had nothing to do except to tick over. It was a lull. Tom Parker spent part of the time living in the past. He went back to Tampa and hung out with old friends like Bob Ross, Paul Wilder, Frank Connors the Irish tenor, and Dave Gardner, the old-time country comedian. Connors's daughter was interested in a show business career and Parker made all the appropriate noises about opening doors in Hollywood.

Parker was also spending time looking toward the future and opening a few doors in Hollywood on his own account. Abe Lastfogel, a senior executive at William Morris, had taken it on himself to introduce the Colonel to the elite of Beverly Hills and Palm Springs. He had shown him the upper crust of movieland and taken him to places like the swank Hillcrest Country Club in West L.A. The Parker vanity lapped it up. This was where the millionaire action was; these people wheeled and dealed and lived like kings. Parker knew he was where he'd wanted to be all his life. It was the final hog heaven.

There was also an eminently practical side to these important entrées. Through Abe Lastfogel he came in contact with the Sinatra clan, the Rat Pack of Dean Martin, Sammy Davis, Jr., Peter Lawford, and Joey Bishop. Parker was quick to realize that if he could somehow get these people to publicly recognize his boy's return, it would be the final cream topping on his plans to make Elvis legitimate. In the past, Sinatra had been disdainful about both Elvis and rock 'n' roll. On the other hand, Sinatra was smart enough to realize there were more ways of dealing with a young contender for your crown than to scorn or ignore him. One tactic might be to have him on your TV show where at least you could control him. After some persuasion, Sinatra took to the scheme. His Timex TV specials were starting to slip in the ratings, and he could use a sensation like the returning Presley. If there was going to be a confrontation with the Colonel's new, improved Elvis, Sinatra might as well have it on his own turf, among his own pals, and on his own terms. Sinatra's terms turned out to be one hundred and twenty-five thousand dollars for six minutes of Elvis. The Colonel accepted but went on to annoy Sinatra by giving away hundreds of free tickets to the show. Despite all his plans, the Colonel had been offered a cheap shortcut to an Elvis comeback special and jumped at it. Suddenly it was apparent that the philosophy in the future would be the same as, if not worse than, it had been in the past. Cheap would still be the key.

The Colonel had also picked up a couple of recreational habits from his new Hollywood associates. Every so often the big boys took off to Las Vegas in somebody's private plane. They'd relax, get loose, maybe drop a few thousand at blackjack or roulette or maybe a whole lot more in a private high-stakes poker game. It may have been beyond the Colonel to relax and get loose, but he discovered that he loved to gamble. The hardened carny let go of everything he knew and started chasing the myth that you can make a fortune in a casino. In his case the contradictions were complete. He already had a fortune and he played in a way that proved he was as turned on by the act of losing as by winning. His addiction would eventually prove to come from deep, dark motivation: Parker lost like a man seeking a gloomy redemption in watching the bucks that so obsessed him going back down the tubes.

When Elvis landed at the McGuire Air Force Base in New Jersey in the middle of a blizzard, he also had a secret that would not have sat well with his new all-American image. He had come home with a dark-haired fourteen-year-old who, in later life, would look uncannily like a female version of himself. She was called Priscilla Beaulieu and she was the adopted daughter of an army major. The move had apparently been made with his full cooperation.

Just two years earlier, Elvis's major rival of the time, Jerry Lee Lewis, had all but wrecked his career by very visibly marrying his thirteen-year-old cousin. On the surface it would appear that Elvis could scarcely fare any better if this particular detail of his domestic arrangements had become public. And yet nobody seemed to care. Pictures were published of Elvis and Priscilla. She had moved into his house and Elvis was putting her through school. The situation wasn't exactly advertised, but it was hardly so covert that a hard-nosed investigative writer couldn't have ferreted out the story. Strangely, nobody seemed particularly interested. It was as though Elvis had become so big that everybody wanted to believe the best of him—nobody would want to hear that John Wayne wore a dress. At the very least, the Colonel might have been expected to be climbing the walls after all the energy he had put into the campaign to clean up Elvis.

Sometime during Elvis's exile in Germany both men seem to have instinctively realized that if the public had so completely been sold on the image, in reality anything was possible. At virtually the same time, but quite independently, both Elvis and the Colonel divorced the truth from the press-release fantasy. For the customers Elvis was the affable, kinda-shy Hollywood heartthrob. Behind closed doors and high walls, and in guarded hotel suites, there were pills, guns, orgies, and an underage concubine. Behind the heartthrob was the down-home Will Rogers supermanager who, in his spare time, was trying his damnedest to get into superhock with the Las Vegas casinos. Star and manager seemed to be pacing each other in their ongoing flirtation with ultimately destructive vices.

10

It was the launch of the new Elvis. The sideburns had gone; the cat clothes had gone; all but a last vestige of the bump, grind, and leer had been steamrollered out of him by the army, and by the grooming for his new role to which the Colonel subjected Elvis just after he was discharged. Initially the product was kept under wraps. There would be no interviews with the press, and no tours. Apart from the Sinatra show, there would be no TV. Elvis made one highly creative pop album, *Elvis Is Back*, and then settled into a routine that Tom Parker appeared to have mapped all the way to the horizon. Elvis was going to be a movie star. It was as simple as that. If Elvis was going to be on the screen all the time, there would be no need for live performances with their complications and over-heads. The fantasy seemed to be that Elvis would be a kind of singing Rock Hudson in a series of light, fluffy comedies.

Parker envisioned Elvis as an entertainment machine, a production line that could turn out three movies a year for the next decade. The machine would be kept rolling clear to 1969. From 1961 to 1969, Elvis performed no live shows, lived in almost complete isolation, and had no contact with his public whatsoever. Even though the sixties was a period of radical, often violent, change in rock 'n' roll, in entertainment, and in the world at large, Elvis stuck to the formula the Colonel had laid down. Little deviation was permitted, and if anyone tried to change the system or convince Elvis that there might be more to the world than three sun 'n' fun pictures a year, it would provoke an immediate, noisy, and negative response from Parker.

At first there were compromises. In 1960, Elvis was permitted to play exactly three live shows. Parker realized he couldn't simply bring the boy out of the army and install him in Hollywood without showing him to the public at all. All three concerts were to be benefits. Two would be held in Memphis and the proceeds would go to local charities; the third would be in Hawaii, to raise funds for the memorial of the battleship *Arizona*. For almost ten years after that, Elvis would not set foot on a stage. For a man rated among the most dynamic live performers of the twentieth century, this policy was little short of criminal.

The benefits appear to have been staged as much to allow the Colonel to show off as to present Elvis to the public. All of Parker's cronies were at the Memphis show, including Memphis mayor Henry Loeb and Tennessee governor Buford Ellington. Parker moved through the backstage crowd, wreathed in a halo of cigar smoke, backslapping and glad-handing the politicians and celebrities. As far as Parker could see, he was king of the world. "Could I get an autograph?"

"My daughter would be so happy to meet Elvis, just for a moment." The Colonel was the one who granted and refused the favors. He was the way; nobody came to Elvis except through him. The Colonel still maintained the nothing-for-nothing rule. For every favor granted, tribute would be exacted.

A couple of weeks later the backslapping became even more intense when Elvis made a nonsinging appearance before a joint session of the Tennessee State Legislature and was honored as a Hero of the Volunteer State. The show in Hawaii was even more of a circus, designed to satisfy something deep in the Colonel's psyche. In January 1961 he announced to the press that he and Elvis wanted to do something special for Hawaii and its people. He had read an editorial in the Los Angeles *Examiner* on Pearl Harbor Day, and he wanted to do something for the brave Americans who had lost their lives in the Japanese attack of December 7, 1941. It was the twentieth anniversary of Pearl Harbor and neither Elvis nor the Colonel wanted it to go unmarked.

Tom Parker held a breakfast meeting with members of the War Memorial Commission. Elvis would give a benefit concert to raise fifty thousand dollars for the *Arizona* memorial fund. There would be four thousand seats, and ringside would cost a hundred bucks apiece. Even the generals had to pay. There was nothing particularly gracious about the Colonel's charity. He loudly told the media how much money he and Elvis were dropping by doing this show. There was fifteen thousand for advertising alone. "I have never worked as hard in my lifetime. If it was my own commercial show, I couldn't have worked harder."

In a way, it was his own show. He was working hard, but he was also having the time of his life. He took particular delight in bullying and humiliating the officers who were sent to liaise with his organization. It was clearly some Beetle Bailey private's daydream of getting his own back on the officers who, once upon a time, had made his life miserable. There was an almost total embargo on favors. The smiling majors, captains, and genuine colonels were uniformly denied autographs, pictures, tickets for their brothers-in-law, or meetings with Elvis. The Colonel, grinning from ear to ear, went right on shaking his head. "No, I'm sorry, that isn't going to be possible. Absolutely not. No." He was having the time of his life. He had the U.S. Army groveling at his feet and the chance of massive revenge for every real or imagined slight he'd suffered while a humble enlisted man. Despite the rejections, the brass kept on coming. Parker had them eating out of his hand. Local DJ Ron Jacob was an onlooker as Parker heaped the humiliation on a particular group of very senior officers.

"The Colonel started snowing on them about how important they were to the security of the world and how patriotic and so on and if they'd line up, why he'd give them a little something from Elvis. So they lined up, all these guys in charge of the Pacific and parts west, and Parker went over to a trunk and carefully, almost secretly, pulled some tiny pictures out and very stingily doled them out, one to each admiral and general."

Minnie Pearl was along on this trip to Hawaii, and as well as watching Parker flaunt his power, she had a number of insights into the unreality of Elvis's situation. "When we arrived at the Hawaiian Village Hotel, we were confronted by hundreds of screaming fans, jammed together, awaiting Elvis's arrival. As our limo stopped, they surged but the police held them back until we started to move through the crowd. They suddenly broke loose and we were literally swept off our feet. I never felt so close to death. I caught a glimpse of Elvis's face and I will never forget it. He had the look of a zombie, a resigned, deadpan, expressionless stare."

During his stay at the Hawaiian Village, Elvis was a virtual prisoner inside his suite. "Elvis never got out of his room except for work. They say he came down in the middle of the night to swim. He couldn't come out during the day. He had the penthouse suite on top of that thing and we'd get out and act crazy and we'd look up there and Elvis would be standing at the window looking down at us. Years later, as word filtered back to Nashville of Elvis's unhappiness and seeming withdrawal, I would think of that day in Hawaii. No wonder he lost touch with reality."

While Parker bathed in a power fantasy that had been born more than a quarter of a century earlier, Elvis stood and stared out the window. There was something less than natural in the juxtaposition of manager and star.

The sky was blue and the cameras were rolling. It was a simple shot. Elvis was to run out of the surf and straight into the camera. It was the eighth day of filming *Blue Hawaii* and everything was running very smoothly. There was the call for silence. Action. The clapper board snapped. Elvis, looking wet, healthy, and desirable, splashed through the waves and onto the wet sand. Suddenly the Colonel was inexplicably in the shot, waving his arms and screaming like a lunatic.

"Stop! Hold everything! Cut! Cut!"

Director Norman Taurog was on his feet and furious.

"What the hell do you think you're doing?"

Parker ignored him. Facing producer Hal Wallis, he pointed to Elvis's waterproof wristwatch.

"Do you remember the terms of Elvis's contract?"

Wallis looked at him stonily but said nothing. Parker raved on.

"That watch Elvis is wearing!"

"What about it?"

"The contract says that Elvis doesn't provide his own clothes. If you want the watch in, you'll have to pay us another twenty-five grand."

For the Colonel, this kind of inane interruption was par for the course. He seemed incapable of team playing and working toward the best possible Elvis Presley product. For him it was a matter of rudeness, petty hustling, and mouthing off at the most inopportune moments. Anecdotes like this one about the watch are normally used to prove what a wild and crazy old guy the Colonel was, always up to his tricks and gags. What nobody appears to have either noticed or considered was the effect these antics had on Elvis. Was he giving of his best work after the Colonel had pulled one of his numbers? How did he feel when he had to stand by and watch his manager shed all dignity and act like a money-grubbing buffoon?

Such considerations clearly didn't trouble Parker. What did it matter if Elvis wasn't giving his best? To the Colonel, *quality* was a dirty word. "We don't want to lose the common touch." The Colonel ought to know; his touch was about as common as it got. He's on record as warning a director on one of Elvis's vehicles, "Now don't you go winning no Oscar with this picture, because we don't have no tuxedo to wear at the celebration."

One of the main targets of Parker's boorish jokes was producer Hal Wallis, another associate of Parker's who refuses to say anything bad about him. Basically, he swallowed Parker's nonsense and used the money he grossed on the quickie Presley pictures to finance more worthwhile films. In public, Wallis has always followed the official party line.

"He [Parker] is a supersalesman. I admire and respect him very much. We are good friends to this day." Insiders, however, relate a different story. "He doesn't tell you, but he didn't like the Colonel one bit." Wallis reportedly told an aide that he hated to do business with Parker. "I'd rather try and close a deal with the devil."

When the Colonel first moved to Hollywood, he made his home in the solid but somewhat staid luxury of the Beverly Wilshire Hotel. Its dark wood, deep pile carpets, heavy antique furniture, and crystal chandeliers were enough of an echo of Old-World European grandeur to make the Colonel and Marie feel they had really arrived. Elvis was less impressed. The Colonel's original scheme was to have Elvis and his entourage also living in the Beverly Wilshire, within easy reach, but it quickly became clear this wasn't going to work out. The hotel couldn't cope with Elvis and his Mafia; in return, Elvis and his Mafia couldn't handle the Beverly Wilshire. They started referring to it as "the old folks' home." There were complaints about the noise and a good deal of gratuitous room-wrecking.

Elvis and entourage had to go. He and his goon squad set themselves up in a house in Bel Air. It rapidly became their West Coast playpen and the parties became legendary. Later, the Colonel would also move, to the millionaire retirement colony of Palm Springs.

If you have to look for one word to provide a key to the string of movies that constitutes Elvis Presley's career through the sixties, it's probably *absurdity;* if not absurdity, certainly *laziness.* When Elvis came out of the army, a lot was going for him in the film world. He appeared to be bankable. All his prearmy pictures had made comfortable profits. He had one movie still to go on a three-picture deal with Hal Wallis, and there was even a certain guarded critical acclaim, not so much for what he'd already done on the screen but for what he might do in the future. A number of people saw a certain potential in Elvis that deserved to be developed. A sensitive manager might have felt it was time to stretch a little and maybe find out what his client could really accomplish. Tom Parker was, of course, the antithesis of the sensitive manager; instead of letting Elvis discover his capabilities, the Colonel engineered things so that in both film and music, Elvis's work would be confined to the cheapest, shallowest formulas. It says a lot for both Elvis's charisma and the blind tolerance of his fans that Parker was able to keep to the formula for so long. Most other entertainers would have committed professional suicide sticking to such a narrow, limiting policy for so long and in spite of all the changes in the outside world.

The best thing to be said about Parker's plan was that it was simple: Elvis would make three films a year. Each film would feature enough tunes to fill an album. Three albums a year were all that RCA needed from Elvis, and thus there would be no need for any recording not related to the films. It was cheap and cheerful and virtually guaranteed to turn out highly inferior product. Such a scheme could only have been hatched by a man who was both lazy and highly insecure. Parker was developing an obsession for long-range planning and a deep hatred of change. When he harangued the flunkies, his wild flights of fancy extended all the way into the seventies: Elvis would go on, always bouncing and grinning, always surrounded by bikinis, maybe clear to the end of the century. If anyone suggested that perhaps times would change, Parker would snarl that you didn't screw around with a winning formula.

Part of Parker's obsession was to keep tying Elvis to long-term deals. *G.I. Blues* was the third and final movie on Hal Wallis's contract, and the Colonel immediately went to work to negotiate a second three-picture contract that would be immediately followed by a further series of three. Even the nature of the films was defined in the contract. Wallis would "present the new, mature Elvis in a series of pictures set in exotic locations."

Elvis was tied to Hal Wallis Productions until 1966.

This deal with Wallis was one of the earliest points where the myth of Colonel Tom Parker's business genius started to unravel. Parker was so eager to get the cash up front that he didn't bother to consider that in the long run, both he and Elvis would have made a great deal more money if each picture had been negotiated separately on the strength of the profits of the preceding ones. Parker may have been fantasizing way into the future, but when he was actually confronted by cash, his instinct was to take the money and run.

It would appear that only a while after he'd closed the deal with Wallis, Parker realized to just what extent Hal Wallis had gotten the better of him. The Colonel, like the sucker who refuses to accept that the play has gone down and belligerently demands a second chance, immediately wanted to reopen negotiations and for months kept badgering Wallis with all kinds of additions and side deals he insisted should be included with the original. Wallis politely fended him off. A deal was a deal and if the Colonel didn't like it, it was just too damn bad; he'd have to live with it. It was around this time that Parker started in earnest with the ludicrous practical jokes at Hal Wallis's expense, as if to punish Wallis for outsmarting him.

Hal Wallis wasn't the only producer with whom Parker did long-term deals. Sam Katzman, at MGM, had the reputation of being a magician who could make big profits out of low-budget pictures. Parker's approach to him was rudimentary. "Instead of making four-million-dollar pictures like we have been, we want to make pictures the way you do it." Katzman didn't need two of the Colonel's heavy conspiratorial winks. "With me being a frugal producer, the Colonel figured we could save a few dollars." With Katzman at the helm, MGM started turning out cheap, formula Elvis pictures as if they were coming off a conveyor belt. *Kissin' Cousins, Harum Scarum,* both were equally cheap and dreadful. An MGM employee was moved to remark that the Elvis movies didn't even need titles. "They could be numbered. They'd still sell." For a while it looked as though the Colonel's crudity and cheapness were actually what was needed. The Elvis fans were proving themselves to be completely indiscriminating. They appeared quite willing to accept the formula garbage and never feel that a movie like *Girls! Girls! Girls!* might be an insult to their taste and intelligence.

As far as the Colonel was concerned, the movie *Flaming Star* was all the confirmation he needed that in all matters pertaining to Elvis, he was the one who ultimately knew best. With *Flaming Star* the critics and the goddamn highbrows got what they wanted. Much against his better judgment he had let producer David Weisbart put Elvis into a class production. The property, a psychological western about a halfbreed

orn between the two sides in a war between ranchers
nd Indians, had originally been offered to Marlon
Brando, but Brando had declined. As second choice,
Elvis was provided with most of what would be
needed to give him a shot at a "serious" movie. The
director was Don Siegel, who had made the original
version of *Invasion of the Body Snatchers* and who
vent on to direct the Clint Eastwood classic *Dirty
Harry*. The supporting cast included John McIntrye,
Dolores Del Rio, Steve Forrest, and Barbara Eden.
Most important of all, aside from the title tune and a
brief banjo and concertina bunkhouse hoedown,
here were no songs. Elvis's acting would stand on its
own. On paper, Elvis was getting the full treatment.
On film, however, it was another matter. Although
Elvis acquitted himself more than adequately, *Flaming Star* simply wasn't a very good movie. The action
ended to flag in scenes where Elvis's character wres-
led with his inner torment. The interplay between
angst and arrows was hardly a happy one, and Elvis
ans stayed away in droves. Apparently they didn't
vant to see Elvis develop into the next James Dean.
They wanted the sun and the fun, the exotic locations,
and the statutory ten songs. Although it didn't actually lose money, *Flaming Star* was a disaster by the
standards of Elvis movies.

Perversely, the Colonel was jubilant. Of course it
rked him to lose money on a picture, but he had
given them enough rope and they'd hanged themselves. The matter of quality in Elvis Presley films had
been dispatched once and for all. *Flaming Star* had
more than vindicated the Colonel's opinion that striv-
ng for quality in an Elvis picture was casting pearls
before swine. From then on there would be no arguments. Above all, there would be no deviations from
the Tom Parker master plan.

The Parker master plan might have made sense if it had just involved simplicity and economic streamlining. But when it was put into practice, many of the Colonel's decisions appeared to be based not even on crude logic but on a strange perversity. He seemed actively to hate the idea of taking the trouble to give the public a quality product. His need to shortchange had grown to psychotic proportions, and he was incapable of missing any chance to behave like a money grubbing boor. The anecdotes are myriad. Director Gene Nelson once sent him a film script for consideration. It was returned with a churlish note. "Thank you for the script, Gene, but if you want an opinion or evaluation of this script, it will cost you an additional twenty-five thousand dollars." One of Parker's favorite boasts was how he and Elvis didn't read scripts "All we want is songs for an album."

He was pathologically unable to resist the temptation of the cheap hustle. When a 20th Century-Fox producer announced he would need two more days of additional filming in order to complete two more songs, the Colonel gave him the fisheye.

"That will cost you seventy-five thousand dollars."

Parker grinned as the producer turned white.

"I tell you what, you got a pair of dice?"

The producer looked at Parker like he was crazy.

"Dice?"

"Yeah, dice. I'll roll you double or nothing. How about that?"

About the only people that the Colonel treated generously were the members of the Elvis Presley Fan Club. Of course, he wasn't above conning them a little, but for the most part his concern was to maintain a loyalty and devotion to Elvis that was almost religious in its intensity. The Colonel, who had started the fan club himself, saw the hardcore fans as his very own private army. They were his troops, miniature promoters out there in the field doing his work for him. They'd call radio stations, write to newspapers, and create an instant crowd for the opening of a new movie. Above all, they would consume any Elvis product put on the market.

The Colonel wasn't above having a squad of flunkies forge Elvis's signature to thousands of supposedly personal letters: "Say, thanks a lot for writing in. I enjoyed your correspondence and hope I will be hearing from you again often." The kicker came in the last line, the order of the day for the troops. "If you get a chance, drop your local disc jockey a card and ask him to spin one of my songs for you. He'll be glad to do it and you'll remember that I'll be singing it just for you!"

In the early sixties, at the peak of Elvis's popularity, the Colonel's people were processing more than thirty thousand fan letters a month. The Colonel rode this section of the operation harder than any other. All fan mail had to be collected whether it was sent to Graceland, the office in Madison, or any of the Hollywood movie studios. Each piece of mail had to be answered; that was the carved-in-stone law. The fan club members were the absolute faithful and they had to be treated accordingly. In all of the Colonel's empire nobody came closer than the fan club to getting something for nothing out of the old man. He organized fan club packages with special, limited-edition records, pictures, gifts, and a constant barrage of "confidential" information about "El." The Colonel probably didn't feel he was giving anything away. The fan club was his grass roots. He constantly reminded movie producers and RCA Records executives that there were a quarter of a million of them and anytime he wanted, he could mobilize them. They were his and he bribed them with color pictures and plastic key rings, most likely feeling he was the one getting the good deal.

"A sure way to debase your merchandise is to give it away," Parker said many times. "I don't believe in overexposure of an artist. I think one of the reasons Elvis is a star is that he hasn't appeared too much in person or on television. Make the fans clamor for a view of the product. I handled Eddy Arnold that way. I am using the same system, if you can call it that, with Presley. It works, I do believe. A typical local example is Hank Snow. Snow isn't overexposed. You don't see him on the TV too much. The result is that when Hank makes a personal appearance tour, people show up at the box office and pay to see Hank sing."

It wasn't often that Tom Parker made a statement of basic philosophy, but when he did, he exhibited such a warped view of the world, it is only reasonable to conclude that he suffered from some deep-seated emotional problems. He appeared actually to fear perfection. The idea of Elvis Presley's giving an ultimate show seemed to fill him with trepidation. If Elvis pulled out all the stops, what would there be left for the future? Parker seemed to look on talent as a limited resource, something that would be depleted by use and might eventually be exhausted. He was afraid that if he let Elvis paint his masterpiece, there would be nothing left.

Nor was Parker able to disguise the fact that he saw Elvis as his ultimate and possibly final meal ticket. Elvis was the goose that laid the golden eggs, but old Tom wasn't content to relax, let Elvis do what he did best, and pick up the eggs at the end of the day. Parker had to sell off the goose one slice at a time. When you strip away the mythology and the legend of the Colonel and examine the bare facts, his master plan let the new Elvis spend ten of what might have been the most productive years of his life churning out some of the most vapid movies this side of the Three Stooges. The process bored Elvis almost to death, but the Colonel persevered, making sure he didn't get important acting parts or deviate from the Presley vehicles. His star was kept away from his public and placed in a position to progressively lose touch with reality.

Looked at in these terms, the Colonel's strategy seems less a master plan than a recipe for disaster. And yet in some bizarre way he was at least initially right. The bond between Elvis and his fans was so strong that rather than fading, the Presley legend grew and grew. It was almost as though Elvis brought out a weird masochism in the mass audience, who seemed prepared to tolerate the shortchange nonsense and the inferior product. No blame was ever attached to Elvis. If anybody wondered why he made such lousy pictures and such cheap, slapdash records, it was put down to some nebulous "people around Elvis" who were making the wrong decisions. No blame attached to Parker either; he was too close to Elvis to be blamed. Why, Elvis and the Colonel were almost like father and son.

It could be argued that the only person responsible for Elvis Presley's appalling career moves was Elvis Presley himself. Beyond the fact that any man is, in the final analysis, in control of his own destiny and that nobody put a gun to Elvis's head and told him he had to take Tom Parker as his manager or die, all the blame for the fall of Elvis Presley has to rest solidly on the shoulders of Colonel Tom. Once we get past the mythology, a pattern starts to emerge. Tom Parker's dealings look absurd only when viewed in the context of serving Elvis's best interests. If we take a second perspective—that the business dealings never *were* in Elvis's best interests but were the self-serving maneuvers of a greedy manager—it all starts to make ugly sense.

We've already seen how Parker lost Elvis both creative advantage and considerable sums of money by tying him to long-term contracts with MGM and Hal Wallis. In music, which should have been the continuing mainstay of his popularity, the deals were, if anything, even more destructive. When the Colonel signed Elvis to the original Hill & Range publishing agreement, nobody pretended that Elvis Presley was a songwriter. He was signed to an arrangement reserved for nonwriting singing stars. It was invented during vaudeville days to give singers a piece of the action on songs they hadn't written but had made popular either by recording them or by featuring them in their acts. The system disappeared only when the second generation of rockers—the Beatles, the Rolling Stones, Bob Dylan, and others—started writing their own songs.

The way it worked was that if anyone wanted to sell a song to Elvis, they had to approach him via Hill & Range. In the sixties it would be through senior executive Freddy Bienstock. The songwriter would have to assign his song to the company, ensuring a cut for both Hill & Range and for Elvis. In the wild-and-woolly early days, Elvis might also have been credited as a co-writer. Marty Lacker, one of the Memphis Mafia, who also wrote songs, had direct experience of the way the approaches to Elvis were guarded.

"Anyone who tried to get a new song to Elvis, without going through his publishing company people, would run into a series of petty hassles. If a new song was presented to the publishing company, it would never reach Elvis unless the writer made unreasonable concessions to the company." He cites an incident in 1974 at the Stax Studios in Memphis that perfectly illustrates how the setup operated. At the start of a recording session Freddy Bienstock had brought a selection of songs that were company copyright. Elvis looked them over and decided he needed two more. Lacker said he had one but the copyright was signed to another company. "Freddy Bienstock, who I feel had resented us for years, looked at me as soon as Elvis was out of the room and said, 'How come you always have songs by that publishing company? Are you making money off what Elvis does?' There were a lot of people in the room at the time, including one of Colonel Parker's assistants, and they all looked at me."

What we seem to have here is not the average recording session where everyone strives for the best possible performance of the best possible song. Here was a gang of courtiers vying not only for the King's attention but also for points on his action.

It's interesting to note that in this bizarre and rarified world the very idea of making money off Elvis had somehow been turned into a crime. It was obvious Parker psychology. The only people allowed to make money on Elvis were himself and a few of the inner circle like Freddy Bienstock. The Memphis Mafia were allowed to hang out. The salaries they were paid were small, but there were the compensatory gifts of cars and gold watches as well as fringe benefits that could be truly mind-boggling. The only absolute prohibition was the cutting of side deals. That kind of initiative could be punished with instant excommunication.

Back in the fifties the Hill & Range songwriting setup worked very well indeed. Hill & Range had under contract such topflight rock 'n' roll songwriters as Jerry Leiber and Mike Stoller, and Doc Pomus and Mort Shuman. When both pairs of collaborators moved on to greener pastures, the company was left with a lot of less gifted writers, such as Sid Tepper, Roy C. Bennet, Bernie Baum, Florence Kaye, Sid Wayne, Randy Starr; the less than distinguished list went on and on. They became a factory that churned out songs that one way or another fitted the sound tracks of the movies.

Here we turn from the Colonel's ineptitude to his aggressive ignorance. Neither the Colonel nor the Aberbach brothers could perceive that the times were achanging. They still believed that they could create trends, they didn't have to bother to observe them. Elvis didn't have to compete. Elvis was Elvis now and forever more. It didn't matter that over in the Brill Building young writers like Carole King, Jerry Goffin, and Cynthia Weil were turning out material infinitely superior to what was coming to Elvis. It also didn't matter that the Beatles, Bob Dylan, and the Rolling Stones were writing and performing truly revolutionary songs of their own, and would soon all but wipe out institutions like Hill & Range. The Colonel and his cronies had their own ideas of how the music business should be run, and not even hard facts were going to change them.

RCA Records, too, drifted into the Parker malaise during the first half of the sixties. They had Elvis, what more did they need? Between 1961 and 1966 they signed hardly any major acts. In terms of record sales, Elvis's closest rival was Harry Belafonte. Only when, in 1966, Elvis began to slide, did they wake up from the dream and go back to work. In 1966 they bought the Monkees from Don Kirshner. In 1967 they signed the Jefferson Airplane and the Youngbloods, and a year later they had José Feliciano.

One of Parker's greatest weaknesses was his surrounding himself with a tiny circle of sychophants who reinforced his narrow ideas and prejudices. His attitude to friendships is summed up in a remark he made to Bitsy Mott. "Bitsy, I trust you more than anybody else, but you have one fault. You make too many friends." It wasn't only a matter of friends. Jean Aberbach noticed that Parker was also extremely nervous about calling in advisers and experts. "He didn't know too much about taxes. He had a lawyer but never people who could help him avoid paying too much, to create situations to save money in a legal way. I guess he had fears."

The few people that he did trust, apart from his flunkies, were either his age or even older. Abe Lastfogel of the William Morris Agency was born in 1898, as was Hal Wallis. Nat Lefkowitz of William Morris and RCA's Steve Sholes were the same age as Parker. In this circle the Colonel felt safe, and he did his best to avoid going outside it. For almost all his career, Elvis was guided by men old enough to be his father, if not his grandfather.

11

In 1982, when the legal fights with the Presley estate were going on, Parker admitted that everything had not gone well in the sixties. According to his lawyer, for approximately six years after Elvis's discharge from the army, the business activities engaged in by Elvis and the Colonel continued to prosper. However, in the latter part of 1966, the public demand for Elvis's motion pictures and records diminished. The public had become enchanted with competing young rock groups which were emerging in this country and overseas. Many of Elvis's motion pictures had, as of that time, not produced box office sales which would give rise to the right to share in profits since the production and other related costs had not been recouped. Those motion pictures that were "in profit" did not produce substantial income. Elvis's value as a motion picture artist had declined. Record sales had also declined during the latter part of 1966.

Elvis wasn't exactly on the skids, but they did seem to be easing their way in under him. The Colonel knew exactly what to do. He negotiated a new contract and put Elvis's car on tour. The contract gave Parker fifty percent of Elvis's profits. It was only logical: if the goose wasn't laying quite as many golden eggs, the Colonel should get a bigger share of what eggs there were. Why should Tom Parker lose money just because his master plan was going wrong?

The car was Elvis's gold Cadillac. It had been restyled for Elvis by Barris Kustom City of North Hollywood. The interior was more like a yacht than a car, and all the accessories were fourteen-carat gold. It had gold-plated bumpers and hand-spun gold hubcaps. Its interior hardwear was all gold, as were such options as the electric razor, the hair clippers, the shoe buffer, the bar, the automatic record player, and the swivel-mounted TV. The dual phones were only gold-plated. The car was finished with forty hand-rubbed coats of a diamond-pearl glitter flake made from crushed diamonds and fish scales flown in from the Orient. As a final touch, the windows were covered by gold lamé drapes. Elvis had had some ridiculous cars, but this was by far the most ridiculous, virtually a complete waste of money that couldn't be driven without starting a riot. While parked, it needed its own security men to keep an eye on it. Each time the fans got close, it sustained a couple of thousand dollars' worth of damage. Finally, Elvis got disgusted and ordered it to be shut away, out of sight in the garage at Graceland. The Colonel decided it was an asset that could be liquidated. He talked RCA into buying it for twenty-four thousand dollars and sending it on the road to promote *Frankie and Johnny*, debatably the all-time low in Elvis movies. Picture postcards of the car bearing the legend "Elvis

Presley's Gold Car on Tour for RCA Victor Records"
were sold at the shopping centers and movie-theater
parking lots where it was put on show. In keeping
with the principle of never giving something for nothing, neither Barris Kustom City nor even Cadillac was
mentioned in the publicity.

As an Elvis surrogate, the car was an unqualified
success, much more so than the movie it was supposed
to be promoting. In Houston alone, in one afternoon
forty thousand people turned up to take a look at it.
One young woman offered to have sex with Gabe
Tucker, who'd been appointed the car's tour manager, if he'd let her sit inside. According to Tucker's
account, he declined. In Atlanta, there was a gala dinner for two hundred and fifty guests at which the car
was the guest of honor.

One of the more serious effects of the failure of their
fortunes in the mid-sixties was that the Colonel found
himself losing control of Elvis. After finishing *Harum
Scarum*—another contender for the title of the worst
Elvis Presley picture—Elvis returned to Memphis. It
was the end of 1965 and he seemed withdrawn and
depressed, anxious to get away from it all. The incident that had sparked what amounted to—at least
from the Colonel's point of view—Elvis's mutiny was
when shooting on the movie was scheduled for
Thanksgiving Day. Elvis had apparently exploded.
What was so goddamn important about these films
that he had to work on a national holiday? Elvis had
walked off the set and gone home to sulk. He absolutely refused to talk to the Colonel. At Christmas he
didn't bother to call him, a break with a tradition that
had been maintained ever since they'd become artist
and manager. Weeks went by and no word came out
of Memphis. The Colonel became progressively more
nervous. Eventually, just as he'd done in the fifties

when Elvis seemed to be slipping away, he took to his bed. In Palm Springs he had an actual hospital bed set up beside the pool. From there he talked angrily on the phone, blaming everybody he could think of for the fact that Elvis couldn't be either whipped or cajoled back into line. Parker told those around him that he hadn't had a heart attack, but nonetheless he let it be known that he was a very sick man. At one point he raved at Lamar Fike, another of the Memphis Mafia:

"How much longer do I have to live? Ten or fifteen years if I'm lucky. I'm gonna live like I wanna! I don't give a shit! I do like I want to! I spend like I want to. I take care of my people. Fuck it! Talk about leave it to somebody—why should I leave it to somebody? Ain't nobody I wanna leave it to!"

This time even the claims of being at death's door didn't move Elvis. He maintained his silence until March 1966, when, at last, he sullenly went back to work.

There seemed to be nothing Tom Parker could do to stop the decline of Elvis Presley. He had tied his star into so many long-term contracts that Elvis's career had taken on a life of its own. The dreadful movies just kept on coming, as though the conveyor belt couldn't be shut down. Not that Parker was trying particularly hard. His main interests seemed to be feathering his own nest and carving himself larger and larger pieces of the pie. Aside from doubling the size of the slice he took out of Elvis's income, he became obsessive about side deals. Movie producers soon became accustomed to the fact that if they were going to get the Colonel's cooperation, they would have to give him some title. He had to be credited as an "adviser," "consultant," or "technical director," and he had to be paid a salary accordingly. He became absolutely shameless about soliciting personal gifts and always charged his office accommodations to either RCA Records or the movie company of the moment.

Even his much publicized "flamboyance" appeared to be running out of control. Business meetings were disrupted by his crude jokes and boorish behavior. They seemed to have become a wall he had built to keep out innovation and new ideas. A TV network executive came to him with an initial offer of fifty thousand dollars for a single prime-time appearance by Elvis. In a typical example of the way Parker treated people, he laughed in the executive's face. "That'll be just fine for me, but how much are you going to give the boy?"

Finally Parker had an idea; it wasn't great, but the Colonel was getting desperate. Perhaps Elvis should get married. This idea came indirectly from Frank Sinatra, who in July 1966 had married Mia Farrow. It was a small, informal ceremony, arranged at short notice and held at the home of Jack Entratter, owner of the Sands Hotel in Las Vegas. There were few guests, just some friends and no family. It's unclear what Parker thought marriage would achieve for Elvis as far as his career was concerned. Maybe he thought he could float a newer, even more mature Elvis, or maybe he simply thought that marriage would somehow stabilize Elvis and make him more malleable.

For five years Elvis had been living in a bizarre relationship with Priscilla Beaulieu that, according to Priscilla's account in her book, *Elvis and Me*, consisted of pills, Polaroids, and playacting but no fully consummated sex. Priscilla's role as live-in Lolita was certainly not publicized, and it's likely that had the fact about her living under Elvis's roof been made widely known, it would have been the scandal of the decade,

particularly during the period when she was underage. A promise had been exacted from Elvis by Priscilla's stepfather, Captain Joseph Beaulieu, when she
had moved into the Presley household at fourteen:
When Priscilla turned twenty-one, Elvis would make
an honest woman of her. Priscilla had come of age in
the summer of 1966 and her stepfather was dropping
strong hints that he'd like to see the bargain kept,
even though the keeping of bargains had never
caused Parker to lose sleep. Maybe somewhere deep
inside, a vestige of Dutch Catholic morality stirred.
More likely, the matter of Priscilla had always made
the Colonel nervous and he would be happy to have
the potentially damaging situation regularized. Whatever the reasons, Parker suddenly became fixated
with the idea of a wedding.

One thing was sure, though: A wedding couldn't
make matters any worse. The shooting of *Clambake*
had depressed the hell out of Elvis. He had grown to
hate the movies that were being foisted on him and
his seeming inability to stop making them. The stress
was starting to show in a number of ways. He was
spending money like water. He had ballooned up to
two hundred and ten pounds. His hairdresser, Larry
Geller, was feeding him all kinds of religious, mystic,
and occult books, and Elvis was becoming decidedly
odd. There were rumors of drug abuse and orgies.
Things culminated when Elvis tripped over a TV cord
in his Bel Air home, hit his head, and gave himself a
serious concussion. The Colonel had always made it
his policy to not involve himself in Elvis's private life,
but now the golden goose, if not killing himself, might
well be severely damaging his ability to earn. It was
time to move.

Even before the marriage idea, Parker had been
toying with a number of other fantasies, all dramatic

grandstand plays that at a stroke would put the Elvis Presley train firmly back on the rails. One of the most outrageous imagined that he and Elvis bid a final flamboyant farewell to show biz at an enormous Hollywood party with thousands of guests. At the climax, Elvis, the Colonel, and the whole crew of retainers would march out to a line of waiting limousines. They would drive away with a police escort flashing lights and wailing sirens, the whole bit. The crowds jamming the sidewalks would be crying and waving. The next morning there would be huge billboards all over town telling the world that "Elvis and the Colonel bid you a fond farewell."

The Colonel believed salvation lay in a stunt, an old carny-style piece of grandiose flimflam that would make everything come out right. Maybe this is another reason why he fixed on a wedding: a fond memory of the phony Ferris wheel weddings back in the carnival in the thirties. The suckers love a weird wedding.

One might have imagined that if the son of Gladys Presley was going to get married while the whole of the world looked on, it would have been done back home in Memphis. The country church, the huge reception, the motorcade of white Cadillacs through the town, and a private plane to a South Sea isle, how about it, Colonel? The suckers may love a weird wedding, but the world appreciates a class act too. If Elvis had been married with dignity and a solid connection to his roots, there wouldn't have been a dry eye in western civilization.

One more time, though, the Colonel proved that a class act was something quite beyond him. Across the planet a couple of million teenage girls had fantasized about how it would be on the day they became Mrs. Elvis Presley. The choir, the flowers, the floating

wn. Parker gave them an eight-minute ceremony
the owner's suite at a Las Vegas casino. It was
ilton Prell's suite in the Aladdin Hotel, Judge David
enoff presiding, and it bordered on sleazy. Once
ain the Colonel appeared to be playing one of his
astly jokes on both Elvis and the world.

The first task was to mobilize the troops and restore
me measure of morale. He did this by cutting back
aff and reducing the salaries of those who were left.
arker came to Elvis's house in Bel Air, settled into
e den, in the middle of the Memphis Mafia, and
arted laying down the law.

"Things are going to change around here. First of
l the payroll is going to be cut back. Elvis has been
ending too much money lately and he has gone
eyond what he can afford. He's going back into the
udio to start a new picture. There's a lot of people
epending on his obligations and I'm depending on
ou to help us."

All through the speech Elvis sat hunched forward,
aring at the carpet. His hair hung down, hiding his
ce. It was his house, but the Colonel was in charge.

"When things get back to normal, the pay cuts will
e restored. We're more than fair, aren't we, Elvis?"

Elvis just grunted. He knew he was being humili-
ed.

There were also some moves in the hierarchy of the
afia. Joe Esposito came back as foreman and Marty
acker was put in charge of "special projects." The
ery first special project was to be Elvis's wedding.

It had all the makings of a nightmare. It started
ore like a piece of espionage than a celebration. The
ight before the wedding, Marty Lacker had rented a
earjet in Palm Springs. It took off under cover of
ight, carrying Elvis, Priscilla, Joe Esposito, his wife,
anie, and George Klein. The media seemed to have

sensed something in the air and the move was made
with the utmost secrecy. The private jet landed in Las
Vegas at three in the morning of May 1. Elvis and
Priscilla drove directly to the Clark County Court
house and collected their marriage license from a
clerk who had been paid not only to be on duty at the
ungodly hour but also to keep his mouth shut.

It's not clear why the Colonel deemed it necessary
to conduct the wedding as though it were something
out of a James Bond movie. What had started out as a
stunt turned into an absurd exercise in cloak-and-dag-
ger. Possibly the strangest performance was the one
that he put on for the inner circle of the Elvis Presley
business empire. On the day before the wedding he
cabled Abe Lastfogel, Harry Brand—the head of publicity at 20th Century-Fox—Grelun Landon and
Harry Jenkins of RCA, and Stan Brossette, the head
PR for MGM. The instruction was to go directly to the
L.A. airport. (Do not pass Go—Do not collect two
hundred dollars.) When they reached LAX there was
a further message: Fly to Las Vegas. Once in Vegas
they were taken to a small, anonymous hotel where
they were told to spend the night. At seven the next
morning a pair of limousines brought the five of them
to the rear entrance of the Aladdin, where they were
quickly smuggled inside and placed in separate rooms
with strict orders not to make phone calls. They did
not attend the ceremony but instead simply sat in
their rooms until the formalities were complete. Only
then did the Colonel officially inform them that Elvis
was married.

Despite Parker's secrecy, the rumor mill was already in operation. Within hours of Elvis and Priscilla's getting their license, Rona Barrett's office was on
the phone wanting to know what was going on. The
media was buzzing with stories that something was

about to happen in the Elvis Presley camp and that it was probably a wedding.

The wretched little ceremony lasted just eight minutes. The guests were kept to a minimum: the Colonel and Marie; Vernon and his wife, Dee; Major Beaulieu and his wife, Anne, and their two children; Billy and Jo Smith; Patsy and Gee Gee Gambill; George Klein, Marty Lacker, and Joe Esposito. Between the ceremony and the breakfast reception, Parker let the press have its crack at Elvis. It was hardly a contest. Elvis seemed awkward and more than a little dazed as he attempted to explain, without too much conviction, why he had held off from marrying Priscilla for so long. "I decided it would be best if I waited till I . . . I really knew for sure. And now I'm really sure." After a few more mumbled answers the Colonel waved the questioners away and gave the floor to the photographers.

The Colonel's patent mean-spiritedness was also quite plainly at work. With the exception of Joe Esposito, the Memphis Mafia was totally excluded from the wedding ceremony and this created considerable resentment. It was as if Parker was trying to divide and rule what he ruled already. Think what you like about the Memphis Mafia, they *were* Elvis's constant companions and closest male friends and there was no doubt they deserved to be at his wedding. Marty Lacker was particularly bitter about the Colonel's maneuverings. "The reason was given that there would not be enough room in the suite where the ceremony was to be held but, as it turned out, there was plenty of room. I don't know who made the decision but I didn't believe it was Elvis—he would not have done that. It was a bad decision."

In her book, *Elvis and Me,* Priscilla has no illusions that it was the Colonel's entire show.

"Elvis and I followed the Colonel's plan but as we raced through the day we both thought that if we had it to do over again, we would have given ourselves more time. We were particularly upset at the way our friends and relatives ended up being shuffled around. The Colonel even told some of the boys that the room was too small to hold most of them and their wives and there wasn't time to change to a bigger room. Unfortunately, by the time Elvis found out, it was too late to do anything."

A few months later Elvis and Priscilla would hold a substitute wedding at Graceland for all the friends who had been slighted at the Colonel's version.

Parker even managed to horn in on the honeymoon and, with seeming contempt for Elvis's wishes or welfare, he quite literally canceled the whole thing. There had been a tentative plan for Elvis and Priscilla to go for a protracted tour of Europe, but the Colonel blustered that this was quite impossible. The Colonel had blanked out Europe a quarter of a century earlier. He had no desire to go to Europe and couldn't even if he did want to, because he had no passport. No one had suggested that the Colonel should go along on the honeymoon, he simply acted as though it was an accepted fact. There was no honeymoon. After the wedding Elvis and Priscilla flew back to Palm Springs in Frank Sinatra's Learjet, and after a couple of days, Elvis went back to work on *Clambake*.

It's hard to imagine how any wedding could have been more calculatedly depressing.

As a family wedding it was miserable; as a publicity stunt it did little more than make Elvis look no-class stupid. There might have been a certain kitsch value in Priscilla's beehive hairdo and the decor of the Aladdin Hotel, but kitsch was hardly what Elvis needed to revitalize his career in the mid-sixties. As long as he still made movies like *Clambake,* there was precious little hope of any positive new direction.

There was more to the Colonel's manipulation of the nuptials than just a sadistic exercise in nastiness. Ever since Elvis's return from the army his world had been split into two distinct, and often warring, camps. On one side were Elvis himself, his father, Priscilla, and the Memphis Mafia. They were the party people. Their function was to keep Elvis amused, and in so doing they were responsible for spending a great deal of his money. The others were the Colonel's troops, who, constantly hectored and bullied by their leader, basically believed that they made Elvis's money and resented the profligate spending that went on at Graceland and the house at Bel Air. When things went well, the two factions coexisted without too much difficulty. When, however, the tide of Elvis's fortunes began to turn, the Parker camp, led by the Colonel himself, began to take some long, hard looks at the Memphis Mafia and their nonstop party. Parker became convinced that the good ole boys really only wasted money and reduced Elvis's productivity. He had never trusted the Memphis Mafia. There had always been the danger of one of them introducing subversive outside ideas, but now it was crucial that if the Colonel was going to turn things around, he would have to get involved himself.

The Colonel realized there was no way he could isolate Elvis from his gang of cronies and retainers. Elvis might be withdrawn, but he wasn't about to live in solitary confinement. The Memphis Mafia had to stay, if only because the Colonel wasn't willing to train a brand-new clutch of playmates for El. He preferred the devil he knew to the devil he didn't, but nevertheless the Mafia had to be cut down to size.

The wedding did exactly that. It was the Colonel's

wedding. The good ole boys were banished to the outer circle. Even Elvis was publicly humiliated. The Memphis Mafia's power source was their direct line to Elvis. If there was something they didn't like, they could complain directly to God. By means of the wedding, the Colonel demonstrated clearly that Elvis wasn't God and that not even the star could tell the manager what to do. Elvis couldn't even choose his own guests; how about that, boys? It was more of the Colonel's confusing but ultimately basic politics. His paranoia constantly pushed him in the direction of turning Elvis into a powerless product.

A great deal has been written about the Memphis Mafia; its members, its structure, and its antics have been thoroughly chronicled and documented. Colonel Parker's army, on the other hand, is a much more shadowy organization, less prone to publicity or semipublic cutups. Nevertheless, it had its own rituals and its own bizarre atmosphere of unreality, which were equal to anything Elvis and his boys could create.

The triple keys to daily life in the world of the Colonel and his army were his cheapness, his delight in power, and his carnival background. Tom Parker didn't have the kind of ego that required him to make any kind of architectural mark. (He didn't feel the need to build the fifty-story Parker Building on Sunset Boulevard. His mentor had been Peazy Hoffman, not Ayn Rand.) Parker didn't even have to lease a prestige suite of offices in somebody else's building: he expected other people to take care of accommodations and overheads. In the sixties he felt that the movie companies owed him, as Elvis Presley's manager, not only a living but also a place to live. In the seventies, it was the Las Vegas hotels.

In the Paramount studios Parker was given a complex of second-floor offices and a permanent guard of Paramount security men. The minute they walked into the place, people were uncomfortably aware of being in the lair of someone with the insecurities of a pack rat. The reception area was crammed with Elvis Presley promotional material. Parker seemed to have copies of every piece of print ever put out on Elvis. The centerpiece was the cardboard jailhouse used for the promotion of *Jailhouse Rock*. Moving further in, a visitor quickly encountered the power fixation. An entire wall housed the Colonel's collection of signed photographs. There were politicians and celebrities, movie stars, governors, senators, even Richard Nixon. Parker seemed at some pains to impress anyone who invaded his sanctuary that he was at one with wealth, glamor, and fame. His private office was in a window-less converted storage room. The walls of this inner sanctum were lined with spurious awards and certificates that certified little except a desperate vanity: there were awards for his "nonartistic" help in the design of the predictable Elvis album artwork, and fictitious honorary titles. As the work of a man who didn't own a passport, there was a certain scary logic in the display.

The inner workings of Parker's army didn't, however, take place in formal offices. Tent shows and carnivals didn't have offices, not even offices in converted storerooms. In the carnival, business took place in the communal cookhouse. Everywhere the Parker caravan came to rest, the carny cookhouse had to be lovingly duplicated. While he was in residence at MGM, they installed a huge mahogany conference table, at which the Colonel and his inner circle would sit and eat and plot. The innate dignity of dark mahogany, however, proved too much for the Colonel. He didn't want to chow down in a bank.

"Those fellows out there don't know anything about a cookhouse."

Gabe Tucker and another of the help, Bob Isenberg, were sent into town to buy a large, heavy-weight oilcloth, something that would stand getting good and greasy. The spectacle of two country boys trying to buy oilcloth caused some consternation in the boutiques of Beverly Hills.

Oilcloth? Were they out of their minds? Nobody had made oilcloth since World War I!

It was uncomfortably close to an episode of *The Beverly Hillbillies,* but Tucker and Isenberg pressed on until they finally dug some up in an old, obscure back-street store. The Colonel's word was law.

The cookhouse was the repository of all the gifts that the Colonel exacted as a tribute from just about anyone who wanted to do business with him. A cookhouse needed a freezer, and word was passed along to RCA that it would be a nice gesture to give the Colonel one next time they wanted to show their appreciation. Almost immediately a giant Whirlpool freezer was installed in the cookhouse, courtesy of RCA. In addition to the freezer, a kitchen sink, a stove, and new plumbing and wiring were all installed at someone else's expense.

Parker liked to eat almost continually. It was a weakness he shared with his client. In the Colonel's case, though, the food was doubly appreciated when it came for free. Just as when he was dogcatcher, the Colonel went to extraordinary lengths to drum up donations of food. Hints that couldn't be refused were dropped on just about everyone in the Elvis industry: it was intimated that business would run a great deal more smoothly if there were regular presentations to the Colonel of the odd case of wine, frozen turkey, or Virginia ham. The cookhouse was cluttered with

crates and boxes and the freezer was always full. Aside
from the food, there were other carny echoes, such as
the famous collection of toy elephants. There were
neon signs and gumball machines. At some point the
Colonel started collecting the kind of huge stuffed
animals they sell on gas station parking lots, and one
side of the cookhouse was taken over by these Day-
Glo monsters. More conventional gifts of clocks, ra-
dios, stereo equipment, TV sets, and ashtrays were
stacked in haphazard piles on chairs and under tables.
Some had never been taken from their original wrap-
pings.

The Colonel had a rule regarding the cookhouse.
Everything had to be in a state of constant readiness
so it could be moved at a moment's notice. It was one
of the Colonel's favorite ploys. If the studio where
he'd taken up residence started to put any kind of
pressure on him, he could stamp and scream, and if he
wanted to make a grandstand play by threatening to
walk out altogether, it helped to know he could be
totally gone in a matter of minutes, lock, stock, and
elephants. He would hold regular moving drills just to
see that everyone was on his toes. When, in 1964, he
did indeed move from Paramount to MGM, he didn't
trust his treasures to a firm of professionals and his
long-suffering staff were expected to do the moving
by themselves.

Life in Parker's army seems to have been seldom
pleasant and now and then to have bordered on the
nightmarish. The Colonel was relentless. He expected
slavish obedience and total punctuality. No matter
how late they might have worked the night before, his
underlings were expected to show up at nine sharp,
ready for the orders of the day. Even during a slack
afternoon he couldn't tolerate inactivity. "Do something." "Look busy." These were the prime direc-

tives. Parker yelled continuously, and expected an equally robust response, army-style: "Yes, sir, Colonel," "Aye, aye, sir."

Bitsy Mott experienced his fair share of Tom Parker–induced stress. "You're on twenty-four hours a day when you're under his wing. It's an awful strain. Of course, he put a strain on himself by trying to be on top of everybody, including his star performer. He did it because it was his way."

And the Colonel had to have it his way one hundred percent of the time. He didn't take kindly to initiative in the ranks. On one occasion Bitsy Mott made what he thought was a helpful suggestion and the Colonel turned on him.

"If we lose money on that, will you pay for it?"

All Mott could do was shrug.

"You know I can't do that."

It wasn't nice when the Colonel was triumphant.

"All right then, we do it my way."

It didn't help that the Colonel needed next to no sleep. Bitsy Mott again: "He could sleep two hours and be as fresh as I would be after eight hours. He's the most active person I've been around. He just never gets tired; he has an abundance of energy. He can just go and go. Sometimes he'd wear me out."

One of the worst for wear on Parker's staff was Tom Diskin, who'd been Parker's mainstay since the pre-Elvis days in the early fifties. Diskin finished up with bleeding ulcers and a serious drinking problem after a two-decade hitch in the Colonel's army. On more than one occasion it involved being kept up all night as a foil and straight man for Parker's endless self-aggrandizing stories.

One of the more often repeated tales was that Parker had some kind of supernatural power. Bitsy

Mott swore that he had ESP. Each time Mott screwed up, Parker seemed to know about it, no matter how Bitsy might try to cover up. If nothing else, the way the story persists does demonstrate that Parker surrounded himself with highly impressionable men who looked upon him with total awe.

The truth seems to be that Parker did have a certain talent for hypnotism. John Hartman was a William Morris trainee sent over for a spell of flunkying in the Colonel's domain. He, for one, maintains that Parker had Elvis under some kind of mind control. To a degree, of course, the Colonel did have control of Elvis's mind, but this was more a matter of brute psychology than any look-deep-into-my-eyes Svengali tricks. The Parker powers of hypnotism were more mundane and didn't extend beyond causing various members of his entourage to flap their arms as if they were chickens, or to bark like dogs.

One of his first subjects/victims was the slow-witted Bevo Bevis. Parker would slowly repeat over and over to Bevo that he was going to sleep, until the man's face went slack and he was open to any suggestion. When he was completely under, Parker would make him perform all kinds of absurd antics for the amusement of assembled cronies and the later humiliation of the unfortunate Bevis. Sonny West, one of Elvis's bodyguards and a longtime cornerstone of the Memphis Mafia, also fell victim to the Colonel's influence when Parker hypnotized him on the set of *Kid Galahad*. The Colonel set Sonny ranting and raving at director Phil Karlson, screaming that he was incompetent and the movie was the worst thing he'd ever been associated with. "Mr. Karlson really thought that he had a nutcase on his hands."

The Colonel also hypnotized West on the set of *Blue Hawaii*. On this occasion the unfortunate bodyguard was forced to behave as though *he* were the Colonel. There were also instances when the Colonel was able to conduct mass hypnosis with a number of the Memphis Mafia. "He would get us down on all fours and tell us that we were dogs and he would have us barking and yelping like dogs and snapping at each other. Then, on a command, he would tell us to attack one dog and that dog would be Lamar [Fike] and we would be all over him, biting and yelping. I know it sounds kind of nutty, but it was lots of crazy fun. The Colonel could be a very funny dude."

"Good piece of ham, huh, Abe? How are you enjoying that, boy?"

It was always the same when Abe Lastfogel came to dinner. The Colonel gleefully cooked up the all-pork menu.

"You want to try the pork chops now, Abe? Real good pork chops. Good and greasy, just like the way you like them."

It said a lot about the power of Elvis Presley that the Jewish Lastfogel would tolerate, time and again, the Colonel's gloating blasphemy. If you called out the Colonel on his cruelty—which, of course, nobody ever did—he'd undoubtedly wave his hands and declare his complete innocence. "Hell, ole Abe can take a joke. There's no harm in it." That Colonel Tom, he could be a really funny dude.

Colonel Tom's being a really funny dude was codified in a totally pointless organization called the Snowman's Club. The Snowman was the antirube, the consummate hustler who could snow anyone. The Colonel had cards printed identifying the owner as a member in good standing. The card was validated with the Colonel's signature and the date was simply listed as "this year." The Colonel dangled these cards in front of the rank and file of his army as the ultimate carrot. If you were in the Snowman's Club, you were in with the Colonel. The Colonel spread rumors that top executives and even presidents were members of the club. He also spread the rumor that it cost a thousand bucks to get *out* of the club.

As the High Potentate Snower, the Colonel freely used the club in his games and manipulations. He issued a *Snowman's Handbook* with nothing in it but chapter headings: "Snowing," "Melting," "Disappearing." One unfortunate was given a card but was left for almost a year without the all-important validating signature; others would be dressed up in cotton-wool snowmen's suits and sent out into the Vegas summer to parade up and down the hot sidewalk.

When somebody asked Jack Kaplan if the Snowman's card was actually worth something, if you could do anything with it, Kaplan just shrugged.

"No."

That may have been the Colonel's intended message.

Despite all the emphasis on hard work, everyone being on their toes, and absolute punctuality, a lot of energy expended by the Colonel's army was devoted to keeping him amused. One way was to allow yourself to become the butt of his jokes, another was to sit and listen to his endless boasting and tall stories. He'd been a circus freak, he'd been a mind reader and a sword swallower. The Colonel would accept no position except the center spot. He wouldn't share attention with anyone. He was like a greedy child who has to have it all. He talked without letup. He didn't want a conversation, he simply wanted an audience. The most contribution anyone was allowed to make was to be offered the briefest confirmation for one of his anecdotes. Bitsy Mott once had to sit and listen for four hours without opening his mouth. Jean Aberbach also sat through some of the interminable rantings. "He liked to be a performer for a small audience. He used to tell stories and he wanted answers from time to time like, 'Wasn't it so?'—'Yes sir, Colonel.'"

The Colonel's bad manners, boorishness, and need to monopolize any conversation probably meant he had no real friends. The men who flattered and humored him, and allowed him to humiliate and bully them, were either his employees, financially dependent on him, or individuals directly involved in the Elvis industry and also financially dependent on him. One way or another, Colonel Tom would purchase himself cronies. It's unlikely that the Colonel even wanted anything close to a friend. Friends required trust and some sort of giving, and these two things the Colonel didn't do. Friends were risky, friends might criticize, friends might point out the deficiencies in his behaviour and business ethics. Friends were almost certainly something the Colonel knew he couldn't afford. The closest he came were the old carnies he employed, like Jack Kaplan. At least they'd known him before he was rich. He seems to have been well aware that companionship was something to be bought and paid for. On one occasion when Gabe Tucker was living in Houston, he got a call from the Colonel at his home in Palm Springs.

"Come out here and help me. I'll pay you two hundred dollars a week to smoke cigars with me."

Tucker, expecting something fairly substantial in the way of problems, dropped everything and drove to the airport. When he got to L.A., the Colonel and Tom Diskin were waiting for him and took him directly to the William Morris office. The Colonel told

Colonel Parker, age 16.

Colonel Tom Parker (née Andreas van Kuijk) is on the left. With him are his father, his brother, and a sister.

The house (stable) of the van Kuijk family in Breda is to the right of the building with "Kon. Erk. Harmonie De Unie." *(All photos from the author's collection)*

Dries in the mountain guard in Hawaii.

Dries as an American soldier, stationed at Fort Shafter in Hawaii. He sent the picture to his friend Cees in Holland.

Johnny J. Jones Exposition in 1932. Parker, who had just joined the circus, is on the far right of the group under "Oriental and European"; he is dressed in a white shirt and cap. *(All photos from the author's collection)*

Colonel Parker, again in Hawaii, but some years later.
(Photo permission John E. Simonds)

Colonel Parker on the road with Elvis, July 1956.

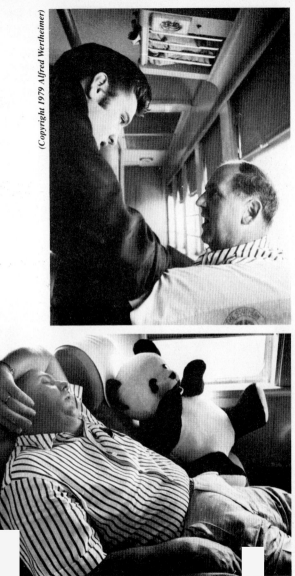

Colonel Tom Parker with a reporter backstage at *The Steve Allen Show*, New York City, July 2, 1956. *(Copyright 1979 Alfred Wertheimer)*

Colonel Parker at work. *(Copyright 1987 Alfred Wertheimer)*

The manager and his star.

Publicity shot of Elvis and the Colonel on the set of *Love Me Tender*. *(AP/Wide World Photos)*

The unedited caption for this 1957 photo reads as follows: "Tom Parker, of Madison, Tenn., beams on protégé Elvis Presley, who doesn't exactly look depressed himself. And why should he? Under Parker's management, the sideburned virtuoso of the mobile hips blossomed into a 20-million-dollar entertainment property (gross, that is) last year. Parker, who's managed many artists before hooking up with his prize bonanza, arranges Presley's personal appearances, TV performances, his movie making, and his swelling fortune. 'We've been good for each other,' says 'Colonel' Tom. As to his sloe-eyed charge: 'He's like most other twenty-one-year-old fellows. He has a few dates, takes care of his folks, and tries hard to live right.' "
(AP/Wide World Photos)

(AP/Wide World Photos)

(Copyright 1979 Alfred Wertheimer)

Wherever he went, the Colonel busied himself handing out photos of Elvis to fans.

Colonel Parker had this rather odd photo of himself printed on buttons, which he handed out to friends. *(The author's collection)*

Elvis and the Colonel and the army.

Colonel Parker caught napping.

(AP/Wide World Photos)

Colonel Parker posed in rare celebrity publicity photos.

(AP/Wide World Photos)

Colonel Parker with Elvis Presley on location for *Change of Habit*. *(The Museum of Modern Art/Film Stills Archive)*

After Elvis's death, Parker continued to sell his star.
(AP/Wide World Photos)

Reputed to be a picture of Colonel Parker dressed up as Santa Claus for a Las Vegas charity.
(AP/Wide World Photos)

Colonel Parker emerged from retirement on the tenth anniversary of Elvis Presley's death. This August 11, 1987, photo was taken in a bedroom of the Elvis Presley Suite at the Las Vegas Hilton, where Parker conducted a rare news conference. *(AP/Wide World Photos)*

the Morris executives that he wanted to employ Tucker for a short while and that they should put him on the payroll. When they finally got to Parker's home, Gabe Tucker discovered to his amazement that the Colonel had been telling the literal truth on the phone. All he wanted from Tucker was someone to keep him company and listen to his stories. He was indeed paying a man to smoke cigars with him.

One of the best-kept secrets in the whole of the Tom Parker mystery is what his home life was like. Marie, his wife, seems to have been the invisible woman. We know she kept cats and kept herself as far in the background as it was possible to be and still retain an identity. That's about the limit of the world's information. Nobody asked Marie Parker how she felt when a good ole boy was flown in all the way from Houston so her husband could have someone to talk to. It may be that nothing is known about the Parker home life because essentially there wasn't one. With the wheeling and dealing, the cookhouse politics, the rambling monologues, and Elvis, the Colonel didn't have time for anything approaching a conventional marriage. He also doesn't appear to have had either mistresses or girlfriends. Maybe the real epitaph to the marriage between Tom Parker and Marie Mott was the lifelong nickname he had for her: "Miz Ree." Phonetically, it was too close to *misery*.

12

"And you listen to me, Bindle! We close the show with 'Silent Night' and that's that. I don't want to hear no more arguments."

The Colonel was fighting a rearguard action but not about to admit it. The TV special was now out of his hands, but that didn't matter. Right to the end he'd go on tossing every possible spanner into the works.

"You hear me, Bindle?"

Steve Binder took a deep breath. Once again he was going to have to explain to the Colonel that the Elvis Presley TV special was not going to close with "Silent Night," or any other Christmas carol, hymn, or sacred song. While he was explaining, he would try and forget that the Colonel was acting disruptive and being generally abusive. He had even twisted Binder's name into the contemptuous "Bindle."

As far as Steve Binder was concerned, the matter was closed. He was the director and Elvis Presley was the star. They'd discussed the matter and had come to a mutually agreeable conclusion. Indeed, Elvis had been quite enthusiastic. The TV special would conclude with a completely new composition, "If I Can Dream." It wasn't a Christmas song, but it did have a certain inspirational message.

At that particular moment Elvis was looking like no help at all. He sat on the sidelines of the argument, hunched over, staring at his shoes as the Colonel blustered on. Suddenly the Colonel played his final trump.

"And the main reason we're going to close the show with 'Silent Night' is because Elvis wants it that way." He turned on Elvis. "Isn't that right, Elvis?"

Elvis silently nodded. He didn't bother to look up. The Colonel grinned sourly at Binder.

"So that's that. 'Silent Night' is in the show."

Satisfied with his victory, the Colonel stalked out of the room. Elvis slowly raised his head.

"That's all right, don't worry about it. We'll take it out."

Steve Binder looked at him in amazement. It scarcely seemed possible that someone of Elvis's stature was afraid to stand up to his manager, even if his career was on the line.

In January 1968, Colonel Parker had announced to the press that Elvis would return to national TV after an absence of close to a decade. Since his induction into the army he had made just one appearance, on the Frank Sinatra show. NBC-TV, with sponsorship from the Singer Sewing Machine Company, would finance and produce a one-hour Elvis Presley special to go out on the air the following Christmas. Even when he made the announcement, the Colonel had a fully formed idea in his head. The Elvis Christmas show was going to be yet another of the Colonel's low-rent creations. Elvis would walk onto a "Christmasy" set, introduce himself, sing twenty-four Christmas tunes, wish everybody happy holidays, and split. The Colonel would pick up the check. If everything went according to plan, there might even be an album out of the show. Elvis's *Christmas Album Volume 2* was a distinct possibility.

As preparations went ahead the Colonel discovered that, for virtually the first time in his association with Elvis, he wasn't going to have things all his own way. NBC had appointed an up-and-coming director, Steve Binder, as both producer and director. Binder had very firm ideas as to what the special was going to be and what it meant to Elvis and, as a feisty outsider who hadn't been brainwashed with the doctrine of the Colonel's infallibility, was quite prepared to fight for those ideas.

"I felt very, very strongly that the television special was Elvis's moment of truth. If he did another MGM movie on the special, he would wipe out his career and he would be known only as that phenomenon who came along in the fifties, shook his hips, and had a great manager. On the reverse side, if he could do a special and prove that he was still number one, he could have a whole rejuvenation thing going. If we could create an atmosphere of making Elvis feel that he was part of the special, that he was creating the special himself, the same way he was originally involved in producing his own records in the old days, before the movies, then we would have a great special. People would really see Elvis Presley, not what the Colonel wanted them to see. I in no way wanted to do a Christmas show full of Christmas songs. I wanted to leave that to the Andy Williamses and Perry Comos. The one thing I knew that I wanted was that

Elvis should say something; let the world in on that great secret, find out what kind of man he really was."

This was possibly the first plain truth that had been voiced around Elvis in six years. Steve Binder was basically everything the Colonel feared. He was from the outside and he wouldn't assume the role of courtier around either Elvis or the Colonel. When he came out with his plans, he wasn't just bucking the Colonel on a single project; he was actively considering what the future might hold for Elvis as a performer. That was something else that hadn't been considered since Elvis had come out of the army. In fact, Binder was actively dismantling both the Colonel's master plan and the Colonel's philosophy. He was about to junk the "new" Elvis, the Colonel's Frankenstein creation that had lurched disastrously through the best part of the sixties. He would dress Elvis in black leather and take him back to his roots in the rocking fifties. "If I Can Dream" may have been the closing number, but the basic spirit of the show was contained in songs like "Guitar Man" and "One Night."

Possibly the unique thing about Binder, though, was that he was challenging Elvis to give his all. A challenge was something else that hadn't been offered to Elvis since he'd been taught to drive a tank. The movies in the sixties had all been made according to the Parker principles: Always leave 'em hungry. Always hold out; never go all the way until you absolutely have to. Do the minimum for the money. Suddenly Elvis was being asked to stretch himself to the limit.

The Colonel may have been powerful, but even he didn't have the clout to fight NBC and the Singer Company when they had their minds made up. Both the network and the sponsor liked Binder's idea and that's what they were going with. There would be no return to the Colonel's concept. About the only weapon the Colonel had was to pull his star out of the production altogether. Although he must have seriously considered this piece of high drama, even the Colonel's ego wasn't desperate enough to make him dump a whole TV special just because he couldn't have his own way.

Not that Colonel Tom could find it within himself to give in gracefully. The run-in over "Silent Night" was only one in a series of petty harassments that continued clear up to showtime, when the Colonel attempted to cause trouble by demanding all the complimentary tickets being handed out to the invited audience, which would be the major part of the live atmosphere of the show. Binder wanted an audience that was young, good-looking, and excited. Parker presumably wanted to use them as rewards for favors and hand them out to his elderly cronies. To any rational person, it was a farcical situation. Here was a major entertainer, with his career quite literally on the line, preparing for an international TV spectacular. One might logically expect that the entertainer's manager would be doing everything he could to smooth the way to make the show the greatest possible success. Instead, Tom Parker, for petty personal reasons, was doing everything he could to sabotage the show. It was practically unthinkable.

As history records, the *Elvis Presley NBC Special* was an unqualified success. In his book *Mystery Train,* rock critic Greil Marcus makes the graphic comment "[it was] the finest music of his life. If there was ever music that bleeds, this was it. Nothing came easy that night and he gave everything that he had—more than anyone knew he had." Elvis Presley the rock 'n' roller was back and the world realized it might be time to take him seriously again. It was a major breakthrough, a complete comeback, achieved without any help from Tom Parker and despite all his machinations and dirty tricks.

Elvis's seeming comeback to reality wasn't simply a matter of the TV special. Elvis himself seemed to have been reenergized. He had taken up the challenge and he had triumphed. There was a whole new future, loaded with possibilities, opening up to him, and Elvis was clearly excited at the prospect. On January 14, 1969, less than two months after the NBC special had been aired to critical raves, Elvis went into American Studios in Memphis and cut a tune called "Suspicious Minds." Just as "Heartbreak Hotel" or "Blue Suede Shoes" had represented the glory years of the fifties and "Do the Clam" had summed up the dire haul through the sixties, "Suspicious Minds" would be associated with his new lease on life in the early seventies. It was a powerful song to which Elvis would do absolute justice. This was the truly mature Elvis. At thirty-four, he was confident of his voice and in the session he was comfortable with the big-sound rock arrangement. It was a piece of work to make the world sit up and take notice. True to form, though, the Colonel did his best to ensure that the whole idea died at birth.

As usual, what should have been purely a recording session started with a protracted bout of song hustling. Lamar Fike came in with a bundle of generally mediocre tunes from Hill & Range. The best of the bunch was a balled titled "Kentucky Rain." "In the Ghetto" came from another source and would be the closest Elvis would come to a protest song. Chips Moman, who owned American Studios, had his own publishing company and one of his writers, Mark James, had come up with a song, "Suspicious Minds," to which Elvis took an immediate shine. The usual triumvirate of the Colonel, Tom Diskin, and Freddy Bienstock were present at the sessions, and when it became clear to them that Elvis was determined to cut the tune, they moved in on Moman and started pressuring him to give them a piece of the publishing rights.

"Hell, Chips, if you really want Elvis to release your tune, you ought to be giving us a taste. Just think how much goddamn money you're going to make. Fifty percent of a fortune is a lot better than a hundred percent of nothing."

Moman, a well-respected producer in his own right flatly refused to see it their way. As far as he was concerned the deal was a simple one. He had a song and Elvis liked it and wanted to record it. There was nothing more to be said. It would be nice for both him and Mark James if Elvis put out their song, but he certainly wasn't about to be giving out any percentage kickbacks in order to see it happen. Once again someone was prepared to stand up to the Colonel.

The Colonel began to threaten and bluster. If there wasn't going to be any piece of the action coming in their direction, there was no way Elvis would be releasing "Suspicious Minds." Chips Moman simply shrugged. The song belonged to him and James and they weren't going to give away any part of it. The Colonel and his cohorts switched the focus of their attack. Maybe Elvis would be an easier target. They tried to break him down.

"Come on, Elvis, you don't need that song. It wasn' like it was any great tune. We've already got 'In the Ghetto' and 'Kentucky Rain.' What do we need to cut this one for?"

Elvis, maybe feeling more on his own turf in the recording studio, dug in his toes and actually stood up to the Colonel. He wanted to do the tune and that wa that. The Colonel growled that the tune would be released over his dead body. Sure, Elvis could record the song, but he'd make damn sure that RCA never put it out. RCA would do what he told them. The situation might have remained deadlocked and "Suspicious Minds" might never have seen the light of day had not RCA boss Harry Jenkins arrived at that point. Jenkins listened to both sides of the argument and to the rough demos of the tune. To him, the answer was obvious.

"Gentlemen, the man is right. This is a good song. It will be a hit record and that's what we're here to cut."

The Colonel continued to bluster, but once again he'd lost and Elvis's career was positively enhanced by his defeat. As well as pointing up the way Elvis was supposed to concentrate on making music while the businessmen around him were turning his recording sessions into a cattle market, this was yet another example of how the Colonel would willingly sacrifice product quality for a fast greasy buck.

The end of a decade is a good time for anyone to take stock of his or her own life, and the Colonel and Elvis were no exceptions. The end of the sixties was obviously a major turning point. One part of Elvis's career was clearly on its last legs, while another showed at least the potential of opening up radical new vistas. His movie career was all but dead. *Change of Habit* had proved to be little more than an unfortunate joke (co-star Mary Tyler Moore—playing a nun— had one scene in which she was raped by teenage hoods). *Charro!*, a substandard Italian-style western, in which Elvis sported a Clint Eastwood Man with No Name three-day growth of beard, was supposed to be a move away from the cotton-candy comedies, but it was so badly made, it wound up going out as half of a drive-in double feature along with *Ghidrah, The*

Three-Headed Monster. In some parts of the country and in Europe, distributors were refusing to take Elvis pictures because they now did such terrible business. One of the last major markets that was still loyal to the Elvis movie was in India, where films liked *Harum Scarum* fitted perfectly with the highly mannered Indian popular cinema.

In the plus column, Steve Binder and the NBC special had pointed Elvis in the obvious direction. If Elvis was to have a career in the seventies, the only way to go was back to rock 'n' roll. Elvis was already demonstrating that he appreciated this and was taking a good deal more care with his recordings. Elvis, and by association, the Colonel, had been given a new lease on life, and it was now up to them to prove what they were going to make of it.

It wasn't going to be easy. Elvis had been completely isolated for an entire decade, and in that time the world, particularly the world of rock 'n' roll, had changed beyond all recognition. The single of "Suspicious Minds" was released during the same month as Woodstock. Later in the same year, the Rolling Stones and the Hell's Angels would preside over killing and mayhem at the Altamont free concert. The hot acts of the time were the Doors, Jimi Hendrix, and the Who, and young Americans were listening to them, between firefights in the jungles of Vietnam. For Elvis, the outside world was alien territory and if he was going to have a place in it, there would have to be some radical rethinking.

In the wake of the NBC special, Elvis could have done just about anything. There was no reason why he shouldn't have headlined a massive Woodstock-style open-air concert. Bob Dylan would do exactly that at England's Isle of Wight Festival. There's little doubt that Bill Graham, the leading rock impresario of the time, would have put on Elvis for as many nights as he wanted at the Fillmores East and West. The Colonel, however, with his famous limited vision, wanted no truck with the new world of contemporary rock. He didn't trust it. What had been good enough for Eddy Arnold was still good enough for Elvis, and he headed straight back to his good-ole-boy cronies in Las Vegas.

The first person the Colonel contacted was the talent booker Tom Miller. Miller was a big fat man with white hair who negotiated with the Vegas casinos on behalf of old-time show-biz establishment figures like Red Skelton and Donald O'Connor. The initial idea was to put Elvis in as the very first act at the brand-new International Hotel. Going to the International would be like keeping it in the family: Kirk Kerkorian, its owner, had been a big wheel at MGM when the Colonel was lording it over his cookhouse there. Alex Shoofey, the general manager, had worked at the Sahara for Milton Prell, Parker's old buddy and the host of Elvis's wedding. It didn't seem as though Tom Parker was particularly thinking about Elvis's future or welfare. He seemed to be working on pure instinct, homing in on the place where he'd feel the most comfortable.

In 1969 the International Hotel was the newest and biggest of the Las Vegas casinos. It had been completed in 1968 and its main room had yet to open. Why shouldn't Elvis do the honors? It would be a prestige event. Then the Colonel got cold feet. He didn't want Elvis making his live comeback in a virgin room. Parker wanted to see another top-class performer go in there first and shake out the bugs. Barbra Streisand opened the International and most reports seem to indicate that she regretted being the first into the new room.

Elvis was scheduled to appear for one week in July

1969, and the buildup to his stage return prompted a frenzy of activity. Elvis's face was plastered all over the city. The Colonel rented every available billboard and took full-page advertisements both in the local Las Vegas papers and in the entertainment trades. With something to promote, the Colonel was back in his element. He was making sure that the name Elvis Presley would blaze across the sky. Not that the Colonel was about to compromise with the current Las Vegas style. Despite the garish neon, the casino hotels did their best to invest their top-line shows with a certain spurious class. The Vegas image was Frank Sinatra or Tony Bennett in a tuxedo, but the Colonel didn't want any part of this. Just because Las Vegas did it their way was no reason, in the Colonel's estimation, to change his own garish carny style of promotion or to relinquish his "common touch." The Colonel's advertising shrieked rather than seduced.

The excitement and ballyhoo was also tempered with a certain amount of trepidation. Elvis was understandably nervous about playing Las Vegas, the one place in the world where he had seriously bombed. It had been fourteen years since then, but he wasn't about to forget the hour of hell he'd gone through when he'd opened at the New Frontier back in the fifties. If he failed this second time around, he knew that his superstar status would be seriously undermined.

The Colonel also had his worries. The opening show was becoming increasingly lavish. Tom Diskin had worked with Elvis to pull together the best possible band and had signed James Burton as lead guitar and band leader. Jerry Scheff was on bass; John Wilkinson, rhythm guitar; Ronnie Tutt on drums; and Larry Muhoberic, piano. In addition to this highly impressive lineup, there was the gospel quartet, the Imperials; the Sweet Inspirations; and a twenty-five-piece orchestra. Initially the Colonel blanched at the expense. The old Elvis had gone onstage with a three- or maybe four-piece group and the Jordanaires. In the end, though, Parker was forced to concede that if you wanted to look like a megastar, you had to spend the money. The Colonel may have been a cheapskate, but he didn't want to look like one in front of all of show business, and the thirty-nine-person ensemble stayed. But the Colonel couldn't resist putting his own hokey stamp on the show. Just as he'd padded the Elvis Presley shows in the fifties with freaks, has-beens, and losers, he insisted that old-time barroom comedian Sammy Shore should open for Elvis at the International.

As the opening night grew closer it was clear that Elvis's return was going to be the show-biz event of the year. Every imaginable celebrity was calling for tickets. The Colonel's own guest list rivaled the Manhattan telephone directory. The final touch was provided when owner Kirk Kerkorian sent his own DC-9 to New York to fly in the entire rock press. This didn't just mean reporters from the daily newspapers and news magazines like *Time* and *Newsweek;* there were also representatives of the new "serious" rock critics from *Rolling Stone* and *Crawdaddy.* For Elvis, the opening at Vegas would be either a new dawn or a swan song. Quite literally, the whole wide world was watching.

As with the NBC special, history has said it all. Elvis pulled off a triumph. In his biography *Elvis,* Jerry Hopkins presents a typical eyewitness account. "Elvis sauntered to center stage, grabbed the microphone from its stand, hit a pose from the fifties—legs braced, knees snapping almost imperceptibly—and before he could begin the show, the audience stopped him cold.

Just as he was about to begin his first song, he was hit in the face with a roar. He looked. All two thousand people were on their feet, pounding their hands together and whistling, many of them standing on their chairs and screaming." Without singing a note, Elvis was getting a standing ovation. As the black-clad Elvis (the white rhinestone jumpsuits were part of the future) roared through his rock 'n' roll hits, slowed the tempo with tunes like "Memories" and "Love Me Tender," premiered "Suspicious Minds," and even dipped into the Beatles' songbook for "Yesterday" and a snatch of "Hey Jude," the Colonel stood tensely in the wings. It was a moment of truth for him too. Out front the capacity crowd had no doubts. That the one-time rock king still deserved the crown. After his initial nervousness, Elvis proved that he was fit, well rehearsed, and totally on top of the show. After the final encore, Red West reported that Parker was shaking with emotion.

The critics were ecstatic. *Billboard*'s front page trumpeted "Elvis Retains Touch in Return to Stage." *Variety* called him a "superstar" and described him as "very much in command of the entire scene." David Dalton, writing in *Rolling Stone,* called Elvis "supernatural, his own resurrection." By the end of July he had played to 101,500 paying customers, with scarcely an empty seat in the house.

The morning after the show Parker met with the International's general manager, Alex Shoofey. The Colonel had Tom Diskin and Bitsy Mott backing him up. They were in the hotel's dining room, sitting at a big round table with a red tablecloth. After some initial small talk and sparring, Shoofey got down to the point. He would like to offer Elvis a five-year contract Elvis would play two months a year—February and

August—at the International. He'd be paid a hundred and twenty-five thousand a week in a deal that would gross Elvis and the Colonel a cool million each year. The Colonel didn't dicker; he practically fell over himself in his eagerness to close.

"Bitsy, give me a pen."

While the astounded Shoofey looked on old Colonel Tom, the world's greatest manager, began scrawling terms on the tablecloth. When he was through, he grinned at Shoofey.

"Okay, there it is. If you want it, sign it."

He held out the pen. Alex Shoofey blinked. Then he took the pen and wrote his signature on the red cloth. The Colonel immediately got to his feet. That was that. He was taking off like a thief from a robbery.

"Bitsy, grab that cloth and bring it to my room."

Later, a grinning Alex Shoofey would tell the press that it "was the best deal made in this town."

According to the legend, the tablecloth deal was a living example of Colonel Tom Parker's downhome genius. He could sit down in a hotel dining room and draw up a million-dollar deal. What a guy! The irony is that although Elvis was guaranteed a million a year for five years, it was considerably less than he might have had if Parker had done some real hard-nosed negotiating. It was a rerun of the Hal Wallis deal. In the course of five years, much lesser stars would play the International Hotel and come out with more than a hundred and twenty-five grand a week. The Colonel hadn't even allowed for the fact of inflation. Considering that Elvis was paying the thirty-nine musicians and singers, it starts to look a lot less than sweet. It was even creatively stupid. Elvis had just struggled to achieve a near-miraculous comeback after years of sloppy repetitive work and being tied to long-term movie contracts. The very next day Colonel Parker, who should have been acting like king of the hill, was so anxious to grab Alex Shoofey's deal that he had to scribble it on a tablecloth. When Shoofey announced that it was "the best deal ever made in this town," he wasn't talking from the Colonel's point of view. The Colonel's unique combination of greed and insecurity had tied Elvis to the Las Vegas world of Sammy Davis and Wayne Newton until the mid-seventies.

It might be an exaggeration to say that Elvis Presley's death warrant was signed on that red tablecloth, but not that much of an exaggeration.

13

It was a ludicrous sight. In front came the security guards holding back the curious onlookers. Behind them was this bulky bald man in a battered fedora, a baggy, old-fashioned suit, and a bow tie. Behind him were three young men in neat dark suits, each carrying a basket of silver dollars. Under the Colonel's direction they all started stuffing money into the slot machines as fast as they could. The old man shouted and gestured with the cane he carried. The word went around the room. Colonel Tom Parker—Elvis Presley's manager—was playing the slot machines! The Colonel was over there playing the slots while Elvis was down in the main lounge doing his show. How about that?

Alex Shoofey made another remark about Tom Parker that wasn't a fraction so widely reported as the one about "the best deal ever made in this town."

"He was one of the best customers we had. He was good for a million dollars a year."

Well before Elvis Presley opened in Las Vegas, Colonel Tom Parker was already a compulsive gambler, which must have been a major factor in his decision to take Elvis to Vegas. The Colonel had gambled most of his life; there are damn few carnies who don't. The carny, however, likes to have an edge and he plays to win. This was certainly Parker's attitude during the making of *King Creole* as he sat by the pool and played poker with Walter Matthau and refused to accept his checks. Somewhere along the line, something had come unhinged. Whatever turns gambling from fun to self-destruction had taken hold of Tom Parker and parted him from his senses. He had lost control and he had acquired a taste for losing. The madness of isolation, wealth, and adulation that pushed Elvis to impossible games with medication seems also to have infected the Colonel and driven him to the crap tables.

The ever-present Bitsy Mott had more than enough experience of Parker's will to lose. "He's got a weakness. When you get him over to the slot machines he'd play those for fun, but when you get him over on the roulette and blackjack tables he plays stupid. In fact, they take off the limit when he comes to the tables. He liked to play craps. He covers the two spot, the three spot, the seven spot, the eleven spot. They give you good odds, but it's ridiculous to bet on them because they don't come up that often. He lost a big lump. I've watched him. . . . He doesn't do it with ignorance, he knows what's going on. Evidently he doesn't mind to lose that money."

Parker's technique with roulette was equally bizarre. He'd cover half the numbers on the table and put extra on the twenty-six because he was born June

26. He'd pass handfuls of money to the people with him. It seemed there was just no way he could lose money fast enough. Estimates of his losses ran between $25,000 and $75,000 a month.

Parker's gambling caused his longtime associate Jean Aberbach to go on record with his only public adverse comment regarding the Colonel.

"His big change came when Elvis started working in Vegas. Before the time they went to Vegas, Colonel Parker was an extremely conservative, extremely friendly family-oriented man. It was almost like Doctor Jekyll and Mister Hyde. He was the most wonderful human being that God created, but once he came to Vegas I couldn't recognize him. From what I read and heard he had become one of the biggest losers of all time. Not only that, also the most consistent loser. Until that time the Colonel did not even want to spend one dollar on anything; he used to hustle everybody, make them pay for everything. All of a sudden, this same person lost up to a million dollars a year. It's unbelievable because in the United States you cannot deduct gambling losses from your income."

Down at the grass roots, someone on the Sahara casino staff referred to him as "our favorite roulette junkie."

In Vegas they're kind to their favorites. As the highest of high rollers, who had an insurance policy against his debts singing in the lounge, Colonel Tom was accorded every privilege. Although Elvis worked at the International only two months in the year, the Colonel set up permanent camp there. He had a three-room suite on the fourth floor. He was guarded twenty-four hours a day and had carte blanche on all services. The hotel staff had instructions never to say no to the Colonel. Even when he went home to Palm Springs, he was still permitted to gamble by phone.

He'd pick a roulette number and the croupier would tell him if he'd won.

"Sorry, Colonel, you just missed it."

He also had an office. All the cookhouse stuff was carefully trucked out from Hollywood. The elephants, the stuffed animals, the pictures of Elvis, the crated-up appliances, and the food. There's a legend that Joseph Stalin had copies of the same room constructed in buildings all over Russia so that no matter what town he was in, he'd always feel at home. Tom Parker seemed to be doing much the same thing.

When the Hilton group bought the International in 1972, it at first seemed the Colonel's antics might no longer be tolerated. Barron Hilton arrived in Vegas determined to do something about Parker and his weird situation. Hilton's determination wilted, however, when some of the old-timers explained to him just how valuable Parker was to the casino. Within a matter of weeks Barron Hilton had done a complete about-face and was pampering the Colonel. He even paid Parker, who would receive fifty thousand dollars a year for "talent and publicity consulting services." What did it matter? It all came back through the tables anyway.

The worst part of the gambling obsession was that it began to eat into Parker's time. Where once the Colonel was a bundle of bellowing energy, he now only went through the motions. He had the same team around him; it was no great problem to make it look like business as usual. The Colonel's day would start with an enormous breakfast—rib-eye steak topped with country ham, fried eggs and bacon, imported cheeses, and hot biscuits. Just before nine he'd either call his office or wander in there. As in Hollywood, the Colonel's army would be expected to be on time and ready to roll.

Unlike in Hollywood, the Colonel wouldn't stay around to watch for long. By ten-thirty he'd be getting twitchy. He'd pick up his cane and announce, "I think we better go down to my casino office." He'd wander off and lose some money and leave the business of the day to the underlings.

After the double whammy of the TV special and the Las Vegas opening, everyone seemed to have plans for Elvis except Tom Parker. In the first flurry of excitement, there was talk about a closed-circuit TV show and another show to be transmitted by satellite from Anaheim Stadium. Both suggestions came to nothing. Steve Binder came up with the idea that Elvis should host a documentary movie about the history of rock 'n' roll. Abe Lastfogel negotiated on behalf of Parker, whose demands were nothing short of revenge on Binder for bucking him over the TV special. Parker wanted a million dollars cash plus fifty percent of the profits and twenty-five percent of the TV sales. He also stipulated that the total cost of the picture should not exceed two million. It didn't matter that Binder had been crucial in creating the momentum for Elvis's comeback and that he might have an equally good concept here. All the Colonel cared about was getting even, punishing the upstart. The point had arrived when Parker's need to gratify his egomania outweighed any other consideration. Binder could do nothing except walk away from the project.

The idea of the documentary film was also in the Colonel's head. It was fairly obvious one. Elvis had pretty much run out of road on any other kind of movie. The Colonel, predictable as ever, went back to the old boys at MGM. It was decided that the movie would follow Elvis through rehearsals and the entire buildup to his 1970 summer season in Las Vegas. Directed by Dennis Sanders and produced by Dale Hutchinson, it was a fascinating insight into the closed world of Elvis Presley but left a good deal to be desired as a movie. It was shot on the cheap and looked it. There was also the somewhat deceptive suggestion that what we were watching was the *first* Presley show in Vegas, rather than the second. *Elvis, That's the Way It Is* gave the impression it was showing the original comeback rather than events of a year later.

The making of the documentary gave the Colonel the excuse to get out and do some old-fashioned promoting, which was, aside from eating and gambling, the only activity that seemed to give him any pleasure. The movie was full of his garish billboards and displays. A huge flag over the entrance of the International declared that this was the "Elvis Summer Festival." The camera dwelled lovingly on the souvenirs, the posters, the scarves, the stuffed toys, the Styrofoam Elvis skimmers.

The movie, however, was only icing on the cake. The Colonel's long-term idea was to put Elvis out on the road and pretty much keep him there. The Colonel was once again establishing a long-range routine, although it had been clearly demonstrated in the sixties to be about the worst thing anyone could do to Elvis Presley. Elvis was an artist who thrived on novelty and challenge. When pushed, he'd rise valiantly to the occasion and summon all his almost superhuman charisma. When any situation shook down to routine and repetition, Elvis rapidly lost interest and contented himself with merely going through the motions.

At first, touring was a new experience and Elvis threw himself into it with considerable enthusiasm. He was seeing his audience again, feeling their re-

sponse, and receiving the performers' instant feed-
back and instant gratification. Touring, however, can
also be a numbing experience, second only to working
on a production line, and the Colonel, anxious to cash
in as much as possible, pitchforked Elvis into it head-
first. In 1971, Elvis played 156 shows. This was twice,
going on three times, what the Rolling Stones might
play during a year when they were on tour. It was a
hell of a strain to put on a man in his mid-thirties
who'd just had a ten-year layoff from the stage.

The danger in all rock 'n' roll touring is basically the
tedium. There is a jolt of the most intense excitement,
which usually lasts for not more than a couple of
hours, depending on the length of the particular artist's act. The rest of the time, the performer is a spare
part whom most of the road crew would rather see
locked up in his own flight case. The temptation is
always to party, and the one thing Elvis Presley
couldn't resist was temptation. Indeed, he carried his
own party with him and, providing he didn't leave the
hotel, he could have pretty much anything he
wanted. Elvis on the road turned into a traveling bac-
chanal of women and pills that, unlike the more public excesses of the Stones, the Who, or Led Zeppelin,
were shielded from press and public by a small army
of security guards.

The disintegration came fast. While Elvis indulged
himself with Quaaludes, Percodan, and cheerleaders,
the Colonel was losing a million bucks a year at the
tables. The empire was clearly out of control.

Things weren't so out of control that the Colonel
couldn't cut himself a new deal with Elvis for a larger
slice of the pie. Relative to record and movie money,
Parker didn't take all that much of what Elvis made
on the road. A long time had elapsed since Elvis had

been on tour, and the Colonel hadn't bothered to
update the contracts when he'd revised everything
else back around the time of the wedding. The over
sight was soon put to rights with yet another of hi
unbelievable documents. On February 4, 1972, the
Colonel sent Elvis the new tour agreements:

The following constitutes our agreement, between
you and Col. Tom Parker, All Star Shows, P.O. Bo
220, Madison, Tenn. with respect to personal ap
pearance tours of the Elvis Presley Show, concer
dates as selected by Col. Parker exclusively.

In consideration for the rendition of our com
plete organizing of tours, handling of all transporta
tion, reservations, talent, tour supervision, packag
ing, show security setup, chartering of aircraft, etc
with Mr. Diskin and his staff, it is understood tha
the deduction of all show-related expenses, includ
ing agency commissions, any bonuses that you ma
decide to distribute at the close of the tours (simila
but not limited to what has been done in the past
all charter transportation, talent costs, personne
and office expenses, telephone and show-related ex
penses from opening till closing, but not includin
any personal expenses, promotion, and advertising
from the total gross receipts received by All Sta
Shows or by Elvis Presley, the remaining balanc
shall be divided: 2/3 to Elvis Presley, 1/3 to All Sta
Shows.

If the above meets with your approval, kindly s
indicate by signing in the space below.

Elvis signed without comment. It didn't occur to
him to wonder why the Colonel took so much troubl
writing up contracts with him when their other busi
ness deals were scrawled on tablecloths. Later ther

would be riders added giving Parker merchandising rights and other fringe benefits, and—exceedingly strange—a clause that made Parker *personally* responsible for the planning and supervision of the shows. At the age of sixty-two, Colonel Tom Parker had committed himself to travel with the tours. It was as though he were lashing himself to the mast. Whatever happened to the good ship *Elvis*, the Colonel was going to be there till the end.

There was just one problem with having Elvis out on the road for half the year. It became almost impossible to get him into the studio. Put crudely, the Colonel now had a star who was either out on tour or out to lunch. This wasn't, however, beyond the Colonel's ingenuity. Elvis would begin cutting a long series of live albums, and RCA's quota could be met without his setting foot in a studio. The Colonel was creating a seventies' live-touring rut that was as deep and damaging as the sixties' movie rut had been.

The irony was that while on the inside the empire was getting set to crumble, to all outward appearances Elvis and the Colonel were still on a fabulous roll. The extensive touring was breaking box-office records and culminated in a mammoth weekend-long extravaganza at New York's Madison Square Garden in June 1972. More than eighty thousand tickets were sold for the four shows, the first time Elvis had played live in the Big Apple. RCA also pulled out all the stops. The live album—*Elvis as Recorded at Madison Square Garden*—which was recorded during the course of the shows, was mixed, pressed, and in the stores within two weeks. Unfortunately, what the album had in speed, it rather lacked in value. No fewer than half the tunes had been released before in live form.

To the outside world Elvis was once again the undisputed King. His white spangled jumpsuits had become as much a pop icon as the gold lamé of the fifties. With America conquered, the next logical move was for Elvis to tour the world. It wasn't just a matter of Europe. Led by Japan, the noncommunist countries of the Far East were also clamoring loudly for appearances by Elvis and, with their new industrial affluence, they had the money to pay for them. Parker's back was being pushed firmly against the wall. Having no reasonable excuse as to why Elvis shouldn't have a blockbuster world tour, all the Colonel could do was duck the issue.

The offers from other countries were very tempting indeed. A British promoter offered a million dollars plus a round-trip private airliner across the Atlantic. The most lavish came from a Japanese promoter whom Alex Shoofey introduced to the Colonel. From the instant the unfortunate man was ushered into his suite at the International, the Colonel treated him with open hostility. He couldn't have been ruder if he were getting even for Pearl Harbor.

"I want two million dollars on my desk by tomorrow. I want you to make sure you cover this whole desk."

The Japanese smiled and made a half bow.

"No problem."

Shoofey backed up the man: His resources were immense; he had at least two million available in American banks. The only problem was that the Colonel didn't appear to be listening. His face had folded into the expression of a petulant child and he was grumbling.

"Don't wanna go to Japan."

Then the Colonel brightened. He'd thought of something. He fixed the Japanese with the fisheye stare.

"Tell you what I would like you to do. I'd like to do a

picture, but you have to come up with a million dollars. That's mine, for *me*. You pay for the movie and everything, and then we'll split the distribution, okay?"

Again the Japanese smiled.

"Okay."

The Colonel was suddenly angry.

"Forget it!"

Shoofey couldn't believe what he was hearing. The Colonel appeared to be taking leave of his senses, doing everything he could to screw up the deal short of punching the promoter. What was the matter with the man? What Shoofey didn't know was that Parker had no passport and was also too paranoid to contemplate Elvis going out of the country without him. He wasn't aware that the Colonel was stonewalling while waiting for a miracle to bail him out.

The get-out came in the unlikely form of Muhammad Ali. His heavyweight title fights were attracting such huge potential audiences that there was no way they could be contained in an arena, even one the size of Madison Square Garden, or restricted to one country. The fight promoters had turned to satellite technology to solve their problem. A live, closed-circuit transmission was relayed from space to all parts of the globe and projected, as it happened, on the screens of movie theaters all across the world. It was the Colonel's ten-year-old science fiction dream come true: one show, and an audience of hundreds of millions. The Colonel, however, wasn't going to cinemas. The live Elvis would be beamed directly to participating national TV networks. Wasn't that as good as a world tour?

Well, maybe . . . Unlike a title fight, there was no "outcome." The concept of a live broadcast was mainly in the mind of the beholder. Did it really matter whether Elvis is singing the song now or three weeks ago? A concert, no matter how spectacular, doesn't have the urgency of a boxing match. The fact that the show is live really offers only the prurient interest of waiting for the performer to make the kind of mistake normally edited out of a prerecorded show.

As the plans went ahead a number of things started to become apparent. The show would be staged in Hawaii, at the Honolulu International Arena. The gate would go to the Kui Lee Cancer Fund. The Colonel had chosen a Hawaiian venue, not because of his affection for the islands, but because Hawaii was the piece of U.S. sovereign territory closest to Japan in terms of time zones. The show, scheduled for January 14, 1973, was to take place at twelve-thirty at night. This was no exotic sop to Elvis's night owl life-style. A broadcast at 12:30 A.M. in Hawaii would play in Japan in the middle-evening TV prime time. The time factor also made it impractical and uneconomical to broadcast the show—now called *Aloha from Hawaii* —in either the United States or Europe. It ceased to look like a bold experiment in high-tech entertainment and more and more like some weird Tom Parker idea of a Japanese tour surrogate. All the rest of the world was getting a TV special from a romantic location. Only a few European countries ran the show the following day. The United States had to wait until April to see it, and in many countries, it wasn't shown until after Elvis's death.

The real kicker came when RCA released the *Aloha from Hawaii* double live album, the second live Elvis album in less than a year and the sixth released since 1969. Although the album went straight into the charts at number one and sold in excess of two million, there was a growing sense of fan resentment at the continuous duplication.

* * *

Back at the ranch, things were not going so well. Elvis's antics on the road had pushed Priscilla first into the arms of her dance teacher and then those of karate instructor Mike Stone. Elvis and Priscilla were separated by the end of 1972 and divorced in Santa Monica in October 1973. It was a shattering blow to Elvis's never particularly resilient ego. He was an international sex symbol, yet he couldn't keep his own wife. His behavior deteriorated as he appeared to stop caring. He retreated into a twilight zone of speed, tranquilizers, and painkillers. There was no one to halt the slide. For years he had lived exclusively in a world where his every whim was indulged and nobody ever said no.

Gone was Parker's paternal dream of Elvis, Priscilla, and their daughter, Lisa Marie, somehow having a place at their family hearth for the poor old Colonel in his final years. It was a preposterous fantasy, but on some deep emotional level, it was all the Colonel had. The alternative was simply to watch himself weaken as he got older and as, one by one, his enemies turned on him—the old bull elephant losing control of his herd as he dies by inches. Somewhere around this point Parker seems to have decided that the *only* defense was money.

If the Colonel had been very different, the year 1973 might have been a last chance to mount a rescue mission to save Elvis from his pills, his boredom, and his cheeseburgers. Elvis could have been dried out, counseled, analyzed, and invested with some career moves that might have rekindled his enthusiasm and self-respect. The Colonel was the Colonel, though, and his only thought was to get the money he needed to protect himself in his old age by taking it from Elvis in quite startling amounts.

The year 1973 was also Elvis's last chance to rescue himself. It was the last time he was still sufficiently in control to cut loose from the Colonel. Certainly the motivation existed, and on at least one occasion there was almost the opportunity. The summer season at the International was a less than happy one. Elvis was in bad shape, taking a lot of drugs and frequently verging on the irrational. On this particular night an incident with the hotel staff had launched Elvis into an extended onstage diatribe against the Hiltons and their organization. When Elvis finally came off the stage, the Colonel raced to the dressing room to deliver the strongest of reprimands. Elvis, however, wasn't having any. He might be behaving like a child, but he wasn't about to be treated like one. He beat the Colonel to the punch and started yelling about the Colonel's gambling. The particular beef seemed to be that they couldn't accept better offers from other hotels because of the Colonel's gambling debts at the International.

"And what about the goddamn MGM Grand? We could be opening that place for a fortune except you got me in hock with the fucking Hiltons!"

"You can't talk to me like that."

"The hell I can't."

"Then I quit."

Elvis sneered.

"You can't quit because you're fired."

"I have quit and I'm calling a press conference in the morning to explain the whole situation."

This was supposed to be the Colonel's parting shot. He stormed out of the dressing room and was waddling angrily down the hall. Elvis stuck his head around the door and yelled after him.

"I'm calling a press conference tonight."

When it came down to it, neither man called the

press. The Colonel retreated into his inner sanctum and began figuring out how much Elvis owed him. During the final years, the Colonel had it organized so that Elvis maintained a running debt to him, in preparation for a moment exactly like this. When the debt totaled several million, the Colonel had the figures delivered to Elvis. If he wanted out, that was what it was going to cost him. For a number of hours it seemed as if Elvis was moving to sever the relationship.

"Hell, daddy, let's pay him what he wants and be done with it."

Attorney Ed Hookstratten was on alert to be ready to move in and take control of the Presley empire once the Colonel had gone. Hookstratten had considerable experience in management, having handled Cary Grant, Glen Campbell, David Merrick, and Joseph Levine. The only serious resistance to firing the Colonel came from Elvis's father, Vernon. Vernon didn't know. Vernon wasn't sure.

"We may not have that much money, son."

In the end, it was Elvis's instability that concluded the incident. Instead of sitting down calmly and planning his route away from the Colonel's domination, he fell apart and went on a week-long rampage during which he swallowed every pill he could get his hands on, fought with the Memphis Mafia, and generally did his best to alienate everyone who was close to him and everyone who might be able to protect him. The nightmare of psychosis culminated with Elvis and the Memphis Mafia rushing out to pick up girls. Elvis was with a pretty teenager and proceeded to get them both overdosed on the cough medicine Hycodan. The girl was out for more than twenty-four hours and there was every possibility she might have sustained brain damage. The moment the still-unconscious teen was carried out of the house on a stretcher, Elvis called the Colonel. It was the Colonel's kind of operation. He'd know what to do. He'd keep it out of the papers and pay off the relatives and square the cops and the hospital staff. The rebellion was all over. The Colonel was back, cleaning up the mess and no doubt gloating. Just look, Elvis couldn't make it through a week on his own. Elvis Presley would never get out from under.

14

There's a hard core of Elvis Presley fans who have no doubts at all: Colonel Tom Parker killed Elvis. They don't mean that the old man put a gun to his head and pulled the trigger, but they feel that Parker was a venal, ignorant, greedy man who, motivated by nothing except his own short-term gain, set up a situation that in the long run couldn't do anything but destroy the star. Another school of thought says that nobody killed Elvis but Elvis himself. No matter how much stress, how much talent, or how much money is involved, a man is, in the final analysis, in control of his own destiny and his self-destruction cannot be blamed on anyone else. There's also a middle path that says, sure, Parker didn't actually kill Elvis Presley, but that is no reason why his conscience should rest easy. Parker was gross, insensitive, and lazy. He appears to have cared no more about Elvis Presley than he did about the trained goat of his youth, the one he sold on impulse when he wanted to show off and take his brothers and sisters to the circus. Parker undercut a considerable amount of his client's talent and deprived the world of much of his potential. If art counts for anything, that should surely be enough to merit a considerable stretch in purgatory.

Possibly the greatest condemnation of Tom Parker lies in the efficiency with which he prepared for Elvis's end but made no effort to help or to find help for the problems dragging him down. Parker may not have expected Elvis actually to drop dead in the bathroom (although it hardly took a clairvoyant to determine that drug intake could easily lead to such a disaster), but he certainly seemed to have decided that the way things were, Elvis's days as a top-line performer were severely numbered. Parker's reaction was swift and totally in character. He set about to bleed Elvis to the last drop while refusing absolutely to turn the artist loose.

The first of the Parker maneuvers, known as the Amazing Buy-out Agreement, was little more than an ugly money-raising scam that was directly detrimental to Elvis's best interests. Through the two decades that Elvis had been signed to RCA, he had cut more than seven hundred songs. The deal was that Parker should sell the masters of these songs—all the songs recorded before March 1973—back to RCA for a single lump sum and relinquish all future royalties. Elvis would receive $2,800,000; the Colonel would get $2,600,000. It was a lot of money, but nothing compared to what Elvis (or his heirs) might have received in a lifetime of royalty payments.

The Colonel's limp rationale for the move was that "the old records don't sell no more." This was patently untrue and could be refuted by a constant stream of compilations, golden hits, boxed sets, and reissues.

Each time Elvis pulled off a major coup—the NBC special, the opening in Las Vegas, or *Aloha from Hawaii*—he attracted brand-new fans who went out and bought his classic work as well as the current releases. The only person who would benefit from a deal of this kind was a manager who believed he wouldn't be holding on to his client for very long.

Blanchard Tual—the court-appointed guardian of Lisa Marie Presley who would, after Elvis's death, wrest control of the Elvis industry away from the Colonel and return it to Lisa Marie and her mother—used the Amazing Buy-out Agreement as one of the cornerstones of his case against Parker. "It was illogical for Elvis to consider selling an almost certain lifetime annuity from his catalogue of almost seven hundred chart songs. On the other hand, the buy-out from the Colonel's point of view was much more appealing. In 1973, Colonel Parker was sixty-three years old, overweight, and recovering from a heart attack."

The Amazing Buy-out Agreement came with a number of side deals for the Colonel designed to grease the way to the sale of the masters. (It has to be remembered that, apart from the Colonel, RCA was the real beneficiary of the deal. Over the years they'd save a fortune in royalties they wouldn't have to pay out to Elvis.) RCA would pay $50,000 over five years to Parker's company, All Star Shows, to "consult and assist in the exploitation of Elvis's merchandising rights." RCA and RCA Record Tours would pay a further $350,000 for "assisting RCA records for planning, promotion, and merchandising in connection with the operation of the tour agreement." A further $350,000 was promised for just "planning promotion and merchandising." When the dust finally settled on the deal with RCA, the Colonel came away with $6,200,000. Elvis came in second with $4,650,000.

Suddenly the manager was making more than the artist.

Jean Aberbach was just one of the Parker circle who noticed that the Colonel had become absolutely shameless in his demands for money. "In his dealings, he was always straight and honest. He just wanted to know one thing: What do I get in advance? Later this changed. He started asking for money for himself."

The next, and even more destructive, move was the formation of the notorious Boxcar Enterprises. Boxcar Enterprises, Inc., with registered offices in Madison, Tennessee, was a partnership among Tom Parker, Tom Diskin, RCA's George Parkhill, Freddy Bienstock, and Elvis. Diskin's sisters, Patti and Mary, were made secretary and treasurer. Parker had a forty-percent share, Bienstock, Diskin, and Parkhill were given fifteen percent each, and Elvis also got fifteen percent. All the Elvis merchandising interests were transferred to Boxcar, which would administer them henceforth. In practical terms, it meant that Elvis received just fifteen percent of his own earnings from the souvenirs and posters that were a major and lucrative part of the Elvis industry.

The sinister overtone to the whole setup was that it was an obvious preparation for Elvis's death. If Elvis died, there would be no more live concerts, no films or TV, and no new records. The souvenir business, on the other hand, might well go through the roof. Boxcar Enterprises would be worth a fortune if, indeed, something happened to Elvis.

None of the Colonel's final maneuvering would have been possible if Elvis hadn't been totally acquiesent. He had to approve and sign every step of the way in both the Amazing Buy-out Agreement and the creation of Boxcar Enterprises. It wasn't that he was just so stoned, he didn't know what was going on (although that may well have been the case). Elvis, by his own bizarre standards, was broke. On paper Elvis was making a fortune, but high operating costs, the financial inroads of the Colonel himself, the support of his entourage, his wild gift-giving—when expensive jewelry and luxury cars were given not only to friends and associates but, now and again, to total strangers— all took their toll. His drug habits weren't cheap and there were the endless sundry bites that mounted and mounted. His father's divorce settlement was a perfect example. That alone was a quarter of a million dollars. There were also the complete bouts of fiscal madness—like the time when Elvis took it into his head to go out buying private planes. Coupled with the Colonel, in his paranoia, never allowing Elvis to seek the advantages of tax shelters or to put his affairs in the hands of a shrewd accountant or tax lawyer, this meant that Elvis constantly lived beyond his means. When the four and a half million came from the various RCA deals, Elvis was probably exceedingly glad to get it and didn't give a thought to what it might mean in the future.

Nineteen seventy-four was the perfect example. Throughout that year Elvis had played a grueling 152 dates. The gross on this was in excess of seven million dollars and yet at the end of the year, Elvis had to dip into his own reserves to the tune of seven hundred thousand just to make ends meet.

It was the middle of the afternoon, August 16, 1977. The Colonel was holding court in his suite in the Dunfey Sheraton Hotel in Portland, Maine. For the next two days Elvis would be playing at the Cumberland Civic Center. The Colonel was leading the advance party, but there wasn't too much to do. The ticket sales looked good and the place was expected to be packed. The phone rang. The Colonel had just been talking on it and he picked it up himself.

"Yeah?"

Joe Esposito's voice came on the line. He was calling from Memphis. Even before the words sank in, the tone sent a chill through the Colonel.

"I don't want you to hear it from a radio bulletin, Colonel."

"Hear what, for Christ's sake?"

"Elvis is dead. We found him in his bathroom about an hour ago, slumped on the floor. We've tried to revive him but we couldn't."

The Colonel took a single deep breath.

"Oh, dear God."

It was the only expression of grief he made. After the single exclamation, he sat in silence for some minutes. Finally he looked up at Lamar Fike, who was in the same room.

"Nothing has changed. This won't change anything."

He reached for the phone. His first call was to Vernon Presley. Suddenly the Colonel was the commander rallying his demoralized troops after a crushing defeat. For Vernon, it was a pep talk. He explained slowly and carefully to the bewildered, grief-stricken father that literally thousands of people would be trying to cash in on the tragedy.

"We must immediately make sure that outsiders cannot exploit the name of Elvis Presley. We can mourn, but a long and inactive period of grief over Elvis will prove disastrous for you, for his daughter, for his estate, for his legend."

Vernon had only one possible reaction: He gave the Colonel an absolutely free hand to carry on exactly as he wished. The next call was to Harry "The Bear"

Geissler, the president of the huge merchandising company of Factors, Inc. They agreed to open negotiations on the Elvis Presley souvenir rights as soon as possible. The Elvis merchandising really was going to go through the roof. The third call was to George Parkhill at RCA to confirm that the record company would pick up all expenses incurred in Portland. After that, the Colonel set the still shocked minions to work. The promoters on the upcoming tour dates had to be informed of the circumstances and arrangements had to be canceled. Everyone had to work.

By nine that evening all the immediate tasks had been accomplished and the Colonel and his inner circle moved down to the hotel dining room. Even in the face of death a man had to eat. Hans Eckert, the hotel manager, came by the table to pay his respects. The Colonel nodded.

"I believe we have it all under control."

He indicated that Eckert should take a seat. All through the ensuing conversation, Elvis's name was never mentioned. The Colonel even steered the talk around to German wines. Anything but Elvis. There was just one gruff comment.

"It's bad it had to end this way."

The very next day, the Colonel sat down with Harry Geissler and finalized the deal with Factors, Inc. Geissler bought the exclusive rights for an advance of one hundred fifty thousand. A royalty rate was set. Parker signed on behalf of Boxcar Enterprises rather than the Presley estate, and the deal was structured so half the proceeds went to Parker directly, half went to Boxcar, and a ten percent commission went to William Morris for putting the two parties together. It basically meant that in the coming souvenir boom, Parker would be taking seventy-eight percent of the proceeds due to Elvis's heirs.

It's likely the Colonel found himself riding a roller coaster bigger than anything he'd ever imagined. Nobody, the Colonel included, had envisioned the extent of the outpouring of shock and grief that followed Elvis's death. People went out and bought his records as though it was an act of faith. Within the first few days, millions of units—not only records but every kind of souvenir—had been moved. In England an entire RCA pressing plant that had been slated for closure was reactivated for a number of months by nothing more than the phenomenal demand for Elvis Presley records. It must have felt as exhilarating as the golden days in the fifties. There was also the same tension and gut-fluttering insecurity. All over the world there was a flood of unauthorized Presley products. Would the Colonel even be able to hold on to his property? His mind was racing and he didn't sleep too much. He was constantly on the phone. Elvis's death was the Colonel's new lease on life, which may have accounted for his somewhat odd behavior at the funeral.

The Colonel arrived as though he was there to organize rather than grieve; at one point, he was dressed in a Hawaiian shirt and a baseball cap. One of his first moves after arriving at Graceland was to take Vernon to one side and make sure he had signed the Factors, Inc. agreement. Parker barely participated in the funeral ceremony. As the limos brought in the mourners and the fans massed outside the gates, he stood to one side of the mansion's pillared entrance, leaning on a car, seemingly deep in thought. He neither offered nor accepted condolences. His main mission appeared to be to ride herd on Vernon and make sure he didn't do anything dumb. As far as the Colonel was concerned, Vernon, the sole executor of the Presley estate, was now his client; and since he held the golden key to everything, he merited the full treatment. Over and over, the Colonel counseled the need for strength.

"His death doesn't change anything. If you show signs of weakness at this moment, everything will fall apart."

The Colonel refused to be a pallbearer. Elvis had supported him for twenty years, but he didn't seem inclined to return the favor. Lamar Fike, Charlie Hodge, Gene Smith, George Klein, Joe Esposito, Billy Smith, Jerry Schilling, and Dr. George Nichopoulos carried the coffin. There was a certain irony in the fact that Nichopoulos—the notorious Dr. Nick—should carry Elvis's body to the grave. He was the one who'd prescribed Elvis and others—including rock 'n' roll madman Jerry Lee Lewis—enough drugs to poison a small town.

The motorcade that took the coffin from Graceland to the Forest Hill Cemetery consisted of a white Cadillac hearse followed by sixteen white limousines and more than fifty cars. The Colonel found himself a seat in one of the limos, but while the final words were spoken over the grave, the Colonel wandered away. He was seen sitting silently on a police motorcycle.

A few days later, after the funeral, the Colonel had the crucial meeting with Vernon at which all the deals made with Elvis would be confirmed and continued. Parker didn't view the meeting with too much trepidation; he'd never had much respect for Vernon. He considered Elvis's father weak and stupid, essentially a pushover, and nothing happened to cause him to revise his opinion. Following the meeting, Vernon sent him a formal letter.

"I am deeply grateful that you have offered to carry on in the same old way, assisting me in any way possible with the problems facing us." All terms and conditions remained the same and Vernon even authorized the Colonel to sign for him. "I will rely on your good judgment to keep the image alive for the many fans and friends."

The Colonel nearly had it all. He had the power of attorney and, with it, total control of the Elvis empire. Apart from paying the estate what amounted to a royalty, Colonel Tom Parker didn't have to be responsible to anyone.

The empire continued without Elvis. The legend seemed to have a life of its own, constantly perpetuating its own intensity. If anything, life was easier for the Colonel with Elvis safely in the grave. There were no freak-outs, no orgies, no paternity suits or overdosed teenagers who had to be hushed up. The Colonel was in the business of licensing icons and shrines. He was virtually in the religious-artifact business, and it suited him fine. Initially he worried about the reaction of Barron Hilton. The International stood to take one of the worst losses that would result from Elvis's death. Presumably, Hilton also held a stack of Colonel Tom's gambling markers. The Colonel's problem was to convince him that there was still a future and that he shouldn't call in Parker's debts or evict him from his fourth-floor suite. Parker had started to look on the Hilton as the hub of the empire, and the idea of being deprived of it filled him with superstitious dread.

A series of Elvis happenings turned the trick. There was the "Elvis Festival" featuring a life-size bronze statue. There was a display of his costumes and a souvenir market. Elvis's ties to the International were milked to the limit, but people kept on coming. They paid the admission, they bought the pictures and posters and souvenirs, and in between times they gambled. That was all Hilton needed to see. The hotel qualified as a place of worship and the pilgrims would flock to it from all over the world. The Colonel kept his suite, his salary, and his perks.

He even went ahead and cut a new deal with RCA. For a nebulously defined consultancy, he was to be paid the sum of $675,000. Since there was no mention made of Elvis Presley in these agreements, no part of the money had to be passed on to Vernon and the estate.

The crowd had paid fifteen dollars a head for the privilege of being there, and conversations dropped away to nothing when Priscilla, Vernon, and little Lisa Marie stepped forward. The three of them pulled on the gold ropes. The red velvet curtain slowly lifted. There was a gasp. Elvis was standing there, life-size, cast in bronze. Those of the crowd with cameras surged forward with flash cubes popping. The Colonel raised his hands, urging the security forward. No photographs; pictures of the statue could be purchased for two dollars.

On Tom Parker's seventieth birthday—June 26, 1979—Vernon died and the situation became extremely complicated. While Vernon was the sole executor of the Presley estate and gave full powers to the Colonel, everything was very simple. The Colonel had it all. With Vernon dead, the matter would have to go to court and new executors would have to be appointed. The idea of any sort of brush with the legal system scared the hell out of the Colonel, but there wasn't a damn thing he could do about it.

As it turned out, the first hearing was relatively painless. The court appointed Priscilla, Joe Hanks—Elvis's former accountant—and the Memphis National Bank of Commerce as "successor co-executors."

They would hold the estate in trust for the eventual heir, Lisa Marie, and watch out for her best interests. It was certainly a more complex setup than the one with Vernon, but nobody appeared to want to make any trouble. The successor co-executors wrote Parker a cordial letter. "We do want things to continue as they have and as set forth in the letter of August 23, 1977 from Vernon Presley as the then executor of the Estate."

In 1980, however, things started to go wrong, virtually by accident. The co-executors went to the probate court in Memphis for approval of the compensation agreement with Colonel Parker. There was no conflict and no dispute. It was supposed to have been merely a rubber-stamp formality, a continuation of a situation that had existed for years. Unfortunately for the Colonel, Judge Joseph Evans had both his doubts and his questions. He was puzzled by the Colonel's fifty-percent commission and other seemingly excessive points in the agreement, and he withheld approval pending a full investigation.

Judge Evans appointed Blanchard Tual, a rising young Memphis lawyer, to "represent and defend the interests of Lisa Marie" and to prepare a detailed report on the agreements between Parker and the estate, on which the judge would base his decision whether or not to approve their continuation. The Colonel must have felt the bottom was falling out of his world. The enemy was inside the gates. His worst nightmare was coming true, and he couldn't do a damn thing to stop it. A lousy probate court judge had brought the walls tumbling down. There was no one to bribe or bully.

In September 1980, Blanchard Tual presented what is now known as the "Original Report," containing the first conclusions while investigations were still going on. Tual recommended that all moneys coming from the Elvis industry would be paid directly to the estate and not to Parker and "that the Court enjoin the Executors from paying Parker any further commissions pending the conclusion of this investigation." Tual asked the court not to approve the fifty-percent commission and withhold approval of any percentage. He also wanted Parker and all his companions to open their books. The Original Report said that the Colonel was "guilty of self-dealing and overreaching and has violated his duty both to Elvis and to the Estate."

Blanchard Tual stated that Parker "handled affairs not in Elvis's but in his own best interest." He described the Colonel's role as follows:

> He had made a great deal of money and received many benefits from those who had to go through Parker to reach Elvis. RCA, William Morris, the motion picture companies, the television networks and the Las Vegas Hotels, all catered to Parker and provided various monetary and non-monetary incentives to keep Parker happy and therefore get Elvis. For example, RCA had always provided Parker with free office space, office supplies, secretaries, etc. Whenever Elvis appeared in Las Vegas, Parker was treated like a king and virtually got everything he wanted, including special gambling privileges. Parker had always had complete free rein with William Morris and, again, whatever he wanted he got.

Tual said that Parker systematically overpowered Elvis. He handled all the money earned by Presley. All income was paid to him or All Star Shows, and Parker would deduct his part and pay the rest to Elvis. He never gave full, annual accountings. Elvis and his

accountants always assumed that his figures were beyond any doubt.

Judge Evans was extremely impressed with Tual's
initial findings, and on December 10, 1980, he ordered that the investigation should be broadened. He
wanted to see the Colonel's tax returns. He wanted to
know why there were six separate agreements when a
single comprehensive one would have been infinitely
preferable. He wanted to know why the percentages
the Colonel negotiated on Elvis's behalf were so much
lower than the industry standards for an artist of his
stature. Why, for example, was Elvis making only half
the points received by the Rolling Stones? One question of particular interest was why the Colonel made
more than Elvis on the Amazing Buy-out Agreement,
and why it was structured so badly that a large
amount of what Elvis made on the deal was taken in
taxes. The judge was also curious as to why the Colonel never questioned RCA's royalty figures when
there was "an industry wide practice of objecting as a
matter of course."

The new Amended Report was filed on July 31,
1981, and it didn't mince words. "Both Parker and
RCA are guilty of collusion, conspiracy, fraud, misrep-
resentation, bad faith and overreaching." The 1973
agreements were called "unethical, fraudulently ob-
tained and against all industry standards."

On August 14, 1981, the probate court in Memphis
adopted most of Blanchard Tual's recommendations.
Judge Evans ordered the estate to stop making payments to Parker and to file a complaint against him to
recover an unspecified amount of money.

The Colonel, now under serious attack, decided
that a bit of good publicity wouldn't hurt. For the first
time since Elvis had died, the Colonel broke his si-

lence. He pleaded innocence to *The Memphis Commercial Appeal.*

"Elvis and Vernon were well pleased with my services and desired to continue them over the years. Detailed explanations were regularly made of the transactions pertaining to Elvis and the companies with which we dealt."

Speaking over the phone from his home in Palm Springs to the *Press-Scimitar,* he criticized Elvis for the very first time. When Elvis was alive, Parker always avoided making negative remarks about him because, as he told his friends, the public takes sides against the manager if he has a dispute with his artists. Now he called Elvis a "moody and headstrong client." He said he always respected Presley, but the problem was that "he had little self-motivation."

"Sometimes it was such a heartache to keep him going. We had to have a way of keeping Elvis going." In his opinion Elvis definitely was not the victim of his manager's manipulations. "Elvis wanted to always make the final decision. And that's the way it was. He had a mind of his own." Parker said that the agreements with RCA were a lot more beneficial to Elvis than Blanchard Tual reported. "This man goes into a rattle about show business. The whole picture isn't there. I feel he has been unjust and unfair to me and the memory of Elvis and his father."

According to the Colonel, RCA approached Elvis with a three million dollar offer in exchange for the seven hundred Presley songs in 1973. He said Elvis and his father were excited about the possibility of selling the royalties and instructed him to negotiate the deal. "When RCA approached us about the buyout, I was not interested. I thought it was a stupid idea to even consider it. I knew there wasn't much coming in, but it could change. I said the money was not enough."

Mel Ilberman, Parker's closest contact with RCA, and former president Rocco Laginestra, told the same story. They said it was RCA's idea to buy the catalogue, but mentioned two million dollars as the sum they offered initially. It still seemed to be an unusual move, because RCA never bought a song catalogue from any other artist. Parker negotiated the amount to five million. But neither the Colonel nor RCA can give an explanation for the buy-out. Parker kept quiet about Elvis's bad condition in March 1973, and said, "Elvis was fully aware of the entire transaction and it was his decision. I had absolutely nothing to hide from Elvis." Parker concluded that Tual's allegations had damaged his relationship with the Presley estate and thought it unlikely that this relationship could be repaired.

In this instance, the Colonel was right. The stage was set for a massive legal battle that the Colonel was almost certain to lose. The reports to the court were so damning, it was a question not of whether he could win back control of the empire but of what he might be able to hang on to. In an unseemly hurry, everyone started to sue everyone else. The estate sued Parker and RCA. RCA, not wishing to be in any way tied to the Colonel as codefendant, sued both the Colonel and the estate. The Colonel brought his own countersuit against the estate.

The Colonel had one single advantage. Although he was no longer receiving an income, he had the money and the estate wanted it. If he stalled and the estate did all the running, it would be the estate that did the bulk of the spending on litigation. If he could string things out for a number of years, he might actually force the estate to the edge of bankruptcy and compel them to make some sort of compromise agreement. The months went by and the Colonel and his lawyers used every delaying tactic available to them. They shuffled jurisdiction from Memphis to New York to California and back again. All the time, the estate seemed to be closing in, and there were many times when they managed to stay only one legal jump ahead. In one particularly tight corner, the Colonel was forced to reveal his darkest and most carefully hidden secret, his stateless background. If he was stateless, the federal court would have no jurisdiction over him.

"I was born in the Netherlands on June 26, 1909, of parents who were lawfully married and Dutch subjects. After I left the Netherlands and emigrated to the United States I enlisted in the United States Army in or about 1929, in which I served until I was discharged in 1933 or 1934. In connection with my enlistment, I was required to and did willingly swear allegiance to the government of the United States of America. I did not seek or obtain the permission of the Dutch government to serve in the United States Army either prior to or after my service. As I am now informed, my failure to seek and receive such permission effected an automatic forfeiture of my Dutch citizenship. I am not a citizen of the United States, having never become a naturalized citizen of this country, or of any other country."

A couple of years earlier, Lamar Fike had remarked "Gee, Colonel, how come you never told us you were a Dutchman?"

The Colonel's answer came back pat.

"You never asked me."

At the start of 1983, the Colonel's strategy began to pay off. The estate's lawyers informed the executors that they were coming up to the point of no return.

The estate was having to pay lawyers in Memphis, New York, and Los Angeles. In order not to lose money, they would have to demand an astronomical sum from Parker, and in the face of such a sum, the Colonel would undoubtedly declare bankruptcy. Even if the Colonel did pay them, the IRS would want sixty percent, so an ultimate profit was impossible. They had a choice: They could either go broke pursuing a principle or they could settle. In June 1983, they settled.

The Colonel would sever all connections with the estate and give up his claim to all future income. In return, he would receive two million dollars (paid in installments of forty thousand dollars per month, concluding in May 1987) from RCA for his "right, title and interest in all Presley-related contracts." The Colonel would also be entitled to fifty percent of all record royalties prior to September 1982. After that, everything would go to the estate.

There were some who might think that the Colonel did better than he deserved. It was surely enough to ensure the old age of a man who was already in his mid-seventies. The agreement, however, seems to have broken Parker. While he was fighting, there was still something to live for, but when the court cases stopped and the adrenaline no longer pumped, there didn't seem to be anything left to hold him up. He went back to Palm Springs and prepared to die. In the main, the army deserted him. Only Bitsy Mott stayed loyal and, after all, he was kin. The Hiltons evicted him from his fourth-floor suite at the International, packing up all his boxes and shipping them to Palm Springs. Worst of all, Elvis had been taken from him. For almost half a lifetime—almost thirty years—he had lived and breathed Elvis Presley. Now there was nothing. He had to go on breathing, but it was without any enthusiasm. The man's face continued to look down at him from the walls of his home, a hundred variations on the same sneering smile. The famous gold lamé suit, designed by Nudie, the one Elvis hated to wear, still hung in one of the closets. That was all he had left, mementos and memories. Without Elvis, without the empire, the industry, the army, and the constant bellowing wheeling-dealing, there was no reason to live. He had dedicated his life to the hustle. He had sacrificed many of the things other men see as the essential to a normal life. He had no children, and his marriage had been a minimal business. All he'd wanted out of life was to be the greatest promoter in the world. He'd lived for the hustle and without it, that life was over.

Elvis and the Colonel—
The Nuts and Bolts

The relationship between artist and manager is essentially one of business. Personalities may intrude, as may prejudices, insecurities, even neuroses. At root, though, it is a matter of balance sheets and bottom lines. The artist is a commodity and the manager is the individual who exploits, markets, and maintains that commodity. In this the performer's manager is no different from the president of a brokerage house or the boss of a construction business. The only true evaluation of the success or failure of the relationship between Elvis Presley and Colonel Tom Parker has to be made on the strength of balance sheets and bottom lines, and on a dispassionate evaluation of the extent to which Parker capitalized on the Presley potential.

Clearly, we will never see the Colonel's balance sheets. A man who has rarely allowed his right hand to know what his left hand was doing certainly isn't going to open his accounts to anyone who hasn't come

armed with, at the very minimum, a court order.
(Even in that extreme circumstance, the result might
be more a cosmetic simulation than the real deal.)
What we do have, however, are the basic workings of
the Elvis industry. His recording sessions, the release
schedules of his movies, and his live concert dates are
a matter of public record. Any serious examination of
these immediately reveals a definite and repeated
pattern.

Up to 1960, things appear as normal as possible,
considering we are witnessing the meteoric rise of
one of the most successful show business phenomena
of all time. The Elvis industry is carried along, virtually by its own momentum. Elvis is in demand everywhere. He records. He stars in four movies. He is on
TV almost all the time: he's practically a regular on
The Ed Sullivan Show. There is a constant flow of
new, quality recordings, and he is able to maintain an
intense schedule of live appearances. Even peripheral
considerations seem to be covered. People are beating a path to the Colonel's door for merchandizing
licenses and product endorsements.

But after Elvis returns from the army, a much more
destructive picture starts to emerge. From 1960 to
1968, Elvis absents himself from the live stage and,
instead, devotes most of his energies to making an
interminable series of cheap formula movies. Even his
recording career becomes subordinate to the needs of
movie making. By far the bulk of his recording sessions are devoted to largely substandard soundtrack
albums. It begins to look as though the Elvis industry
—with the Colonel firmly in charge—is no longer capable of operating on more than one front at once.
The results stop just short of disaster. Elvis is given
another chance, but only because of the public's
scarcely rational reserves of goodwill. And still no-

body expresses any serious doubts about the Colonel's ability. In such a situation in any normal corporation, where huge areas of company resources have been completely neglected, the shareholders would clamor for the board's removal. Unfortunately, Elvis had no shareholders to look out for him, and the Colonel went on just as before.

The Colonel might be forgiven if Elvis's great comeback of the late sixties had put an end to the pattern that had lasted for most of that decade. Unfortunately, it can be easily seen that this is not the case. After the huge, two-year blaze of energy that was the Elvis renaissance, the same pattern of lazy thinking, corner-cutting, and neglect sets in again. This time it's not a concentration on movies. Nobody wants a re-make of *Clambake*. About the only Elvis Presley films the public will buy are documentaries of live concerts and archive footage. This time around, everything else takes a backseat to concerts and touring. It's the complete reverse of what went on during most of the sixties, but very soon the same malaise can be seen to set in. The other assets of the Elvis industry are again neglected. Original recording sessions are replaced by the taping of shows, and the fans are expected to go out and buy a stream of live albums that frequently duplicate each other. Very quickly, stagnation and boredom set in on the part of both artist and public. This time, there is no burst of energy and no magical comeback.

The Elvis Presley Recording Sessions: 1954 to 1977

There can be really no argument that Elvis Presley's music was the backbone of his career, and yet for significant portions of that career, the content and quality of the music was consistently ignored. This becomes all too apparent when one reads through the chronology of the times when Elvis went into the studios and of the songs he recorded.

There is no way to fault the sessions that took place between 1956 and 1958, for both Sun and RCA. Elvis recorded regularly, his material was excellent, and he worked with a crack band honed to a fine edge by constant touring. Elvis gave his best and nobody interfered with him. Even after he came out of the army, the initial recordings, particularly those of March and April 1960 that gave the world the *Elvis Is Back* album, were equal to—and some cases surpassed—those that had gone before. By 1963, however, it started to become clear that as a recording artist, Elvis had begun to slide. The greater part of his time in the studio was spent cutting material for movie soundtracks and soundtrack albums.

The kind of material that went into the Elvis movies was a problem all by itself. Although Elvis was a supreme ballad singer, he had made his reputation as a pioneer of straight-ahead rock 'n' roll. But the Colonel seemed to distrust the delinquent wildness of rock and continually steered his client toward being an all-round entertainer. Nowhere was his manipulation more evident than in the music that went into the movies. Hard rockabilly was all but eliminated in favor of light show tunes and sappy beat ballads. Whether this strategy was right or wrong can be debated. What can't be disputed was that even by the standards of the most lightweight Hollywood musical, the songs in the Elvis movies of the sixties were mediocre if not awful. Nobody seemed to take the trouble to ensure that Elvis become a great all-round entertainer. The prevailing attitude appeared to be that the fans were ultimately gullible and that just about anything went.

The movie music was cut on the cheap and in the shortest possible time. In all of 1964, Elvis spent just four days in the recording studio. Even when he did get into the studio, the tracks were cut in minimal time and, from the evidence of the resulting records, with equally minimal care. The session of February 24, 1965—when Elvis laid down ten tracks for the movie *Harum Scarum* in a single day—proved to be the rule rather than the exception. An added irony was that such slapdash work was being done at the very time when everyone around Elvis Presley should have been acutely aware that new bands like the Beatles and the Rolling Stones were starting to breathe down their man's neck.

The picture suddenly changed in the first months of 1969. For the first time in fourteen years, Elvis was in a Memphis recording studio and turning out some of the best work of his career. He still recorded fast, using pretty much the same methods he'd used in the fifties. In these sessions, quality wasn't sacrificed. It seemed that when Elvis was putting his heart into his work, and when the Colonel and the rest of the entourage weren't attempting to push him in unfamiliar or uncomfortable directions, he was able to realize completely his creative potential.

It would be wrong to think that Elvis's work at the

end of the sixties and the start of the seventies was a
single blaze of glory that immediately deteriorated
into his obesity, drug abuse, and eventual death. Elvis
kept up the good work with serious recording stints
clear through 1973. The only noticeable drop-off was
in the quality of the songs being cut, which has to be a
direct result of Parker's business practices regarding
song publishing, as well as his almost pathological
need to try and get a piece of any song Elvis recorded.
Respected songwriters were simply not prepared to
give the Colonel a kickback from their earnings to
ensure that Elvis cut their tunes. It actually wasn't
until 1974 that the real rot began to set in. In that
year, Elvis did no recording at all. In 1975, he put in
just one two-day session. From then on, recordings
were halfhearted and spasmodic. Elvis had lost interest and the Colonel, far from moving heaven and
earth to get his client back on the track, seemed more
than content to package live recordings and reissues.
By 1975, the Colonel was treating Elvis Presley the
recording star as though he were already dead.

1954

July 1954		Sun studio, Memphis
	I Love You Because	G2WB 1086
U-128	*That's All Right [Mama]*	F2WB 8040
U-129	*Blue Moon of Kentucky*	F2WB 8041
	Blue Moon	F2WB 8117

September 1954		Sun studio, Memphis
U-130	*I Don't Care if the Sun Don't Shine*	F2WB 8042
U-131	*Good Rockin' Tonight*	F2WB 8043
	Just Because	F2WB 8118

December 1954		Sun studio, Memphis
U-140	*Milkcow Blues Boogie*	F2WB 8044
U-141	*You're a Heartbreaker*	F2WB 8045

1955

January 1955		Sun studio, Memphis
	I'll Never Let You Go	F2WB 8116

February 1955		
U-143	*Baby, Let's Play House*	F2WB 8046
U-156	*Mystery Train*	F2WB 8001

July 1955

U-142	*I'm Left, You're Right, She's Gone*	F2WB 8047
U-157	*I Forgot to Remember to Forget*	F2WB 8000
U-131	*Tryin' to Get to You*	F2WB 8039

1956

January 10–11, 1956		**RCA Nashville studio**
G2WB 0208	*I Got a Woman*	January 10, 1956
G2WB 0209	*Heartbreak Hotel*	January 10, 1956
G2WB 0210	*Money Honey*	January 10, 1956
G2WB 0211	*I'm Counting on You*	January 11, 1956
G2WB 0218	*I Was the One*	January 11, 1956

MUSICIANS:

Lead guitar—Scotty Moore
Guitar—Chet Atkins
Guitar—Elvis
Bass—Bill Black

Vocal—Gordon Stoker
Vocal—Ben and Brock Speer

Drums—D. J. Fontana
Piano—Floyd Cramer

January 30–31 and February 3, 1956		RCA New York studio
G2WB 1230	Blue Suede Shoes	January 30, 1956
G2WB 1231	My Baby Left Me	January 30, 1956
G2WB 1232	One-sided Love Affair	January 30, 1956
G2WB 1233	So Glad You're Mine	January 30, 1956
G2WB 1254	I'm Gonna Sit Right Down and Cry	January 31, 1956
G2WB 1255	Tutti Frutti	January 31, 1956
G2WB 1293	Lawdy, Miss Clawdy	February 3, 1956
G2WB 1294	Shake, Rattle and Roll	February 3, 1956

MUSICIANS:

Lead guitar—Scotty Moore
Guitar—Elvis
Bass—Bill Black

Drums—D. J. Fontana
Piano—Shorty Long

April 11, 1956		RCA Nashville studio
G2WB 0271	I Want You, I Need You, I Love You	April 11, 1956

MUSICIANS:

Lead guitar—Scotty Moore
Guitar—Chet Atkins
Guitar—Elvis
Bass—Bill Black
Drums—D. J. Fontana
Piano—Marvin Hughes

Vocal—Gordon
Stoker
Vocal—Ben
and Brock
Speer

July 2, 1956

**RCA New York
studio**

G2WB 5935	*Hound Dog*	July 2, 1956
G2WB 5936	*Don't Be Cruel*	July 2, 1956
G2WB 5937	*Any Way You Want Me*	July 2, 1956

MUSICIANS:

Lead guitar—Scotty Moore
Guitar—Elvis
Bass—Bill Black
Drums—D. J. Fontana

Piano—Shorty
Long
Vocal—The
Jordanaires

August 1956

Hollywood

G2WB 4767	*Love Me Tender*
G2WB 7260	*We're Gonna Move*
G2WB 7223	*Poor Boy*
G2WB 7225	*Let Me*

BACKING: Ken Darby's Trio

September 1–3, 1956		Radio Recorders, Hollywood
G2WB 4920	Playing for Keeps	September 1, 1956
G2WB 4921	Love Me	September 1, 1956
G2WB 4922	Paralyzed	September 1, 1956
G2WB 4923	How Do You Think I Feel	September 1, 1956
G2WB 4924	How's the World Treating You	September 1, 1956
G2WB 4925	When My Blue Moon Turns to Gold Again	September 2, 1956
G2WB 4926	Long Tall Sally	September 2, 1956
G2WB 4927	Old Shep	September 2, 1956
G2WB 4928	Too Much	September 2, 1956
G2WB 4929	Anyplace Is Paradise	September 3, 1956
G2WB 4930	Ready Teddy	September 3, 1956
G2WB 4931	First in Line	September 3, 1956
G2WB 4932	Rip It Up	September 3, 1956

MUSICIANS:

Lead guitar—Scotty Moore
Guitar—Elvis
Bass—Bill Black
Drums—D. J. Fontana
   Elvis played piano on *Old Shep.*

Piano—
Unknown
Vocal—
Jordanaires

December 9, 1956

Sun studio, Memphis

Unreleased	*Big Boss Man*	December 9, 1956
Unreleased	*Blueberry Hill*	December 9, 1956
Unreleased	*I Won't Have to Cross the Jordan Alone*	December 9, 1956
Unreleased	*Island of Golden Dreams*	December 9, 1956
Unreleased	*That Old Rugged Cross*	December 9, 1956
Unreleased	*Peace in the Valley*	December 9, 1956

MUSICIANS:

Guitar and vocal—Carl Perkins
Guitar and vocal—Johnny Cash
Piano and vocal—Elvis

Piano and vocal—
Jerry Lee Lewis

1957

January 12–13 and 19, 1957		**Radio Recorders, Hollywood**
H2WB 0253	*I Believe*	January 12, 1957
H2WB 0254	*Tell Me Why*	January 12, 1957
H2WB 0255	*Got a Lot o' Livin' to Do*	January 12, 1957
H2WB 0256	*All Shook Up*	January 12, 1957
H2WB 0257	*Mean Woman Blues*	January 13, 1957
H2WB 0258	*Peace in the Valley*	January 13, 1957
H2WB 0259	*I Beg of You*	January 13, 1957
H2WB 0260	*That's When Your Heartaches Begin*	January 13, 1957
H2WB 0261	*Take My Hand, Precious Lord*	January 13, 1957
H2WB 0282	*It Is No Secret*	January 19, 1957
H2WB 0283	*Blueberry Hill*	January 19, 1957
H2WB 0284	*Have I Told You Lately That I Love You?*	January 19, 1957

| H2WB 0285 | *Is It So Strange* | January 19, 1957 |

MUSICIANS:

Lead guitar—Scotty Moore	Piano—Dudley
Guitar—Elvis	Brooks
Bass—Bill Black	Vocal—
Drums—D. J. Fontana	Jordanaires

| **February 23–24, 1957** | **Radio Recorders, Hollywood** |

H2WB 0259	*I Beg of You*	February 23, 1957
H2WB 0414	*Don't Leave Me Now*	February 23, 1957
H2WB 0415	*One Night*	February 23, 1957
H2WB 0416	*True Love*	February 23, 1957
H2WB 0417	*I Need You So*	February 23, 1957
H2WB 0418	*Loving You*	February 24, 1957
H2WB 0419	*When It Rains, It Really Pours*	February 24, 1957

MUSICIANS:

Lead guitar—Scotty Moore	Piano—Dudley
Guitar—Elvis	Brooks
Bass—Bill Black	Vocal—
Drums—D. J. Fontana	Jordanaires

February–March 1957 **Hollywood**

H2WB 2193 *Teddy Bear*
H2WB 2194 *Lonesome Cowboy*
H2WB 2195 *Party*
H2WB 2196 *Hot Dog*
H2WB 2197 *Loving You*
H2WB 2198 *Got a Lot o' Livin' to Do*

MUSICIANS:

Lead guitar—Scotty Moore Vocal—
Guitar—Elvis Jordanaires
Bass—Bill Black
Drums—D. J. Fontana

May 2, 1957 **MGM studios, Culver City, California**

H2WB 6777 *Young and Beautiful* May 2, 1957
H2WB 6778 *Treat Me Nice* May 2, 1957
H2WB 6779 *Jailhouse Rock* May 2, 1957
H2WB 6780 *Jailhouse Rock* May 2, 1957
H2WB 6781 *I Want to Be Free* May 2, 1957
H2WB 6782 *Baby, I Don't Care* May 2, 1957
H2WB 6783 *Don't Leave Me Now* May 2, 1957

MUSICIANS

Lead guitar—Scotty Moore
Guitar—Elvis
Bass—Bill Black
Drums—D. J. Fontana

Piano—
Mike Stoller
Vocal—
Jordanaires

September 5–7, 1957

**Radio
Recorders,
Hollywood**

H2PB 5523	*Treat Me Nice*	September 5, 1957
H2PB 5524	*My Wish Came True*	September 5, 1957
H2PB 5525	*Blue Christmas*	September 5, 1957
H2PB 5526	*White Christmas*	September 6, 1957
H2PB 5527	*Here Comes Santa Claus*	September 6, 1957
H2PB 5528	*Silent Night*	September 6, 1957
H2PB 5529	*Don't*	September 6, 1957
H2PB 5530	*O Little Town of Bethlehem*	September 7, 1957
H2PB 5531	*Santa, Bring My Baby Back*	September 7, 1957
H2PB 5532	*Santa Claus Is Back in Town*	September 7, 1957
H2PB 5533	*I'll Be Home for Christmas*	September 7, 1957

MUSICIANS:

Lead guitar—Scotty Moore
Guitar—Elvis
Bass—Bill Black
Piano—Dudley Brooks
Drums—D. J. Fontana

Vocal—Millie
Kirkham,
Jordanaires

1958

January 1958   **Hollywood**

J2PB 3603	*Hard-headed Woman*
J2PB 3604	*T-R-O-U-B-L-E*
J2PB 3605	*New Orleans*
J2PB 3606	*King Creole*
J2PB 3607	*Crawfish*
J2PB 3608	*Dixieland Rock*
J2PB 3609	*Lover Doll*
J2PB 3610	*Don't Ask Me Why*
J2PB 3611	*As Long As I Have You*
J2PB 3612	*King Creole*
J2PB 3613	*Young Dreams*
J2PB 4228	*Steadfast, Loyal and True*

MUSICIANS:

Lead guitar—Scotty Moore
Guitar—Elvis
Bass—Bill Black

Drums—D. J.
Fontana
Vocal—
Jordanaires

January 23, 1958		**Radio Recorders, Hollywood**
J2WB 0178	*My Wish Came True*	January 23, 1958
J2WB 0179	*Doncha' Think It's Time*	January 23, 1958

MUSICIANS:

Lead guitar—Scotty Moore	Piano—Dudley Brooks
Guitar—Elvis	Vocal—Jordanaires
Bass—Bill Black	
Drums—D. J. Fontana	

February 1, 1958		**Radio Recorders, Hollywood**
J2WB 0178	*My Wish Came True*	February 1, 1958
J2WB 0179	*Doncha' Think It's Time*	February 1, 1958
J2WB 0180	*Your Cheatin' Heart*	February 1, 1958
J2WB 0181	*Wear My Ring Around Your Neck*	February 1, 1958

MUSICIANS:

Lead guitar—Scotty Moore	Drums—D. J. Fontana
Guitar—Elvis	Vocal—Jordanaires
Bass—Bill Black	
Guitar—H. J. Timbrell	
Piano—Dudley Brooks	

June 11–12, 1958		RCA Nashville studio
J2WB 3253	*I Need Your Love Tonight*	June 11, 1958
J2WB 3254	*A Big Hunk o' Love*	June 11, 1958
J2WB 3255	*Ain't That Loving You, Baby*	June 11, 1958
J2WB 3256	*A Fool Such as I*	June 11, 1958
J2WB 3257	*I Got Stung*	June 12, 1958

MUSICIANS:

Lead guitar—Hank Garland	Bongos—
Guitar—Chet Atkins	Murrey
Guitar—Elvis	Harman
Bass—Bob Moore	Vocal—
Drums—D. J. Fontana	Jordanaires
	Piano—Floyd Cramer

(The Jordanaires: Gorden Stoker, Neil Matthews, Hoyt Hawkins, Ray Walker)

1960

March 20–21, 1960		RCA Nashville studio
L2WB 0081	*Make Me Know It*	March 20, 1960
L2WB 0082	*Soldier Boy*	March 20, 1960

L2WB 0083	*Stuck on You*	March 21, 1960
L2WB 0084	*Fame and Fortune*	March 21, 1960
L2WB 0085	*A Mess of Blues*	March 21, 1960
L2WB 0086	*It Feels So Right*	March 21, 1960

MUSICIANS:

Lead guitar—Scotty Moore
Guitar—Elvis
Bass—Bob Moore
Bass—Hank Garland
Drums—D. J. Fontana

Drums—
Murrey
Harman
Piano—Floyd
Cramer
Vocal—
Jordanaires

April 3–4, 1960   **RCA Nashville studio**

L2WB 0098	*Fever*	April 3, 1960
L2WB 0099	*Like a Baby*	April 3, 1960
L2WB 0100	*It's Now or Never*	April 3, 1960
L2WB 0101	*The Girl of My Best Friend*	April 4, 1960
L2WB 0102	*Dirty, Dirty Feeling*	April 4, 1960
L2WB 0103	*Thrill of Your Love*	April 4, 1960
L2WB 0104	*I Gotta Know*	April 4, 1960
L2WB 0105	*Such a Night*	April 4, 1960
L2WB 0106	*Are You Lonesome Tonight?*	April 4, 1960

L2WB 0107	*The Girl Next Door Went Awalking*	April 4, 1960
L2WB 0108	*I Will Be Home Again*	April 4, 1960
L2WB 0109	*Reconsider, Baby*	April 4, 1960

MUSICIANS:

Lead guitar—Hank Garland
Guitar—Scotty Moore
Guitar—Elvis
Bass—Bob Moore
Drums—D. J. Fontana
Drums—Murrey Harman

Piano—Floyd Cramer
Tenor sax—Homer (Boots) Randolph
Vocal—Jordanaires

April–June 1960   **Hollywood**

| L2PW 3678 | *Tonight Is So Right for Love* *What's She Really Like* *Frankfort Special* |
| L2PW 3681 | *Wooden Heart* *G.I. Blues* *Pocketful of Rainbows* *Shoppin' Around* *Big Boots* *Didja Ever* *Blue Suede Shoes* |

	Doin' the Best I Can	
WPA1 8124	*Tonight's All Right for Love*	

Vocal—Jordanaires

August 12, 1960		**Hollywood**
M2PB 1986	*Summer Kisses, Winter Tears*	
M2PB 1987	*Flaming Star*	
M2PB 1988	*A Cane and a High Starched Collar*	

Vocal—Jordanaires

October 30–31, 1960		**RCA Nashville studio**
L2WB 0373	*Milky White Way*	October 30, 1960
L2WB 0374	*His Hand in Mine*	October 30, 1960
L2WB 0375	*I Believe in the Man in the Sky*	October 30, 1960
L2WB 0376	*He Knows Just What I Need*	October 30, 1960
L2WB 0377	*Surrender*	October 30, 1960
L2WB 0378	*Mansion Over the Hilltop*	October 31, 1960
L2WB 0379	*In My Father's House*	October 31, 1960
L2WB 0380	*Joshua Fit the Battle*	October 31, 1960

L2WB 0381	*Swing Down, Sweet Chariot*	October 31, 1960
L2WB 0382	*I'm Gonna Walk Dem Golden Stairs*	October 31, 1960
L2WB 0383	*If We Never Meet Again*	October 31, 1960
L2WB 0384	*Known Only to Him*	October 31, 1960
L2WB 0385	*Crying in the Chapel*	October 31, 1960
L2WB 5001	*Working on the Building*	October 31, 1960

November 1960		**Hollywood**
L2PB 5381	*Lonely Man*	
L2PB 5382	*I Slipped, I Stumbled, I Fell*	
L2PB 5383	*Wild in the Country*	
L2PB 5384	*In My Way*	
L2PB 5385	*Forget Me Never*	

1961

March 12–13, 1961		**RCA Nashville studio**
M2WW 0567	*I'm Comin' Home*	March 12, 1961
M2WW 0568	*Gently*	March 12, 1961

M2WW 0569	*In Your Arms*	March 12, 1961
M2WW 0570	*Give Me the Right*	March 12, 1961
M2WW 0571	*I Feel So Bad*	March 12, 1961
M2WW 0572	*It's a Sin*	March 13, 1961
M2WW 0573	*I Want You with Me*	March 13, 1961
M2WW 0574	*There's Always Me*	March 13, 1961
M2WW 0575	*Starting Today*	March 13, 1961
M2WW 0576	*Sentimental Me*	March 13, 1961
M2WW 0577	*Judy*	March 13, 1961
M2WW 0578	*Put the Blame on Me*	March 13, 1961

MUSICIANS:

Lead guitar—Hank Garland
Piano—Floyd Cramer
Tenor sax—Homer (Boots) Randolph

Vocal—
Jordanaires

June 25–26, 1961

RCA Nashville studio

M2WW 8854	*Kiss Me Quick*	June 25, 1961
M2WW 8858	*That's Someone You Never Forget*	June 25, 1961
M2WW 8859	*I'm Yours*	June 26, 1961

| M2WW 8860 | *His Latest Flame* | June 26, 1961 |
| M2WW 8861 | *Little Sister* | June 26, 1961 |

Vocal—Jordanaires

April 1961   **Hollywood**

M2PB 2984	*Blue Hawaii*
M2PB 2985	*Almost Always True*
M2PB 2986	*Aloha Oe*
M2PB 2987	*No More*
M2PB 2988	*Can't Help Falling in Love*
M2PB 2989	*Rock-a-hula Baby*
M2PB 2990	*Moonlight Swim*
M2PB 2991	*Ku-u-i-po*
M2PB 2992	*Ito Eats*
M2PB 2993	*Slicin' Sand*
M2PB 2994	*Hawaiian Sunset*
M2PB 2995	*Beach Boy Blues*
M2PB 2996	*Island of Love*
M2PB 2997	*Hawaiian Wedding Song*
M2PB 3038	*Steppin' Out of Line*

Vocal—Jordanaires

July 5, 1961   **RCA Nashville studio**

| M2WW 0878 | *Sound Advice* | July 5, 1961 |

Follow That Dream	July 5, 1961
Angel	July 5, 1961
What a Wonderful Life	July 5, 1961
I'm Not the Marrying Kind	July 5, 1961

MUSICIANS:

Lead guitar—Hank Garland
Piano—Floyd Cramer
Tenor sax—Homer (Boots) Randolph

Vocal—Jordanaires

October 15–16, 1961   **RCA Nashville studio**

M2WW 1002	*For the Millionth and the Last Time*	October 15, 1961
M2WW 1003	*Good Luck Charm*	October 15, 1961
M2WW 1004	*Anything That's Part of You*	October 15, 1961
M2WW 1005	*I Met Her Today*	October 16, 1961

Vocal—Jordanaires

October–November, 1961   **Hollywood**

N2PB 3131	*King of the Whole Wide World*

	This Is Living	
	Riding the	
	Rainbow	
N2PB 3134	*Home Is*	
	Where the	
	Heart Is	
	I Got Lucky	
	A Whistling	
	Tune	

Vocal—Jordanaires

1962

March 18–19, 1962		**RCA Nashville studio**
N2WW 0685	*Something Blue*	March 18, 1962
N2WW 0686	*Gonna Get Back Home Somehow*	March 18, 1962
N2WW 0687	*Easy Question*	March 18, 1962
N2WW 0688	*Fountain of Love*	March 18, 1962
N2WW 0689	*Just for Old Time Sake*	March 18, 1962
N2WW 0690	*Night Rider*	March 18, 1962
N2WW 0691	*You'll Be Gone*	March 18, 1962
N2WW 0692	*I Feel That I've Known You Forever*	March 19, 1962

N2WW 0693	*Just Tell Her Jim Said Hello*	March 19, 1962
N2WW 0694	*Suspicion*	March 19, 1962
N2WW 0695	*She's Not You*	March 19, 1962

Vocal—Jordanaires

March 1962   **Hollywood**

N2PB 3272	*Girls! Girls! Girls!*
N2PB 3273	*I Don't Wanna Be Tied*
N2PB 3274	*Where Do You Come From*
N2PB 3275	*I Don't Want To*
N2PB 3276	*We'll Be Together*
N2PB 3277	*A Boy Like Me, a Girl Like You*
N2PB 3278	*Earth Boy*
N2PB 3279	*Return to Sender*
N2PB 3280	*Because of Love*
N2PB 3281	*Thanks to the Rolling Sea*
N2PB 3282	*Son of the Shrimp*
N2PB 3283	*The Walls Have Ears*
N2PB 3288	*We're Comin' In Loaded*

WPA1 8122   *Mama*
Vocal—Jordanaires   Vocal—Amigos

October 1962   **Hollywood**

PPA3 2717   *Happy Ending*
PPA3 2722   *How Would*
            You Like to Be
PPA3 2724   *One Broken*
            Heart for Sale
PPA3 2725   *They Remind*
            Me Too Much
            of You
PPA3 2726   *Relax*
PPA3 2719   *Beyond the*
            Bend
PPA3 2718   *I'm Falling in*
            Love Tonight
PPA3 2721   *Take Me to the*
            Fair
PPA3 2720   *Cotton Candy*
            Land
PPA3 2723   *A World of*
            Our Own
Vocal—Mello Men

1963

January 20, 1963   **Hollywood**

PPA3 4423   *Fun in*   January 20,
            Acapulco   1963
PPA3 4424   *Vino, Dinero y*   January 20,
            Amor   1963

PPA3 4425	*Mexico*	January 20, 1963
PPA3 4426	*El Toro*	January 20, 1963
PPA3 4427	*Marguerita*	January 20, 1963
PPA3 4428	*The Bullfighter Was a Lady*	January 20, 1963
PPA3 4429	*No Room to Rhumba in a Sports Car*	January 20, 1963
PPA3 4430	*I Think I'm Gonna Like It Here*	January 20, 1963
PPA3 4431	*Bossa Nova Baby*	January 20, 1963
PPA3 4432	*You Can't Say No in Acapulco*	January 20, 1963
PPA3 4433	*Guadalajara*	January 20, 1963

Vocal—Jordanaires   Vocal—Amigos

May 26–27, 1963   **RCA Nashville studio**

PPA4 2290	*Echoes of Love*	May 26, 1963
PPA4 2291	*Please Don't Drag That String Around*	May 26, 1963
PPA4 2292	*Devil in Disguise*	May 26, 1963
PPA4 2293	*Never Ending*	May 26, 1963
PPA4 2294	*What Now, What Next, Where To*	May 26, 1963
PPA4 2295	*Witchcraft*	May 26, 1963

PPA4 2296	*Finders Keepers, Losers Weepers*	May 26, 1963
PPA4 2297	*Love Me Tonight*	May 26, 1963
PPA4 0303	*Long Lonely Highway*	May 27, 1963
PPA4 0304	*Blue River*	May 27, 1963
PPA4 0305	*Western Union*	May 27, 1963
PPA4 0306	*Slowly but Surely*	May 27, 1963

Vocal—Jordanaires

July 7 and 9, 1963   **Hollywood**

RPA3 0234	*Viva Las Vegas*
RPA3 0235	*What'd I Say*
	I Need Somebody to Lean On
	C'mon, Everybody
	If You Think I Don't Need You
	Today, Tomorrow and Forever
SPA1 6898	*Santa Lucia*
WPA1 8023	*Night Life*
WPA1 8024	*Yellow Rose of Texas/The Eyes of Texas*
WPA1 8025	*Do the Vega*
	The Lady Loves Me

Vocal—Jordanaires

Vocal—Jubilee
Four

Vocal—Carol Lombard Quartet

October 11, 1963		**Hollywood**
RPA3 0218	*Kissin' Cousins* (number 2)	October 11, 1963
RPA3 0219	*Kissin' Cousins*	October 11, 1963
RPA3 0220	*Barefoot Ballad*	October 11, 1963
RPA3 0221	*Catchin' on Fast*	October 11, 1963
RPA3 0222	*Once Is Enough*	October 11, 1963
RPA3 0223	*One Boy, Two Little Girls*	October 11, 1963
RPA3 0224	*Smokey Mountain Boy*	October 11, 1963
RPA3 0225	*Tender Feeling*	October 11, 1963
RPA3 0226	*There's Gold in the Mountains*	October 11, 1963
RPA3 0227	*Anyone*	October 11, 1963

Vocal—Jordanaires

1964

January 12, 1964		**RCA Nashville studio**
RPA4 1004	*Memphis, Tennessee*	January 12, 1964

| RPA4 1005 | *Ask Me* | January 12, 1964 |
| RPA4 1006 | *It Hurts Me* | January 12, 1964 |

Vocal—Jordanaires

January 1964   **Hollywood**

RPA3 5264	*Big Love, Big Heartache*
RPA3 5265	*Wheels on My Heels*
RPA3 5266	*Carny Town*
RPA3 5267	*Hard Knocks*
RPA3 5268	*It's a Wonderful World*
RPA3 5269	*It's Carnival Time*
RPA3 5270	*Little Egypt*
RPA3 5271	*One-track Heart*
RPA3 5272	*Poison Ivy League*
RPA3 5273	*Roustabout*
RPA3 5274	*There's a Brand New Day on the Horizon*

Vocal—Jordanaires

June 5 and July 8, 1964   **Hollywood**

| SPA3 2001 | *Girl Happy* | June 5, 1964 |
| SPA3 2002 | *Spring Fever* | July 8, 1964 |

SPA3 2003	*Fort Lauderdale Chamber of Commerce*	June 5, 1964
SPA3 2004	*Startin' Tonight*	June 5, 1964
SPA3 2005	*Wolf Call*	June 5, 1964
SPA3 2006	*Do Not Disturb*	July 8, 1964
SPA3 2007	*Cross My Heart and Hope to Die*	July 8, 1964
SPA3 2008	*The Meanest Girl in Town*	July 8, 1964
SPA3 2009	*Do the Clam*	June 5, 1964
SPA3 2010	*Puppet on a String*	July 8, 1964
SPA3 2011	*I've Got to Find My Baby*	July 8, 1964

Vocal—Jordanaires
Vocal—Carol Lombard Trio

Vocal—Jubilee Four

1965

February 24, 1965		**Hollywood**
SPA3 6751	*Go East, Young Man*	February 24, 1965
SPA3 6752	*Shake That Tambourine*	February 24, 1965
SPA3 6753	*Golden Coins*	February 24, 1965
SPA3 6754	*So Close, Yet So Far*	February 24, 1965

SPA3 6755	*Harum Holiday*	February 24, 1965
SPA3 6756	*Mirage*	February 24, 1965
SPA3 6757	*Animal Instinct*	February 24, 1965
SPA3 6758	*Kismet*	February 24, 1965
SPA3 6759	*Hey, Little Girl*	February 24, 1965
SPA3 6760	*Wisdom of the Ages*	February 24, 1965
SPA3 6761	*My Desert Serenade*	February 24, 1965

May 13–15, 1965	**United Artists Recording Studio, Los Angeles**

SPA3 7374	*Come Along*
SPA3 7375	*Petunia, the Gardener's Daughter*
SPA3 7376	*Chesay*
SPA3 7377	*What Every Woman Lives For*
SPA3 7378	*Frankie and Johnny*
SPA3 7379	*Look Out, Broadway*
SPA3 7380	*Beginner's Luck*

SPA3 7381	*Down by the Riverside/ When the Saints Go Marching In*	
SPA3 7382	*Shout It Out*	
SPA3 7383	*Hard Luck*	
SPA3 7384	*Please Don't Stop Loving Me*	
SPA3 7385	*Everybody Come Aboard*	
July 19, 1965		**Paramount Recording Studio, Hollywood**
TPA3 3834	*Queenie Wahine's Papaya*	July 19, 1965
TPA3 3835	*Paradise, Hawaiian Style*	July 19, 1965
TPA3 3836	*A Dog's Life*	July 19, 1965
TPA3 3837	*Drums of the Islands*	July 19, 1965
TPA3 3838	*This Is My Heaven*	July 19, 1965
TPA3 3839	*Scratch My Back*	July 19, 1965
TPA3 3840	*Stop Where You Are*	July 19, 1965
TPA3 3841	*Stop Where You Are*	July 19, 1965

TPA3 3842	*House of Sand*	July 19, 1965
TPA3 3843	*Datin'*	July 19, 1965
TPA3 3844	*Sand Castles*	July 19, 1965

Vocal—Jordanaires

1966

February 21, 1966   **Hollywood**

TPA3 5305	*Stop, Look and Listen*	February 21, 1966
TPA3 5306	*Adam and Evil*	February 21, 1966
TPA3 5307	*All That I Am*	February 21, 1966
TPA3 5308	*Never Say Yes*	February 21, 1966
TPA3 5309	*Am I Ready*	February 21, 1966
TPA3 5310	*Beach Shack*	February 21, 1966
TPA3 5311	*Spinout*	February 21, 1966
TPA3 5312	*Smorgasbord*	February 21, 1966
TPA3 5313	*I'll Be Back*	February 21, 1966

MUSICIANS:

Guitar—James Burton
Bass—Bob Moore
Drums—Murrey Harman

Piano—Floyd Cramer
Vocal—Jordanaires

May 25–28, 1966		RCA Nashville studio
TPA4 0908	*Run On*	May 25, 1966
TPA4 0909	*How Great Thou Art*	May 25, 1966
TPA4 0910	*Stand by Me*	May 26, 1966
TPA4 0911	*Where No One Stands Alone*	May 26, 1966
TPA4 0912	*Down in the Alley*	May 26, 1966
TPA4 0913	*Tomorrow Is a Long Time*	May 26, 1966
TPA4 0914	*Love Letters*	May 25, 1966
TPA4 0915	*So High*	May 27, 1966
TPA4 0916	*Farther Along*	May 27, 1966
TPA4 0917	*By and By*	May 27, 1966
TPA4 0918	*In the Garden*	May 27, 1966
TPA4 0919	*Beyond the Reef*	May 27, 1966
TPA4 0920	*Somebody Bigger Than You and I*	May 27, 1966
TPA4 0921	*Without Him*	May 27, 1966
TPA4 0922	*If the Lord Wasn't Walking by My Side*	May 28, 1966
TPA4 0923	*Where Could I Go But to the Lord*	May 28, 1966
TPA4 0924	*Come What May*	May 28, 1966
TPA4 0925	*Fools Fall in Love*	

MUSICIANS:

Guitar—Harold Bradley	Organ—David Briggs
Guitar—Chip Young	Organ—Henry Slaughter
Guitar—Scotty Moore	Steel guitar—Millie Kirkham
Bass—Bob Moore	Vocal—Jordanaires
Bass and harmonica—Charlie McCoy	Vocal—Imperial Quartet
Drums—Murrey Harman, D. J. Fontana	
Piano—Floyd Cramer	

(The Imperial Quartet: Jake Hess, Jim Murray, Gary McSpadden, Amond Morales)

June 10, 1966		RCA Nashville studio
TPA4 0982	*Indescribably Blue*	June 10, 1966
TPA4 0983	*I'll Remember You*	June 10, 1966
TPA4 0984	*If Every Day Was Like Christmas*	June 10, 1966

June 26, 1966		Hollywood
UPA3 3934	*Double Trouble*	June 26, 1966
UPA3 3935	*Baby, If You'll Give Me All of Your Love*	June 26, 1966
UPA3 3936	*Could I Fall in Love*	June 26, 1966

UPA3 3937	*Long-legged Girl*	June 26, 1966
UPA3 3938	*City by Night*	June 26, 1966
UPA3 3939	*Old MacDonald*	June 26, 1966
UPA3 3940	*I Love Only One Girl*	June 26, 1966
UPA3 3941	*There Is So Much World to See*	June 26, 1966
UPA3 3942	*It Won't Be Long*	June 26, 1966

Vocal—Jordanaires

September 26, 1966		**Paramount Recording Studio, Hollywood**
UPA3 3805	*Easy Come, Easy Go*	September 26, 1966
UPA3 3806	*The Love Machine*	September 26, 1966
UPA3 3807	*Yoga Is as Yoga Does*	September 26, 1966
UPA3 3808	*You Gotta Stop*	September 26, 1966
UPA3 3809	*Sing, You Children*	September 26, 1966
UPA3 3810	*I'll Take Love*	September 26, 1966
WPA1 8027	*She's a Machine*	September 26, 1966

Vocal—Jordanaires

1967

February 21, 1967		RCA Nashville studio
UPA3 8443	*Clambake*	February 21, 1967
UPA3 8444	*Who Needs Money*	February 21, 1967
UPA3 8445	*A House That Has Everything*	February 21, 1967
UPA3 8446	*Hey, Hey, Hey*	February 21, 1967
UPA3 8447	*The Girl I Never Loved*	February 21, 1967
UPA3 8448	*How Can You Lose What You Never Had*	February 21, 1967
UPA3 8449	*You Don't Know Me*	February 21, 1967
UPA4 2753	*Confidence*	February 21, 1967

MUSICIANS:

Guitar—Grady Martin
Guitar—Harold Bradley
Bass—Bob Moore
Drums—Murrey Harman
Steel guitar—Pete Drake

Piano—Floyd Cramer
Vocal—Jordanaires
Vocal—Millie Kirkham

June 19, 1967		**Hollywood**
WPA1 1022	*There Ain't Nothing Like a Song*	June 19, 1967
WPA1 1023	*Your Time Hasn't Come Yet, Baby*	June 19, 1967
WPA1 1024	*Five Sleepy Heads*	June 19, 1967
WPA1 1025	*Who Are You?*	June 19, 1967
WPA1 1026	*Speedway*	June 19, 1967
WPA1 1027	[No information available]	June 19, 1967
WPA1 1028	*Suppose*	June 19, 1967
WPA1 1029	*Let Yourself Go*	June 19, 1967
WPA1 1030	*He's Your Uncle, Not Your Dad*	June 19, 1967

Vocal—Jordanaires

September 10–12, 1967		**RCA Nashville studio**
UPA4 2765	*Guitar Man*	September 10, 1967
UPA4 2766	*Big Boss Man*	September 10, 1967
UPA4 2767	*Mine*	September 11, 1967
UPA4 2768	*Singing Tree*	September 11, 1967
UPA4 2769	*Just Call Me Lonesome*	September 11, 1967

UPA4 2770	*High-heel Sneakers*	September 11, 1967
UPA4 2771	*You Don't Know Me*	September 11, 1967
UPA4 2772	*We Call on Him*	September 11, 1967
UPA4 2773	*You'll Never Walk Alone*	September 11, 1967
UPA4 2774	*Singing Tree*	September 12, 1967

MUSICIANS:

Lead guitar—Scotty Moore
Lead guitar—Jerry Reed
Guitar—Grady Martin
Bass—Bob Moore
Drums—Murrey Harman
Piano—Floyd Cramer
Harmonica—Charlie McCoy

Steel guitar—
Pete Drake
Vocal—Millie
Kirkham
Vocal—
Jordanaires

Jerry Reed appears on 2765 only.

October 4, 1967　　　　　　　　**Hollywood**

WPA1 1001	*Goin' Home*	October 4, 1967
WPA1 1002	*Stay Away*	October 4, 1967
WPA1 8026	*All I Needed Was the Rain*	October 4, 1967
ZPA4 1054	*Stay Away, Joe*	October 4, 1967
ZPA4 1055	*Dominique*	October 4, 1967

Vocal—Jordanaires

1968

January 15–17, 1968		RCA Nashville studio
WPA4 1800	*Too Much Monkey Business*	January 15, 1968
WPA4 1807	*U.S. Male*	January 17, 1968
March 11, 1968		MGM Sound Studio, Hollywood
WPA1 5766	*Almost in Love*	March 11, 1968
WPA1 5766	*A Little Less Conversation*	March 11, 1968
WPA1 5768	*Wonderful World*	March 11, 1968
WPA1 5769	*Edge of Reality*	March 11, 1968
WPA1 8022	*Mama*	
WPA1 8023	*Night Life*	
WPA1 8024	*Yellow Rose of Texas/The Eyes of Texas*	
WPA1 8025	*Do the Vega*	
WPA1 8026	*All I Needed Was the Rain*	
WPA1 8027	*She's a Machine*	
WPA1 8124	*Tonight's All Right for Love*	

June 27 and 29, 1968   Burbank
Studios,
Burbank

WPA1 8028	*Tiger Man*
WPA1 8031	*Lawdy, Miss Clawdy*
WPA1 8032	*Baby, What You Want Me to Do*
WPA1 8033	*Heartbreak Hotel*
WPA1 8034	*Hound Dog*
WPA1 8035	*All Shook Up*
WPA1 8036	*Can't Help Falling in Love*
WPA1 8037	*Jailhouse Rock*
WPA1 8038	*Love Me Tender*
WPA1 8042	*Blue Christmas*
WPA1 8043	*One Night*
WPA1 8044	*Memories*
WPA1 8116	*Are You Lonesome Tonight?*
WPA1 8118	*Love Me*
WPA1 8119	*Tryin' to Get to You*
	That's All Right
	It Hurts Me
	Let Yourself Go

*When My Blue
Moon Turns to
Gold Again
Blue Suede
Shoes
Don't Be Cruel
If I Can
Dream
Trouble
Blue Moon of
Kentucky
Santa Claus Is
Back in Town
Are You
Lonesome
Tonight?
Baby, What
You Want Me
to Do*

MUSICIANS:

Guitar—Scotty Moore	Drums—D. J.
Guitar—Elvis	Fontana
Guitar—Charlie Hodge	

June 30, 1968		Burbank Studios, Burbank
WPA1 8029	*If I Can Dream*	June 30, 1968
WPA1 8030	*Trouble*	June 30, 1968
WPA1 8039	*Where Could I Go But to the Lord*	June 30, 1968

WPA1 8040	*Up Above My Head*	June 30, 1968
WPA1 8041	*Saved*	June 30, 1968
WPA1 8045	*Nothingville*	June 30, 1968
WPA1 8046	*Big Boss Man*	June 30, 1968
WPA1 8047	*Guitar Man*	June 30, 1968
WPA1 8048	*Little Egypt*	June 30, 1968

MUSICIANS:

Lead guitar—Tommy Tedesco
Guitar—Mike Deasy
Bass—Larry Knectal
Drums—Hal Blaine
Piano and organ— Don Randi
Vocal— Blossoms
(The Blossoms: Darlene Love, Jean King, and Fanita James)

July 7, 1968   Hollywood

| WPA1 8091 | *Charro!* | July 7, 1968 |

October 15, 1968   Hollywood

XPA1 3976	*Clean Up Your Own Back Yard*	October 15, 1968
XPA1 3978	*Almost*	October 15, 1968
	Swing Down, Sweet Chariot	October 15, 1968
	Aura Lee	October 15, 1968
	Sign of the Zodiac	October 15, 1968

1969

January 13–16 and 20–23, 1969		American Studios, Memphis
XPA5 1142	*Long Black Limousine*	January 13, 1969
XPA5 1143	*This Is the Story*	January 13, 1969
XPA5 1144	*Come Out, Come Out*	January 14, 1969
XPA5 1145	*Wearin' That Loved-on Look*	January 14, 1969
XPA5 1146	*You'll Think of Me*	January 14, 1969
XPA5 1147	*I'm Movin' On*	January 15, 1969
XPA5 1148	*A Little Bit of Green*	January 15, 1969
XPA5 1149	*Don't Cry, Daddy*	January 15, 1969
XPA5 1150	*Poor Man's Gold*	January 15, 1969
XPA5 1151	*Inherit the Wind*	January 16, 1969
XPA5 1152	*Mama Liked the Roses*	January 16, 1969
XPA5 1153	*My Little Friend*	January 16, 1969
XPA5 1154	*In the Ghetto*	January 21, 1969
XPA5 1155	*Gentle on My Mind*	January 15, 1969

XPA5 1156	*Rubberneckin'*	January 20, 1969
XPA5 1157	*Hey, Jude*	January 22, 1969
XPA5 1158	*From a Jack to a King*	January 21, 1969
XPA5 1159	*Without Love*	January 21, 1969
XPA5 1160	*I'll Hold You in My Heart*	January 23, 1969
XPA5 1161	*I'll Be There*	January 23, 1969
XPA5 1227	*Suspicious Minds*	

MUSICIANS:

Guitar and electric sitar—Reggie Young
Guitar and bass—Tommy Cogbill
Bass—Mike Leech
Drums—Gene Chrisman
Piano—Bobby Emmons
Organ—Glen Spreen
Vocal—Jeannie Green
Vocal—Mary and Ginger Holladay
Horn—Wayne Jackson
Horn—Bob Taylor
Horn—Ed Logan
Memphis Strings

| **February 17–22, 1969** | **American Studios, Memphis** |
| XPA5 1265 | *True Love Travels on a Gravel Road* | February 17, 1969 |

XPA5 1266	*Stranger in My Own Home Town*	February 17, 1969
XPA5 1267	*And the Grass Won't Pay No Mind*	February 18, 1969
XPA5 1268	*Power of My Love*	February 18, 1969
XPA5 1269	*After Loving You*	February 18, 1969
XPA5 1270	*Do You Know Who I Am*	February 19, 1969
XPA5 1271	*Kentucky Rain*	February 19, 1969
XPA5 1272	*Only the Strong Survive*	February 20, 1969
XPA5 1273	*It Keeps Right On A-hurtin'*	February 20, 1969
XPA5 1274	*Any Day Now*	February 21, 1969
XPA5 1275	*If I'm a Fool*	February 21, 1969
XPA5 1276	*The Fair's Moving On*	February 21, 1969
XPA5 1277	*Memory Revival*	February 22, 1969
XPA5 1278	*Who Am I?*	February 22, 1969

March 5–6, 1969   **MCA Studio, Hollywood**

ZPA4 1054	*Stay Away, Joe*	October 4, 1969 [mixed]

ZPA4 1055	*Let's Forget About the Stars*	[date uncertain] March 5–6, 1969
ZPA4 1056	*Have a Happy*	March 5–6, 1969
ZPA4 1057	*Let's Be Friends*	March 5–6, 1969
ZPA4 1058	*Change of Habit*	March 5–6, 1969
ZPA4 1957	*Let Us Pray*	September 22, 1969 [mixed]
August 22–26, 1969		**Recorded at the International Hotel, Las Vegas**
XPA5 2309	*I Got a Woman*	August 22, 1969
XPA5 2310	*All Shook Up*	August 22, 1969
XPA5 2311	*Love Me Tender*	August 22, 1969
XPA5 2312	*Suspicious Minds*	August 22, 1969
XPA5 2313	*Words*	August 22, 1969
XPA5 2314	*Johnny B. Goode*	August 22, 1969
XPA5 2315	*Runaway*	August 22, 1969
XPA5 2316	*Are You Lonesome Tonight?*	August 25, 1969

XPA5 2317	*Jailhouse Rock/Don't Be Cruel*	August 25, 1969
XPA5 2318	*Yesterday/Hey, Jude*	August 25, 1969
XPA5 2319	*Memories*	August 25, 1969
XPA5 2320	*I Can't Stop Loving You*	August 25, 1969
XPA5 2374	*In the Ghetto*	August 25, 1969
XPA5 2375	*What'd I Say*	August 25, 1969
XPA5 2376	*Inherit the Wind*	August 25, 1969
XPA5 2377	*Rubberneckin'*	August 24, 1969
XPA5 2378	*This Is the Story*	August 24, 1969
XPA5 2379	*Can't Help Falling in Love*	August 24, 1969
XPA5 2380	*Heartbreak Hotel*	August 24, 1969
XPA5 2381	*My Babe*	August 24, 1969
XPA5 2382	*Funny How Time Slips Away*	August 26, 1969
XPA5 2383	*Blue Suede Shoes*	August 26, 1969
XPA5 2384	*Hound Dog*	August 26, 1969
XPA5 2385	*Baby, What You Want Me to Do*	August 26, 1969

| XPA5 2386 | *Mystery Train/ Tiger Man* | August 26, 1969 |

MUSICIANS:

Lead guitar—James Burton
Guitar—John Wilkinson
Guitar and vocal—Charlie Hodge
Bass—Jerry Scheff
Drums—Ronnie Tutt
Piano—Larry Muhoberac
Vocal—Millie Kirkham

Vocal—Sweet Inspirations
Vocal—Imperial Quartet
Joe Guercio Orchestra

(The Sweet Inspirations: Emily Houston, Myrna Smith, Sylvia Shenwell, Estelle Brown)

1970

February 16–19, 1970		International Hotel, Las Vegas
ZPA5 1286	*All Shook Up*	February 16, 1970
ZPA5 1287	*In the Ghetto*	February 16, 1970
ZPA5 1288	*Suspicious Minds*	February 16, 1970
ZPA5 1289	*Proud Mary*	February 17, 1970
ZPA5 1290	*See See Rider*	February 17, 1970
ZPA5 1291	*Let It Be Me*	February 17, 1970

ZPA5 1292	*Don't Cry, Daddy*	February 17, 1970
ZPA5 1293	*Sweet Caroline*	February 18, 1970
ZPA5 1294	*Release Me*	February 18, 1970
ZPA5 1295	*Kentucky Rain*	February 18, 1970
ZPA5 1296	*Long Tall Sally*	February 18, 1970
ZPA5 1297	*Walk a Mile in My Shoes*	February 18, 1970
ZPA5 1298	*Polk Salad Annie*	February 18, 1970
ZPA5 1299	*I Can't Stop Loving You*	February 18, 1970
ZPA5 1300	*The Wonder of You*	February 19, 1970

MUSICIANS:

Lead guitar—James Burton
Guitar—John Wilkinson
Guitar and vocal—Charlie Hodge
Bass—Jerry Scheff
Drums—Ronnie Tutt
Piano—Glenn D. Hardin
Vocal—Millie Kirkham

Vocal—Sweet Inspirations
Vocal—Imperial Quartet
Joe Guercio Orchestra

June 4–8, 1970		**RCA Nashville studio**
ZPA4 1593	*Twenty Days and Twenty Nights*	June 4, 1970
ZPA4 1594	*I've Lost You*	June 4, 1970

ZPA4 1595	*I Was Born About 10,000 Years Ago*	June 4, 1970
ZPA4 1596	*The Sound of Your Cry*	June 4, 1970
ZPA4 1597	*The Fool*	June 4, 1970
ZPA4 1598	*Little Cabin on the Hill*	June 4, 1970
ZPA4 1599	*Cindy, Cindy*	June 4, 1970
ZPA4 1600	*Bridge over Troubled Water*	June 5, 1970
ZPA4 1601	*Got My Mojo Working/Keep Your Hands*	June 5, 1970
ZPA4 1602	*How the Web Was Woven*	June 5, 1970
ZPA4 1603	*It's Your Baby, You Rock It*	June 5, 1970
ZPA4 1604	*Stranger in the Crowd*	June 5, 1970
ZPA4 1605	*I'll Never Know*	June 5, 1970
ZPA4 1606	*Mary in the Morning*	June 5, 1970
ZPA4 1607	*It Ain't No Big Thing*	June 6, 1970
ZPA4 1608	*You Don't Have to Say You Love Me*	June 6, 1970
ZPA4 1609	*Just Pretend*	June 6, 1970
ZPA4 1610	*This Is Our Dance*	June 6, 1970
ZPA4 1613	*Life*	June 6, 1970
ZPA4 1614	*Heart of Rome*	June 6, 1970
ZPA4 1615	*When I'm Over You*	June 7, 1970

ZPA4 1616	*I Really Don't Want to Know*	June 7, 1970
ZPA4 1617	*Faded Love*	June 7, 1970
ZPA4 1618	*Tomorrow Never Comes*	June 7, 1970
ZPA4 1619	*The Next Step Is Love*	June 7, 1970
ZPA4 1620	*Make the World Go Away*	June 7, 1970
ZPA4 1621	*Funny How Time Slips Away*	June 7, 1970
ZPA4 1622	*I Washed My Hands in Muddy Water*	June 7, 1970
ZPA4 1623	*Love Letters*	June 7, 1970
ZPA4 1624	*There Goes My Everything*	June 8, 1970
ZPA4 1625	*If I Were You*	June 8, 1970
ZPA4 1626	*Only Believe*	June 8, 1970
ZPA4 1627	*Sylvia*	June 8, 1970
ZPA4 1628	*Patch It Up*	June 8, 1970

MUSICIANS:

Lead guitar—James Burton
Guitar—Chip Young
Bass—Norbert Putnam
Drums—Jerry Carrigan
Piano—David Briggs
Harmonica—Charlie McCoy
Vocal—Millie Kirkham
Vocal—Jeannie Green
Vocal—Mary and Ginger Holladay
Vocal—Jordanaires
Vocal Imperial Quartet
Vocal—Nashville Edition

July–August 1970

MGM Recording Studio, Los Angeles

*Words
The Next Step
Is Love
Polk Salad
Annie
That's All
Right
Little Sister
What'd I Say
Stranger in the
Crowd
How the Web
Was Woven
I Just Can't
Help Believing
You Don't
Have to Say
You Love Me*

MUSICIANS:

Lead guitar—James Burton
Guitar—John Wilkinson
Guitar—Charlie Hodge
Bass—Jerry Scheff

Drums—
Ronnie Tutt
Piano—Glenn
D. Hardin

August 1970	International Hotel, Las Vegas

Bridge over Troubled Water
You've Lost That Lovin' Feelin'
Mary in the Morning
Polk Salad Annie

August 10, 1970	International Hotel, Las Vegas

That's All Right	August 10, 1970
I've Lost You	August 10, 1970
Patch It Up	August 10, 1970
Love Me Tender	August 10, 1970
You've Lost That Lovin' Feelin'	August 10, 1970
Sweet Caroline	
I Just Can't Help Believing	
Tiger Man	
Bridge over Troubled Water	

> *Heartbreak
> Hotel
> One Night
> Blue Suede
> Shoes
> All Shook Up
> Polk Salad
> Annie
> Can't Help
> Falling in Love*

August 13–15, 1970		**International Hotel, Las Vegas**
ZPA5 1862	*I Just Can't Help Believing*	August 13, 1970
ZPA5 1863	*Patch It Up*	August 13, 1970
ZPA5 1864	*You've Lost That Lovin' Feelin'*	August 14, 1970
ZPA5 1865	*I've Lost You*	August 14, 1970
ZPA5 1866	*Bridge over Troubled Water*	August 15, 1970

MUSICIANS:

Lead guitar—James Burton
Guitar—John Wilkinson
Guitar and vocal—Charlie Hodge
Bass—Jerry Scheff
Drums—Ronnie Tutt
Piano—Glenn D. Hardin
Vocal—Millie Kirkham

Vocal—Sweet Inspirations
Vocal—Imperial Quartet
Joe Guercio Orchestra

September 9, 1970		Veterans Coliseum, Phoenix, Arizona
	Mystery Train/ Tiger Man	September 9, 1970

MUSICIANS:

Lead guitar—James Burton
Guitar—John Wilkinson
Guitar and vocal—Charlie Hodge
Bass—Jerry Scheff
Piano—Glenn D. Hardin
Vocal—Kathy Westmoreland

Vocal—Sweet Inspirations
Joe Guercio Orchestra

September 22, 1970		**RCA Nashville studio**
ZPA4 1797	*Snowbird*	September 22, 1970
ZPA4 1798	*Where Did They Go, Lord*	September 22, 1970
ZPA4 1799	*Whole Lotta Shakin' Goin' On*	September 22, 1970
ZPA4 1800	*Rags to Riches*	September 22, 1970

MUSICIANS:

Lead guitar—Edward Hinton
Guitar—Chip Young
Bass—Norbert Putnam
Drums—Jerry Carrigan
Organ—Charlie McCoy

Vocal—Jeannie Green
Vocal—Jordanaires
Piano—David Briggs

1971

March 15, 1971		RCA Nashville studio
APA4	*The First Time Ever I Saw Your Face*	March 15, 1971
APA4	*Amazing Grace*	March 15, 1971
APA4	*Early Mornin' Rain*	March 15, 1971
APA4	*For Lovin' Me*	March 15, 1971

MUSICIANS:

Lead guitar—James Burton
Guitar—Chip Young
Bass—Norbert Putnam
Drums—Jerry Carrigan
Piano—David Briggs
Harmonica—Charlie McCoy
Vocal—Millie Kirkham
Vocal—Jeannie Green

Vocal—Mary and Ginger Holladay
Vocal—Imperial Quartet
Vocal—Nashville Edition

May 15–21, 1971		RCA Nashville studio
APA4 1259	*Miracle of the Rosary*	May 15, 1971
APA4 1260	*It Won't Seem Like Christmas*	May 15, 1971

APA4 1261	*If I Get Home on Christmas Day*	May 15, 1971
APA4 1262	*Padre*	May 15, 1971
APA4 1263	*Holly Leaves and Christmas Trees*	May 15, 1971
APA4 1264	*Merry Christmas, Baby*	May 15, 1971
APA4 1265	*Silver Bells*	May 15, 1971
APA4 1266	*I'll Be Home on Christmas Day*	May 16, 1971
APA4 1267	*On a Snowy Christmas Night*	May 16, 1971
APA4 1268	*Winter Wonderland*	May 16, 1971
APA4 1269	*Don't Think Twice, It's All Right*	May 16, 1971
APA4 1270	*O Come, All Ye Faithful*	May 16, 1971
APA4 1271	*The First Noel*	May 16, 1971
APA4 1272	*The Wonderful World of Christmas*	May 16, 1971
APA4 1273	*Help Me Make It Through the Night*	May 16, 1971
APA4 1274	*Until It's Time for You to Go*	May 17, 1971
APA4 1275	*Lead Me, Guide Me*	May 17, 1971
APA4 1276	*Fools Rush In*	May 18, 1971

APA4 1277	*He Touched Me*	May 18, 1971
APA4 1278	*I've Got Confidence*	May 18, 1971
APA4 1279	*An Evening Prayer*	May 18, 1971
APA4 1280	*Seeing Is Believing*	May 19, 1971
APA4 1281	*A Thing Called Love*	May 19, 1971
APA4 1282	*It's Still Here*	May 19, 1971
APA4 1283	*I'll Take You Home Again, Kathleen*	May 19, 1971
APA4 1284	*I Will Be True*	May 19, 1971
APA4 1285	*I'm Leavin'*	May 20, 1971
APA4 1286	*We Can Make the Morning*	May 20, 1971
APA4 1287	*It's Only Love*	May 20, 1971
APA4 1288	*Love Me, Love the Life I Lead*	May 21, 1971

MUSICIANS:

Lead guitar—James Burton
Guitar—Chip Young
Bass—Norbert Putnam
Drums—Jerry Carrigan
Piano—David Briggs
Harmonica—Charlie McCoy
Vocal—Millie Kirkham
Vocal—Ginger Holladay
Vocal—Temple Riser
Vocal—Imperial Quartet

June 8–9, 1971　　　　**RCA Nashville studio**

| APA4 1289 | *Until It's Time for You to Go* | June 8, 1971 |

APA4 1290	*Put Your Hand in the Hand*	June 8, 1971
APA4 1291	*Reach Out to Jesus*	June 8, 1971
APA4 1292	*He Is My Everything*	June 8, 1971
APA4 1293	*There Is No God But God*	June 9, 1971
APA4 1294	*I John*	June 9, 1971
APA4 1295	*The Bosom of Abraham*	June 9, 1971
APA4 1296	*I'll Be Home for Christmas*	June 9, 1971

MUSICIANS:

Lead guitar—James Burton
Guitar—Chip Young
Bass—Norbert Putnam
Drums—Jerry Carrigan
Drums—Kenneth Buttrey
Piano—David Briggs
Organ—Glen Spreen
Harmonica—Charlie McCoy

Vocal—Millie Kirkham
Vocal—June Page
Vocal—Sonja Montgomery
Vocal—Imperial Quartet

1972

February 14–17, 1972   **Hilton Hotel, Las Vegas**

| BPA5 1142 | *Never Been to Spain* | February 14, 1972 |
| BPA5 1143 | *You Gave Me a Mountain* | February 15, 1972 |

BPA5 1144	*A Big Hunk o' Love*	February 15, 1972
BPA5 1145	*It's Impossible*	February 16, 1972
BPA5 1146	*The Impossible Dream*	February 16, 1972
BPA5 1147	*An American Trilogy*	February 17, 1972

MUSICIANS:

Lead guitar—James Burton
Guitar—John Wilkinson
Guitar and vocal—Charlie Hodge
Bass—Jerry Scheff
Drums—Ronnie Tutt
Piano—Glenn D. Hardin
Vocal—Kathy Westmoreland

Vocal—Sweet Inspirations
Vocal—J. D. Sumner and the Stamps
Joe Guercio Orchestra

(The Sweet Inspirations: Myrna Smith, Sylvia Shenwell, Estelle Brown)
(J. D. Sumner and the Stamps: J. D. Sumner, Donnie Sumner, Bill Baize, Ed Enoch, Richard Staborn)

March 27–29, 1972		**MGM Recording Studio, Los Angeles**
BPA3 1149	*Separate Ways*	March 27, 1972
BPA3 1150	*For the Good Times*	March 27, 1972
BPA3 1151	*Where Do I Go from Here*	March 27, 1972

BPA3 1257	*Burning Love*	March 28, 1972
BPA3 1258	*Fool*	March 28, 1972
BPA3 1259	*Always on My Mind*	March 29, 1972
BPA3 1260	*It's a Matter of Time*	March 29, 1972

MUSICIANS:

Lead Guitar—James Burton
Guitar—John Wilkinson
Bass—Emory Gordy
Drums—Ronnie Tutt
Piano—Glenn D.Hardin

Vocal—J. D. Sumner
and the Stamps

April 9, 1972	Coliseum, Hampton Roads, Virginia
April 10, 1972	Coliseum, Richmond, Virginia
April 18, 1972	Convention Center, San Antonio, Texas

Johnny B. Goode
See See Rider
Polk Salad Annie
Proud Mary
Never Been to Spain

Burning Love
Love Me
Tender
Until It's Time
for You to Go
Suspicious
Minds
Bridge over
Troubled Water
Funny How
Time Slips
Away
American
Trilogy
I Got a Woman
A Big Hunk o'
Love
You Gave Me a
Mountain
Lawdy, Miss
Clawdy
Can't Help
Falling in Love

MUSICIANS:

Lead guitar—James Burton
Guitar—John Wilkinson
Guitar and vocal—Charlie
Hodge
Bass—Jerry Scheff
Drums—Ronnie Tutt
Piano—Glenn D. Hardin
Vocal—Kathy Westmoreland

Vocal—Sweet
Inspirations
Vocal—J. D.
Sumner
and the Stamps
Joe Guercio
Orchestra

All of these were live recordings from the April tour.

> *For the Good Times*
> *Lead Me,*
> *Guide Me*
> *Bosom of*
> *Abraham*
> *I John*

MUSICIANS:

Piano and vocal—Charlie Hodge
Vocal—Sweet Inspirations
Vocal—J. D. Sumner and the Stamps

June 10, 1972		Madison Square Garden, New York
BPA5 6797	*Also Sprach Zarathustra*	June 10, 1972
BPA5 6774	*That's All Right*	June 10, 1972
BPA5 6775	*Proud Mary*	June 10, 1972
BPA5 6776	*Never Been to Spain*	June 10, 1972
BPA5 6777	*You Don't Have to Say You Love Me*	June 10, 1972
BPA5 6778	*You've Lost That Lovin' Feelin'*	June 10, 1972
BPA5 6779	*Polk Salad Annie*	June 10, 1972

BPA5 6780	*Love Me*	June 10, 1972
BPA5 6781	*All Shook Up*	June 10, 1972
BPA5 6782	*Heartbreak Hotel*	June 10, 1972
BPA5 6783	*Teddy Bear/ Don't Be Cruel*	June 10, 1972
BPA5 6794	Introductions by Elvis	June 10, 1972
BPA5 6784	*The Impossible Dream*	June 10, 1972
BPA5 6785	*Hound Dog*	June 10, 1972
BPA5 6786	*Suspicious Minds*	June 10, 1972
BPA5 6787	*For the Good Times*	June 10, 1972
BPA5 6788	*American Trilogy*	June 10, 1972
BPA5 6789	*Funny How Time Slips Away*	June 10, 1972
BPA5 6790	*I Can't Stop Loving You*	June 10, 1972
BPA5 6791	*I Can't Stop Loving You*	June 10, 1972
BPA5 6792	*Can't Help Falling in Love*	June 10, 1972
BPA5 6793	Closing	June 10, 1972

MUSICIANS:

Lead guitar—James Burton
Guitar—John Wilkinson
Guitar and vocal—Charlie Hodge
Bass—Jerry Scheff

Vocal—Sweet Inspirations
Vocal—J. D. Sumner and the Stamps

Drums—Ronnie Tutt
Piano—Glenn D. Hardin
Vocal—Kathy Westmoreland

Joe Guercio
Orchestra

1973

	January 14, 1973	H.I.C. Arena, Hawaii
CPA5 4723	*Also Sprach Zarathustra*	January 14, 1973
CPA5 4724	*See See Rider*	January 14, 1973
CPA5 4725	*Burning Love*	January 14, 1973
CPA5 4726	*Something*	January 14, 1973
CPA5 4727	*You Gave Me a Mountain*	January 14, 1973
CPA5 4728	*Steamroller Blues*	January 14, 1973
CPA5 4729	*My Way*	January 14, 1973
CPA5 4730	*Love Me*	January 14, 1973
CPA5 4731	*Johnny B. Goode*	January 14, 1973
CPA5 4732	*It's Over*	January 14, 1973
CPA5 4733	*Blue Suede Shoes*	January 14, 1973
CPA5 4734	*I'm So Lonesome I Could Cry*	January 14, 1973

CPA5 4735	*I Can't Stop Loving You*	January 14, 1973
CPA5 4736	*Hound Dog*	January 14, 1973
CPA5 4737	*What Now, My Love*	January 14, 1973
CPA5 4738	*Fever*	January 14, 1973
CPA5 4739	*Welcome to My World*	January 14, 1973
CPA5 4740	*Suspicious Minds*	January 14, 1973
CPA5 4741	Introductions by Elvis	January 14, 1973
CPA5 4742	*I'll Remember You*	January 14, 1973
CPA5 4743	*Long Tall Sally/Whole Lotta Shakin' Goin' On*	January 14, 1973
CPA5 4744	*American Trilogy*	January 14, 1973
CPA5 4745	*A Big Hunk o' Love*	January 14, 1973
CPA5 4746	*Can't Help Falling in Love*	January 14, 1973
CPA5 4747	Closing vamp	January 14, 1973
CPA5 4756	*Blue Hawaii*	January 14, 1973
CPA5 4757	*Ku-u-i-po*	January 14, 1973
CPA5 4758	*No More*	January 14, 1973
CPA5 4759	*Hawaiian Wedding Song*	January 14, 1973

CPA5 4760	*Early Mornin' Rain*	January 14, 1973

MUSICIANS:

Lead guitar—James Burton
Guitar—John Wilkinson
Guitar and vocal—Charlie Hodge
Bass—Jerry Scheff
Piano—Glenn D. Hardin
Vocal—Kathy Westmoreland

Vocal—Sweet Inspirations
Vocal—J. D. Sumner and the Stamps

(J. D. Sumner and the Stamps: J. D. Sumner, Donnie Sumner, Bill Baize, Ed Enoch, Ed Wideman)

July 21–25, 1973		**Stax Recording Studio, Memphis**
CPA5 4761	*If You Don't Come Back*	July 21, 1973
CPA5 4762	*Three Corn Patches*	July 21, 1973
CPA5 4763	*Take Good Care of Her*	July 21, 1973
CPA5 4764	*Find Out What's Happening*	July 22, 1973
CPA5 4765	*I've Got a Thing About You, Baby*	July 22, 1973
CPA5 4766	*Just a Little Bit*	July 22, 1973
CPA5 4767	*Raised on Rock*	July 23, 1973
CPA5 4768	*For Ol' Times Sake*	July 23, 1973
CPA5 4769	*Girl of Mine*	July 24, 1973

CPA5 4770	*Good, Bad, but Beautiful*	July 24, 1973
CPA5 4771	*Color My Rainbow*	July 25, 1973
CPA5 4772	*Sweet Angeline*	July 25, 1973
CPA5 4773	*The Wonders You Perform*	July 25, 1973

MUSICIANS:

Lead guitar—James Burton
Guitar—Reggie Young
Guitar—Johnny Christopher
Bass—Tommy Cogbill
Drums—Jerry Carrigan
Drums—Ronnie Tutt
Piano—Bobby Wood
Organ—Bobby Emmons
Vocal—Kathy Westmoreland
Vocal—Jeannie Green
Vocal—Mary and Ginger Holladay
Vocal—J. D. Sumner and the Stamps

September 24, 1973		**Elvis's home, Palm Springs**
CPA5 4774	*I Miss You*	September 24, 1974
CPA5 4775	*Are You Sincere*	September 24, 1974

Vocal—Voice
(Voice: Donnie Sumner, Tim Batey, Sherril Nielson)

| **December 10–16, 1973** | | **Stax Studio, Memphis** |
| CPA5 1617 | *I Got a Feelin' in My Body* | December 10, 1973 |

CPA5 1618	It's Midnight	December 10, 1973
CPA5 1619	You Asked Me To	December 11, 1973
CPA5 1620	If You Talk in Your Sleep	December 11, 1973
CPA5 1621	Mr. Songman	December 12, 1973
CPA5 1622	Thinking About You	December 12, 1973
CPA5 1623	Love Song of the Year	December 12, 1973
CPA5 1624	Help Me	December 12, 1973
CPA5 1625	Loving Arms	December 13, 1973
CPA5 1626	Good-time Charlie's Got the Blues	December 13, 1973
CPA5 1627	Talk About the Good Times	December 14, 1973
CPA5 1628	Promised Land	December 15, 1973
CPA5 1629	Your Love's Been a Long Time Coming	December 15, 1973
CPA5 1630	My Boy	December 15, 1973
CPA5 1631	There's a Honky Tonk Angel	December 15, 1973
CPA5 1632	If That Isn't Love	December 15, 1973
CPA5 1633	Spanish Eyes	December 16, 1973

| CPA5 1634 | *She Wears My Ring* | December 16, 1973 |

MUSICIANS:

Lead guitar—James Burton
Guitar—Johnny Christopher
Bass—Norbert Putnam
Drums—Ronnie Tutt
Piano and organ—David Briggs
Piano—Pete Hullin
Vocal—Kathy Westmoreland
Vocal—Jeannie Green

Vocal—Mary Holladay
Vocal—Susan Pilkington
Vocal—J. D. Sumner and the Stamps
Vocal—Voice

1974

March 20, 1974		Mid-South Coliseum, Memphis
DPA5 0903	*See See Rider*	March 20, 1974
DPA5 0904	*I Got a Woman*	March 20, 1974
DPA5 0905	*Love Me*	March 20, 1974
DPA5 0906	*Tryin' to Get to You*	March 20, 1974
DPA5 0907	*All Shook Up*	March 20, 1974
DPA5 0908	*Steamroller Blues*	March 20, 1974
DPA5 0909	*Teddy Bear/ Don't Be Cruel*	March 20, 1974

DPA5 0910	*Love Me Tender*	March 20, 1974
DPA5 0911	*Long Tall Sally/Whole Lotta Shakin' Goin' On/Your Mama Don't Dance/Flip, Flop, Fly/ Jailhouse Rock/Hound Dog*	March 20, 1974
DPA5 0912	*Fever*	March 20, 1974
DPA5 0913	*Polk Salad Annie*	March 20, 1974
DPA5 0914	*Why Me, Lord*	March 20, 1974
DPA5 0915	*How Great Thou Art*	March 20, 1974
DPA5 0916	*Suspicious Minds*	March 20, 1974
DPA5 0917	Introductions by Elvis	March 20, 1974
DPA5 0918	*Blueberry Hill/I Can't Stop Loving You*	March 20, 1974
DPA5 0919	*Help Me*	March 20, 1974
DPA5 0920	*An American Trilogy*	March 20, 1974
DPA5 0921	*Let Me Be There*	March 20, 1974
DPA5 0926	*My Baby Left Me*	March 20, 1974

DPA5 0927	*Lawdy, Miss Clawdy*	March 20, 1974
DPA5 0928	*Funny How Time Slips Away*	March 20, 1974
DPA5 0929	*Can't Help Falling in Love*	March 20, 1974
DPA5 0930	Closing vamp	March 20, 1974

MUSICIANS:

Lead guitar—James Burton
Guitar—John Wilkinson
Guitar and vocal—Charlie Hodge
Bass—Duke Bardwell
Piano—Glenn D. Hardin
Vocal—Kathy Westmoreland
Vocal—Sweet Inspirations

Vocal—J. D. Sumner and the Stamps
Vocal—Voice
Joe Guercio Orchestra

1975

May 10–12, 1975   **Hollywood**

EPA3 1594	*Fairytale*	May 10, 1975
EPA3 1595	*Green, Green Grass of Home*	May 10, 1975
EPA3 1596	*I Can Help*	May 10, 1975
EPA3 1597	*And I Love You So*	May 10 and 11, 1975
EPA3 1598	*Susan When She Tried*	May 10 and 11, 1975
EPA3 1599	*T-R-O-U-B-L-E*	May 10 and 11, 1975

EPA3 1600	*Woman Without Love*	May 11 and 12, 1975
EPA3 1601	*Shake a Hand*	May 11 and 12, 1975
EPA3 1602	*Bringing It Back*	May 11 and 12, 1975
EPA3 1603	*Pieces of My Life*	May 12, 1975

MUSICIANS:

Lead guitar—James Burton
Piano—Glenn D. Hardin
Guitar—John Wilkinson
Guitar—Charlie Hodge
Drums—Ronnie Tutt
Clarinet—David Briggs

Bass—Duke Bardwell
Vocal—Voice
Vocal—Mary and Ginger Holladay

1976

Release Date: January 1976

April 11, 1956; September 5, 1957; April 3, 1960; April 4, 1960; May 25, 1966

Recording Locations: Texas, Nashville, and Hawaii

EPA3 2742	*Harbor Lights*	
EPA5 2744	Interview with Elvis	
G2WB 0270	*I Want You, I Need You, I Love You*	April 11, 1956

WPA1 8117	*Blue Suede Shoes*	NBC TV show, 1968
H2PB 5525	*Blue Christmas*	September 5, 1957
H2WB 6779	*Jailhouse Rock*	May 2, 1957
L2WB 0100	*It's Now or Never*	April 3, 1960
SPA3 6743	*Cane and a High Starched Collar*	February 9, 1961
EPA3 2743	Presentation of Awards to Elvis	March 25, 1961
CPA5 4756	*Blue Hawaii*	
L2WB 0105	*Such a Night*	April 4, 1960
WPA1 8120	*Baby, What You Want Me to Do*	NBC TV show, 1968
TPA4 0909	*How Great Thou Art*	May 25, 1966
WPA1 8029	*If I Can Dream*	NBC TV show, 1968

MUSICIANS:

Guitar—Elvis, Scotty Moore, Chet Atkins, Hank Garland, Charlie Hodge; Harold Bradley, Chip Young, Jerry Stembridge (on TPA4 0909)
Steel guitar—Pete Drake (on TPA4 0909)
Bass—Bill Black, Bob Moore, Charlie McCoy
Saxophone—Homer (Boots)

Vocals—J. D. Sumner and the Stamps; Imperial Quartet; Jordanaires; Ben Speer; Brock Speer; Gordon Stoker; Millie Kirkham; Neil

Randolph, Rufus Long
Piano—Marvin Hughes,
Dudley Brooks, Floyd
Cramer,
Henry Slaughter,
Mike Stoller
Drums—D. J. Fontana,
Murrey Harman

Matthews, Jr.;
Hoyt Hawkins;
Hugh Jarrett;
Raymond
Walker; Jake
Hess; Charles
S. Nielsen;
Gary
McSpadden;
Amond
Morales; June
Page; Dolores
Edgin

Release Date: March 1976

Recording Location: Sun studio, Memphis

F2WB 8040	*That's All Right*	July 1954
F2WB 8041	*Blue Moon of Kentucky*	July 1954
F2WB 8042	*I Don't Care If the Sun Don't Shine*	September 1954
F2WB 8043	*Good Rockin' Tonight*	September 1954
F2WB 8044	*Milkcow Blues Boogie*	December 1954
F2WB 8045	*You're a Heartbreaker*	December 1954
F2WB 8046	*Baby, Let's Play House*	February 1955

F2WB 8047	*I'm Left, You're Right, She's Gone*	July 1955
F2WB 8001	*Mystery Train*	February 1955
F2WB 8000	*I Forgot to Remember to Forget*	July 1955
F2WB 8116	*I'll Never Let You Go*	January 1955
G2WB 1086	*I Love You Because* (first version)	July 1954
F2WB 8039	*Tryin' to Get to You*	July 1955
F2WB 8117	*Blue Moon*	July 1954
F2WB 8118	*Just Because*	September 1954
G2WB 1087	*I Love You Because* (second version)	July 1954

February 2–8, 1976		**Memphis**
FWA5 0665	*Bigger They Are, Harder They Fall*	February 2–3, 1976
FWA5 0667	*The Last Farewell*	February 2–3, 1976
FWA5 0668	*Solitaire*	February 3–4, 1976
FWA5 0670	*I'll Never Fall in Love Again*	February 4–5, 1976
FWA5 0671	*For the Heart*	February 5–6, 1976

FWA5 0672	*Hurt*	February 5–6, 1976
FWA5 0673	*Danny Boy*	February 5–6, 1976
FWA5 0674	*Never Again*	February 6–7, 1976
FWA5 0675	*Love Coming Down*	February 6–7, 1976
FWA5 0676	*Blue Eyes Crying in the Rain*	February 7–8, 1976
FWA5 0678	*She Thinks I Still Care*	February 2–3, 1976
FWA5 0679	*Moody Blue*	February 3–4, 1976

MUSICIANS:

Lead guitar—James Burton
Piano—Glenn D. Hardin
Guitar—John Wilkinson
Guitar—Charlie Hodge
Drums—Ronnie Tutt
Electric piano —David Briggs
Bass—Jerry Scheff

On *Blue Eyes Crying in the Rain:* Piano—David Briggs; Electric piano—Bobby Emmons; Bass—Norbert Putnam; Electric guitar—Billy Sanford; Vocals—J. D. Sumner and the Stamps, Ed Hill, Larry Strickland, Kathy Westmoreland, Myrna Smith

Release Date: 1976

January 15, 1969; February 18, 1970; June 7, 1970; May 17, 1971; May 20, 1972; January 14, 1973
Recording Locations: Memphis, Las Vegas,

		Nashville, New York, and Hawaii
XPA5 1155	*Gentle on My Mind*	January 15, 1969
ZPA5 1294	*Release Me (and Let Me Love Again)*	February 18, 1970
ZPA4 1616	*I Really Don't Want to Know*	June 7, 1970
ZPA4 1620	*Make the World Go Away*	June 7, 1970
APA3 1273	*Help Me Make It Through the Night*	May 17, 1971
BPA5 6788	*For the Good Times*	May 20, 1972
CPA5 4734	*I'm So Lonesome I Could Cry*	January 14, 1973
CPA5 4739	*Welcome to My World*	January 14, 1973
	I Can't Stop Loving You	June 10, 1972

MUSICIANS:

Guitar—James Burton, John Wilkinson, Charlie Hodge; Reggie Young (on XPA5 1155); Jerry Stembridge (on APA3 1273) Piano—Glenn D. Hardin, David Briggs;

Organ—Bobby Emmons Vocals—J. D. Sumner and the Stamps, Imperial Quartet,

Ronnie Milsap (on
XPA5 1155)
Drums—Ronnie Tutt;
Kenneth
Buttrey (on APA3 1273)
Bass—Jerry Scheff;
Norbert Putnam (on
APA3 1273); Tommy Cogbill
(on XPA5 1155)

Jordanaires,
Jeannie Green,
Mary and
Ginger
Holladay,
Millie
Kirkham,
Sandra P.
Robinson

1977

Release Date: June 1977

March 20, 1974; October 29–31, 1976; April 25, 1977	**Recording Locations: Memphis; Murfreesboro, Tennessee; Saginaw, Michigan**
DPA5 0926	*Let Me Be There*	March 20, 1974
FWA5 1048	*It's Easy for You*	October 29, 1977
FWA5 1049	*Way Down*	October 29, 1976
FWA5 1051	*There's a Fire Below*	October 30, 1976
FWA5 1052	*He'll Have to Go*	October 31, 1976
GWA5 2574	*If You Love Me*	April 25, 1977
GWA5 2575	*Little Darlin'*	April 25, 1977
GWA5 2576	*Unchained Melody*	April 25, 1977

MUSICIANS:

Lead guitar—James Burton
Guitar—John Wilkinson
Guitar—Charlie Hodge
Guitar—Jerry Stembridge
Bass—Jerry Scheff
Bass—Duke Bardwell (on DPA5 0926)
Piano—Sonny Brown
Piano—Glenn D. Hardin (on DPA5 0926)
Electric piano—David Briggs
Drums—Ronnie Tutt

Vocals—J. D. Sumner, Ed Enoch, Ed Hill, Larry Strickland, Kathy Westmoreland, Myrna Smith, Sherril Nielson, Gary Buckles, Estelle Brown, Sylvia Shenwell

Elvis Presley Live Concerts 1969–1977

The record of Elvis's live shows prior to his being drafted into the army is not complete enough to show any logical pattern except one of meteoric success. This was the period when he rose from playing lounges, honky-tonks, and county fairs to filling major theaters and ballparks. Between 1955 and 1958, Elvis worked almost all the time. If he wasn't touring, he was recording or making movies. It was the kind of schedule any would-be star would kill for. After the army, though, a new and unfortunately much more destructive picture began to emerge. For an entire decade Elvis played no live shows. Finally, he returned for a season at the International Hotel in Las Vegas in 1969. From that point on, he played well over a hundred shows every year until his death. Although going to work one day in three may appeal to someone who works nine to five, it is, in fact, a grueling ordeal for a topline entertainer. Compare Elvis's touring with that of the Rolling Stones during the same period when, after a seventy-day tour of the United States, they might well take a full year off.

Although it would be a mistake to say that Elvis was being worked to death, and although in the first few years after his comeback, he took a very obvious delight in being close to his audience again, the strain eventually started to take its toll. There can be little doubt that the constant touring contributed to the physical and mental decay of Elvis Presley during the last three years of his life. Much of the responsibility for this relentless work load has to rest with the Colonel. As we have seen, to cover his own debts he was preselling Elvis to promoters for drastically reduced amounts of money.

1969	**Shows**	
7/26/69–8/28/69	Las Vegas—	
	International	57

1970		
1/26/70–2/23/70	Las Vegas—	
	International	57
2/27/70–3/1/70	Houston—	
	Astrodome	6
8/10/70–9/7/70	Las Vegas—	
	International	58
9/9/70	Phoenix	1
9/10/70	St. Louis	1
9/11/70	Detroit	1

9/12/70	Miami	1
9/13/70	Tampa (aft. & eve.)	2
9/14/70	Mobile	1
11/10/70	Oakland	1
11/11/70	Portland, Oreg.	1
11/12/70	Seattle	1
11/13/70	San Francisco	1
11/14/70	Los Angeles— Forum (aft. & eve.)	2
11/15/70	San Diego	1
11/16/70	Oklahoma City	1
11/17/70	Denver	1
	TOTAL FOR 1970	137

1971

1/26/71–2/23/71	Las Vegas— Hilton	57
7/20/71–8/2/71	Lake Tahoe, Nev. — Sahara	28
8/9/71–9/6/71	Las Vegas— Hilton	57
11/5/71	Minneapolis	1
11/6/71	Cleveland (2 shows)	2
11/7/71	Louisville	1
11/8/71	Philadelphia	1
11/9/71	Baltimore	1
11/10/71	Boston	1
11/11/71	Cincinnati	1
11/12/71	Houston	1

11/13/71	Dallas (2 shows)	2
11/14/71	Tuscaloosa	1
11/15/71	Kansas City, Mo.	1
11/16/71	Salt Lake City	1
	TOTAL FOR 1971	156

1972

1/26/72–2/23/72	Las Vegas— Hilton	57
4/5/72	Buffalo	1
4/6/72	Detroit	1
4/7/72	Dayton	1
4/8/72	Knoxville (aft. & eve.)	2
4/9/72	Hampton Roads, Va. (aft. & eve.)	2
4/10/72	Richmond	1
4/11/72	Roanoke	1
4/12/72	Indianapolis	1
4/13/72	Charlotte	1
4/14/72	Greensboro	1
4/15/72	Macon (aft. & eve.)	2
4/16/72	Jacksonville (aft. & eve.)	2
4/17/72	Little Rock	1
4/18/72	San Antonio	1
4/19/72	Albuquerque	1

6/9/72	New York, Madison Square Garden	1
6/10/72	New York, Madison Square Garden (aft. & eve.)	2
6/11/72	New York, Madison Square Garden	1
6/12/72	Fort Wayne	1
6/13/72	Evansville	1
6/14/72–6/15/72	Milwaukee	2
6/16/72	Chicago (aft. & eve.)	2
6/17/72	Chicago (aft. & eve.)	1
6/18/72	Fort Worth	1
6/19/72	Wichita	1
6/20/72	Tulsa	1
8/4/72–9/4/72	Las Vegas— Hilton	63
11/8/72	Lubbock	1
11/9/72	Tucson	1
11/10/72	El Paso	1
11/11/72	Oakland	1
11/12/72–11/13/72	San Bernardino	2
11/14/72–11/15/72	Long Beach	2
11/17/72	Honolulu	1

11/18/72	Honolulu (aft. & eve.)	2
	TOTAL FOR 1972	164

1973

1/12/73	H.I.C. Arena, Hawaii— rehearsal for *Aloha from Hawaii via Satellite* show	1
1/14/73	H.I.C. Arena, Hawaii— *Aloha from Hawaii* show	1
1/26/73–2/23/73	Las Vegas— Hilton (sick for 3 shows)	54
4/22/73	Phoenix	1
4/23/73–4/24/73	Anaheim	2
4/25/73	Fresno (aft. & eve.)	2
4/26/73	San Diego	1
4/27/73	Portland, Oreg.	1
4/28/73	Spokane (aft. & eve.)	2
4/29/73	Seattle (aft. & eve.)	2
4/30/73	Denver	1
5/5/73–5/20/73	Lake Tahoe, Nev. — Sahara	

	(finished on 5/16/73, sick)	25
6/20/73	Mobile	1
6/21/73	Atlanta	1
6/22/73	Uniondale, N.Y. —Nassau Coliseum	1
6/23/73	Uniondale, N.Y. —Nassau Coliseum (aft. & eve.)	2
6/24/73	Uniondale, N.Y. —Nassau Coliseum	1
6/25/73–6/26/73	Pittsburgh	2
6/27/73	Cincinnati	1
6/28/73	St. Louis	1
6/29/73	Atlanta (aft. & eve.)	2
6/30/73	Atlanta (aft. & eve.)	2
7/1/73	Nashville	1
7/2/73	Oklahoma City	1
8/6/73–9/3/73	Las Vegas— Hilton	59
	TOTAL FOR 1973	168

1974

1/26/74–2/9/74	Las Vegas— Hilton	29
3/1/74–3/2/74	Tulsa	2

3/3/74	Houston—Astrodome (aft. & eve.)	2
3/4/74	Monroe, La.	1
3/5/74	Auburn, Ala.	1
3/6/74	Montgomery	1
3/7/74–3/8/74	Monroe, La.	2
3/9/74	Charlotte	1
3/10/74	Roanoke	1
3/11/74	Hampton Roads, Va.	1
3/12/74	Richmond	1
3/13/74	Greensboro	1
3/14/74	Murfreesboro, Tenn.	1
3/15/74	Knoxville (aft. & eve.)	2
3/16/74	Memphis (aft. & eve.)	2
3/17/74	Memphis	1
3/18/74	Richmond	1
3/19/74	Murfreesboro, Tenn.	1
3/20/74	Memphis (aft. & eve.)	2
3/21/74	Memphis	1
5/10/74	San Bernardino	1
5/11/74	Los Angeles—Forum (aft. & eve.)	2
5/12/74	Fresno	1
5/16/74–5/26/74	Lake Tahoe, Nev.—Sahara	22
6/15/74	Fort Worth (aft. & eve.)	2

6/16/74	Fort Worth (aft. & eve.)	2
6/17/74–6/18/74	Baton Rouge	2
6/19/74	Amarillo	1
6/20/74	Des Moines	1
6/21/74	Cleveland	1
6/22/74	Providence (aft. & eve.)	2
6/23/74	Philadelphia (aft. & eve.)	2
6/24/74	Niagara Falls, N.Y.	1
6/25/74	Columbus, Ohio	1
6/26/74	Louisville	1
6/27/74	Bloomington, Ind.	1
6/28/74	Milwaukee	1
6/29/74	Kansas City, Mo. (aft. & eve.)	2
6/30/74	Omaha (aft. & eve.)	2
7/1/74	Omaha	1
7/2/74	Salt Lake City	1
8/19/74–9/2/74	Las Vegas— Hilton (2 canceled)	27
9/27/74–9/28/74	College Park, Md.	2
9/29/74	Detroit	1
9/30/74–10/1/74	South Bend	2
10/2/74–10/3/74	St. Paul	2
10/4/74	Detroit	1
10/5/74	Indianapolis	1
10/6/74	Dayton	1

10/7/74	Wichita	1
10/8/74	San Antonio	1
10/9/74	Abilene, Tex.	1
10/10/74–10/14/74	Lake Tahoe, Nev.—Sahara	8
	TOTAL FOR 1974	152

1975

3/18/75–4/1/75	Las Vegas— Hilton	29
4/23/75	Mobile	1
4/24/75	Macon	1
4/25/75	Jacksonville	1
4/26/75	Tampa (aft. & eve.)	2
4/27/75	Lakeland, Fla. (aft. & eve.)	2
4/28/75	Lakeland, Fla.	1
4/29/75	Murfreesboro, Tenn.	1
4/30/75–5/2/75	Atlanta	3
5/3/75	Monroe, La.	1
5/4/75	Lake Charles	1
5/5/75	Jackson, Miss.	1
5/6/75–5/7/75	Murfreesboro, Tenn.	2
5/30/75	Huntsville	1
5/31/75	Huntsville (aft. & eve.).	2
6/1/75	Huntsville	1
6/2/75	Mobile (aft. & eve.)	2
6/3/75	Tuscaloosa	1

6/4/75–6/5/75	Houston	2
6/6/75	Dallas	1
6/7/75	Shreveport (aft. & eve.)	2
6/8/75	Jackson, Miss. (aft. & eve.)	2
6/9/75	Jackson, Miss.	2
6/10/75	Memphis	1
7/8/75	Oklahoma City	1
7/9/75	Terre Haute	1
7/10/75	Cleveland	1
7/11/75	Charleston, W.Va.	1
7/12/75	Charleston, W.Va. (aft. & eve.)	2
7/13/75	Niagara Falls, N.Y. (aft. & eve.)	2
7/14/75–7/15/75	Springfield, Mass.	2
7/16/75–7/17/75	New Haven	2
7/18/75	Cleveland	1
7/19/75	Uniondale, N.Y. —Nassau Coliseum (aft. & eve.)	2
7/20/75	Norfolk (aft. & eve.)	2
7/21/75	Greensboro	1
7/22/75–7/24/75	Asheville	3
8/18/75–8/20/75	Las Vegas— Hilton (closed through illness)	5

12/2/75–12/15/75	Las Vegas— Hilton	17
12/31/75	Pontiac, Mich.	1
	TOTAL FOR 1975	106

1976

3/17/76–3/19/76	Johnson City, Tenn.	3
3/20/76	Charlotte	1
3/21/76	Cincinnati	1
3/22/76	St. Louis	1
4/22/76	Omaha	1
4/23/76	Denver	1
4/24/76	San Diego	1
4/25/76	Long Beach	1
4/26/76	Seattle	1
4/27/76	Spokane	1
5/27/76	Bloomington, Ind.	1
5/28/76	Ames, Iowa	1
5/29/76	Oklahoma City	1
5/30/76	Odessa, Tex.	1
5/31/76	Lubbock	1
6/1/76	Tucson	1
6/2/76	El Paso	1
6/3/76	Fort Worth	1
6/4/76–6/6/76	Atlanta	3
6/25/76	Buffalo	1
6/26/76	Providence	1
6/27/76	Largo, Md. (aft. & eve.)	2
6/28/76	Philadelphia	1
6/29/76	Richmond	1

6/30/76	Greensboro	1
7/1/76	Baton Rouge	1
7/2/76	Fort Worth	1
7/3/76	Tucson	1
7/4/76	Tulsa	1
7/5/76	Memphis	1
7/23/76	Louisville	1
7/24/76	Charleston, W.Va. (aft. & eve.)	2
7/25/76	Syracuse	1
7/26/76	Rochester	1
7/27/76	Syracuse	1
7/28/76	Hartford	1
7/29/76	Springfield, Mass.	1
7/30/76	New Haven	1
8/1/76	Hampton Roads, Va.	1
8/2/76	Charlottesville	1
8/27/76	San Antonio	1
8/28/76	Houston	1
8/29/76	Mobile	1
8/30/76	Tuscaloosa	1
8/31/76	Macon	1
9/1/76	Jackson, Miss.	1
9/2/76	Tampa	1
9/3/76	St. Petersburg	1
9/4/76	Lakeland, Fla.	1
9/5/76	Jacksonville	1
9/6/76	Huntsville	1
9/7/76–9/8/76	Pine Bluff	2
10/14/76–10/15/76	Chicago	2
10/16/76	Duluth	1
10/17/76	Minneapolis	1

10/18/76	Sioux Falls, S.Dak.	1
10/19/76	Madison	1
10/20/76	South Bend	1
10/21/76	Kalamazoo	1
10/22/76	Champaign	1
10/23/76	Cleveland	1
10/24/76	Evansville	1
10/25/76	Fort Wayne	1
10/26/76	Dayton	1
10/27/76	Carbondale, Ill.	1
11/24/76	Reno	1
11/25/76	Eugene	1
11/26/76	Portland, Oreg.	1
11/27/76	Eugene	1
11/28/76–11/29/76	San Francisco	2
11/30/76	Anaheim	1
12/2/76–12/12/76	Las Vegas— Hilton	15
12/27/76	Wichita	1
12/28/76	Dallas	1
12/29/76	Birmingham	1
12/30/76	Atlanta	1
12/31/76	Pittsburgh	1
	TOTAL FOR 1976	100

1977

2/12/77	Miami	1
2/13/77	St. Petersburg	1
2/14/77	West Palm Beach	1
2/15/77	Orlando	1
2/16/77	Montgomery	1

2/17/77	Augusta	1
2/18/77	Columbia, S.C.	1
2/19/77	Johnson City, Tenn.	1
2/20/77	Charlotte	1
3/23/77	Phoenix	1
3/24/77	Amarillo	1
3/25/77–3/26/77	Norman, Okla.	2
3/27/77	Abilene, Tex.	1
3/28/77	Austin	1
3/29/77–3/30/77	Alexandria, La.	2
4/21/77	Greensboro	1
4/22/77	Detroit	1
4/23/77	Toledo	1
4/24/77	Ann Arbor	1
4/25/77	Saginaw	1
4/26/77	Kalamazoo	1
4/27/77	Milwaukee	1
4/28/77	Green Bay	1
4/29/77	Duluth	1
4/30/77	St. Paul	1
5/1/77–5/2/77	Chicago	2
5/3/77	Saginaw	1
5/20/77	Knoxville	1
5/21/77	Louisville	1
5/22/77	Largo, Md.	1
5/23/77	Providence	1
5/24/77	Augusta, Maine	1
5/25/77	Rochester, N.Y.	1
5/26/77–5/27/77	Binghampton, N.Y.	2
5/28/77	Philadelphia	1
5/29/77	Baltimore	1
5/30/77	Jacksonville	1
5/31/77	Baton Rouge	1
6/1/77	Macon	1

6/2/77	Mobile	1
6/17/77	Springfield, Mo.	1
6/18/77	Kansas City, Mo.	1
6/19/77	Omaha	1
6/20/77	Lincoln, Nebr.	1
6/21/77	Rapid City, S. Dak.	1
6/22/77	Sioux Falls, S. Dak.	1
6/23/77	Des Moines	1
6/24/77	Madison, Wis.	1
6/25/77	Cincinnati	1
6/26/77	Indianapolis	1
	TOTAL FOR 1977	54

Elvis Presley Discography 1954–1977

During his lifetime, Elvis Presley released 105 singles and 65 albums.

SUN 45 RPM AND 78 RPM SINGLES

1. Sun 209   August 1954
   That's All Right [Mama]/Blue Moon of Kentucky

2. Sun 210   October 1954
   Good Rockin' Tonight/I Don't Care if the Sun Don't Shine

3. **Sun 215** January 1955
Milkcow Blues Boogie/You're a Heartbreaker

4. **Sun 217** May 1955
*I'm Left, You're Right, She's Gone/Baby, Let's
Play House*

5. **Sun 223** August 1955
Mystery Train/I Forgot to Remember to Forget

RCA 45 RPM AND 78 RPM SINGLES

1. **RCA 6357** November 1955
Mystery Train/I Forgot to Remember to Forget

2. **RCA 6380** November 1955
*That's All Right [Mama]/Blue Moon of
Kentucky*

3. **RCA 6381** November 1955
*Good Rockin' Tonight/I Don't Care if the Sun
Don't Shine*

4. **RCA 6382** November 1955
Milkcow Blues Boogie/You're a Heartbreaker

5. **RCA 6383** November 1955
*I'm Left, You're Right, She's Gone/Baby, Let's
Play House*

6. **RCA 6420** January 1956
Heartbreak Hotel/I Was the One

7. **RCA 6540** May 1956
*I Want You, I Need You, I Love You/My Baby
Left Me*

8. **RCA 6604** July 1956
Hound Dog/Don't Be Cruel

9. **RCA 6636** September 1956
   Blue Suede Shoes/Tutti Frutti

10. **RCA 6637** September 1956
    I'm Counting on You/I Got a Woman

11. **RCA 6638** September 1956
    *I'll Never Let You Go/I'm Gonna Sit Right
    Down and Cry
    over You*

12. **RCA 6639** September 1956
    Tryin' to Get to You/I Love You Because

13. **RCA 6640** September 1956
    Blue Moon/Just Because

14. **RCA 6641** September 1956
    Money Honey/One-sided Love Affair

15. **RCA 6642** September 1956
    Shake, Rattle and Roll/Lawdy, Miss Clawdy

16. **RCA 6643** September 1956
    Love Me Tender/Any Way You Want Me

17. **RCA 6800** January 1957
    Too Much/Playing for Keeps

18. **RCA 6870** March 1957
    *All Shook Up/That's When Your Heartaches
    Begin*

19. **RCA 7000** June 1957
    Teddy Bear/Loving You

20. **RCA 7035** September 1957
    Jailhouse Rock/Treat Me Nice

21. **RCA 7150** December 1957
    Don't/I Beg of You

22. **RCA 7240**   April 1958
*Wear My Ring Around Your Neck/Doncha'
Think It's Time*

23. **RCA 7280**   June 1958
Hard-headed Woman/Don't Ask Me Why

24. **RCA 7410**   October 1958
I Got Stung/One Night

25. **RCA 7506**   March 1959
A Fool Such as I/I Need Your Love Tonight

26. **RCA 7600**   June 1959
A Big Hunk o' Love/My Wish Came True

27. **RCA 7740**   March 1960
Stuck on You/Fame and Fortune

28. **RCA 7777**   July 1960
It's Now or Never/A Mess of Blues

29. **RCA 7810**   November 1960
Are You Lonesome Tonight?/I Gotta Know

30. **RCA 7850**   February 1961
Surrender/Lonely Man

31. **RCA 7880**   May 1961
I Feel So Bad/Wild in the Country

32. **RCA 7908**   August 1961
Little Sister/His Latest Flame

33. **RCA 7968**   November 1961
Can't Help Falling in Love/Rock-a-hula Baby

34. **RCA 7992**   February 1962
*Good Luck Charm/Anything That's Part of
You*

35. **RCA 8041**   July 1962
    She's Not You/Just Tell Her Jim Said Hello

36. **RCA 8100**   October 1962
    Return to Sender/Where Do You Come From

37. **RCA 8134**   January 1963
    One Broken Heart for Sale/They Remind Me Too Much of You

38. **RCA 8188**   July 1963
    Devil in Disguise/Please Don't Drag That String Around

39. **RCA 8243**   October 1963
    Bossa Nova Baby/Witchcraft

40. **RCA 8307**   February 1964
    Kissin' Cousins/It Hurts Me

41. **RCA 0639**   April 1964
    Kiss Me Quick/Suspicion

42. **RCA 8360**   May 1964
    Viva Las Vegas/What'd I Say

43. **RCA 8400**   July 1964
    Such a Night/Never Ending

44. **RCA 8440**   September 1964
    Ain't That Loving You, Baby/Ask Me

45. **RCA 0720**   November 1964
    Blue Christmas/Wooden Heart

46. **RCA 8500**   March 1965
    Do the Clam/You'll Be Gone

47. **RCA 0643**   April 1965
    Crying in the Chapel/I Believe in the Man in the Sky

48. **RCA 8585**   May 1965
(Such an) Easy Question/It Feels So Right

49. **RCA 8657**   August 1965
I'm Yours/(It's a) Long Lonely Highway

50. **RCA 0650**   October 1965
Puppet on a String/Wooden Heart

51. **RCA 0647**   November 1965
Blue Christmas/Santa Claus Is Back in Town

52. **RCA 8740**   January 1966
Tell Me Why/Blue River

53. **RCA 0651**   February 1966
Joshua Fit the Battle/Known Only to Him

54. **RCA 0652**   February 1966
Milky White Way/Swing Down, Sweet Chariot

55. **RCA 8780**   March 1966
Frankie and Johnny/Please Don't Stop Loving Me

56. **RCA 8870**   June 1966
Love Letters/Come What May

57. **RCA 8941**   October 1966
Spinout/All That I Am

58. **RCA 8950**   November 1966
If Every Day Was Like Christmas/How Would You Like to Be

59. **RCA 9056**   January 1967
Indescribably Blue/Fools Fall in Love

60. **RCA 9115**   May 1967
Long-legged Girl (with the Short Dress On)/ That's Someone You Never Forget

61. **RCA 9287**   August 1967
    There's Always Me/Judy

62. **RCA 9341**   September 1967
    Big Boss Man/You Don't Know Me

63. **RCA 9425**   January 1968
    Guitar Man/High-heel Sneakers

64. **RCA 9465**   March 1968
    U.S. Male/Stay Away

65. **RCA 9600**   April 1968
    You'll Never Walk Alone/We Call on Him

66. **RCA 9547**   May 1968
    Let Yourself Go/Your Time Hasn't Come Yet, Baby

67. **RCA 9610**   September 1968
    A Little Less Conversation/Almost in Love

68. **RCA 9670**   October 1968
    If I Can Dream/Edge of Reality

69. **RCA 9731**   March 1969
    Memories/Charro!

70. **RCA 0130**   April 1969
    How Great Thou Art/His Hand in Mine

71. **RCA 9741**   April 1969
    In the Ghetto/Any Day Now

72. **RCA 9747**   June 1969
    Clean Up Your Own Back Yard/The Fair Is Moving On

73. **RCA 9764**   August 1969
    Suspicious Minds/You'll Think of Me

74. **RCA 9768**   November 1969
    Don't Cry, Daddy/Rubberneckin'

75. **RCA 9791**   January 1970
    Kentucky Rain/My Little Friend

76. **RCA 9835**   May 1970
    The Wonder of You/Mama Liked the Roses

77. **RCA 9873**   July 1970
    I've Lost You/The Next Step Is Love

78. **RCA 9916**   October 1970
    You Don't Have to Say You Love Me/Patch It Up

79. **RCA 9960**   December 1970
    I Really Don't Want to Know/There Goes My Everything

80. **RCA 9980**   March 1971
    Rags to Riches/Where Did They Go, Lord

81. **RCA 9985**   May 1971
    Life/Only Believe

82. **RCA 9998**   August 1971
    I'm Leavin'/Heart of Rome

83. **RCA 1017**   October 1971
    It's Only Love/The Sound of Your Cry

84. **RCA 0572**   November 1971
    Merry Christmas, Baby/O Come, All Ye Faithful

85. **RCA 0619**   January 1972
    Until It's Time for You to Go/We Can Make the Morning

86. **RCA 0651**   March 1972
    He Touched Me/The Bosom of Abraham

87. **RCA 0672**   April 1972
    *An American Trilogy/The First Time Ever I
    Saw Your Face*

88. **RCA 0769**   August 1972
    Burning Love/It's a Matter of Time

89. **RCA 0815**   November 1972
    Always on My Mind/Separate Ways

90. **RCA 0910**   March 1973
    Fool/Steamroller Blues

91. **RCA 0088**   September 1973
    Raised on Rock/For Ol' Times Sake

92. **RCA 0196**   January 1974
    *Take Good Care of Her/I've Got a Thing About
    You, Baby*

93. **RCA 0280**   May 1974
    Help Me/If You Talk in Your Sleep

94. **RCA 10074**   October 1974
    It's Midnight/Promised Land

95. **RCA 10191**   January 1975
    My Boy/Thinking About You

96. **RCA 10278**   April 1975
    T-R-O-U-B-L-E/Mr. Songman

97. **RCA 10401**   October 1975
    Bringing It Back/Pieces of My Life

98. **RCA 10601**   March 1976
    Hurt/For the Heart

99. **RCA 10857**   December 1976
    Moody Blue/She Thinks I Still Care

100. RCA 10998 June 1977
  Way Down/Pledging My Love

RCA 45 RPM EXTENDED-PLAY ALBUMS

1. RCA EPB-1254 March 1956
  Elvis Presley
Side 1: *Blue Suede Shoes; I'm Counting on You*
Side 2: *I Got a Woman; One-sided Love Affair*
Side 3: *Tutti Frutti; Tryin' to Get to You*
Side 4: *I'm Gonna Sit Right Down and Cry; I'll Never Let You Go*

2. RCA EPA-747 March 1956
  Elvis Presley
Side 1: *Blue Suede Shoes; Tutti Frutti*
Side 2: *I Got a Woman; Just Because*

3. RCA EPA-821 May 1956
  Heartbreak Hotel
Side 1: *Heartbreak Hotel; I Was the One*
Side 2: *Money Honey; I Forgot to Remember to Forget*

4. RCA EPA-830 September 1956
  Shake, Rattle and Roll
Side 1: *Shake, Rattle and Roll; I Love You Because*
Side 2: *Blue Moon; Lawdy, Miss Clawdy*

5. RCA EPA-965 October 1956
  Any Way You Want Me
Side 1: *Any Way You Want Me; I'm Left, You're Right, She's Gone*
Side 2: *I Don't Care if the Sun Don't Shine; Mystery Train*

6. RCA EPA-940 September 1956
   The Real Elvis
Side 1: *Don't Be Cruel; I Want You, I Need You, I
   Love You*
Side 2: *Hound Dog; My Baby Left Me*

7. RCA EPA-5120 (Gold Standard) April 1961
   The Real Elvis
This is the first of Elvis's Gold Standard EPs. It
features the same songs as EPA-940.

8. RCA EPA-992 November 1956
   Elvis, Volume I
Side 1: *Rip It Up; Love Me*
Side 2: *When My Blue Moon Turns to Gold Again;
   Paralyzed*

9. RCA EPA-4006 December 1956
   Love Me Tender
Side 1: *Love Me Tender; Let Me*
Side 2: *Poor Boy; We're Gonna Move*

10. RCA EPA-993 December 1956
   Elvis, Volume II
Side 1: *So Glad You're Mine; Old Shep*
Side 2: *Ready Teddy; Anyplace Is Paradise*

11. RCA EPA-994 January 1957
   Strictly Elvis
Side 1: *Long Tall Sally; First in Line*
Side 2: *How Do You Think I Feel; How's the World
   Treating You*

12. RCA EPA-1-1515 June 1957
   Loving You, Volume I
Side 1: *Loving You; Party*
Side 2: *(Let Me Be Your) Teddy Bear; True Love*

13. RCA EPA-2-1515 June 1957
   Loving You, Volume II

Side 1: *Lonesome Cowboy; Hot Dog*
Side 2: *Mean Woman Blues; Got a Lot o' Livin' to Do!*

14. RCA EPA-4041　　　　　September 1957
　Just for You
Side 1: *I Need You So; Have I Told You Lately That I Love You*
Side 2: *Blueberry Hill; Is It So Strange*

15. RCA EPA-4054　　　　　April 1957
　Peace in the Valley
Side 1: *(There'll Be) Peace in the Valley (for Me); It Is No Secret (What God Can Do)*
Side 2: *I Believe; Take My Hand, Precious Lord*

16. RCA EPA-5121 (Gold Standard)　　April 1961
　Peace in the Valley
This was the second Gold Standard EP. It featured the same songs as EPA-4054.

17. RCA EPA-4108　　　　　November 1957
　Elvis Sings Christmas Songs
Side 1: *Santa, Bring My Baby Back (To Me); Blue Christmas*
Side 2: *Santa Claus Is Back in Town; I'll Be Home for Christmas*

18. RCA EPA-4114　　　　　November 1957
　Jailhouse Rock
Side 1: *Jailhouse Rock; Young and Beautiful*
Side 2: *I Want to Be Free; Don't Leave Me Now; Baby, I Don't Care*

19. RCA EPA-4319　　　　　October 1958
　King Creole, Volume I
Side 1: *King Creole; New Orleans*
Side 2: *As Long As I Have You; Lover Doll*

20. **RCA EPA-5122 (Gold Standard)**   April 1961
    King Creole, Volume I

21. **RCA EPA-4321**   ·   October 1958
    King Creole, Volume II
    Side 1: *Trouble; Young Dreams*
    Side 2: *Crawfish; Dixieland Rock*

22. **RCA EPA-4325**   March 1959
    Elvis Sails
    Side 1: Press interviews with Elvis
    Side 2: More press interviews with Elvis

23. **RCA EPA-5157 (Gold Standard)**   April 1961
    Elvis Sails

24. **RCA EPA-4340**   November 1958
    Christmas with Elvis
    Side 1: *White Christmas; Here Comes Santa Claus*
    Side 2: *O Little Town of Bethlehem; Silent Night*

25. **RCA EPA-5088 (Gold Standard)**   April 1961
    A Touch of Gold, Volume I
    Side 1: *Hard-headed Woman; Good Rockin'*
         Tonight
    Side 2: *Don't; I Beg of You*

26. **RCA EPA-5101 (Gold Standard)**   April 1961
    A Touch of Gold, Volume II
    Side 1: *Wear My Ring Around Your Neck; Treat Me*
         Nice
    Side 2: *One Night; That's All Right*

27. **RCA EPA-5141 (Gold Standard)**   April 1961
    A Touch of Gold, Volume III
    Side 1: *All Shook Up; Don't Ask Me Why*
    Side 2: *Too Much; Blue Moon of Kentucky*

28. **RCA-4368**   May 1962
    Follow That Dream

Side 1: *Follow That Dream; Angel*
Side 2: *What a Wonderful Life; I'm Not the Marrying Kind*

29. RCA EPA-4371 September 1962
Kid Galahad
Side 1: *King of the Whole Wide World; This Is Living; Riding the Rainbow*
Side 2: *Home Is Where the Heart Is; I Got Lucky; A Whistling Tune*

30. RCA EPA-4382 July 1964
Viva Las Vegas
Side 1: *If You Think I Don't Need You; I Need Somebody to Lean On*
Side 2: *C'mon, Everybody; Today, Tomorrow and Forever*

31. RCA EPA-4383 July 1965
Tickle Me
Side 1: *I Feel That I've Known You Forever; Slowly but Surely*
Side 2: *Night Rider; Put the Blame on Me; Dirty, Dirty Feeling*

32. RCA EPA-4387 May 1967
Easy Come, Easy Go
Side 1: *Easy Come, Easy Go; The Love Machine; Yoga Is as Yoga Does*
Side 2: *You Gotta Stop; Sing, You Children; I'll Take Love*

RCA 33$\frac{1}{3}$ RPM LONG-PLAYING ALBUMS

1. LPM-1254 April 1956
Elvis Presley
Side 1: *Blue Suede Shoes; I'm Counting on You; I Got a Woman; One-sided Love Affair; I Love You Because; Just Because*

Side 2: *Tutti Frutti; Tryin' to Get to You; I'm Gonna Sit Right Down and Cry; I'll Never Let You Go; Blue Moon; Money Honey*

2. LPM-1382 October 1956
Elvis
Side 1: *Rip It Up; Love Me; When My Blue Moon Turns to Gold Again; Long Tall Sally; First in Line; Paralyzed*
Side 2: *So Glad You're Mine; Old Shep; Ready Teddy; Anyplace Is Paradise; How's the World Treating You; How Do You Think I Feel*

3. LPM-1515 July 1957
Loving You
Side 1: *Mean Woman Blues; (Let Me Be Your) Teddy Bear; Loving You; Got a Lot o' Livin' to Do; Lonesome Cowboy; Hot Dog; Party*
Side 2: *Blueberry Hill; True Love; Don't Leave Me Now; Have I Told You Lately That I Love You?; I Need You So*

4. LOC-1035 (DELETED) November 1957
Elvis' Christmas Album
Side 1: *Santa Claus Is Back in Town; White Christmas; Here Comes Santa Claus; I'll Be Home for Christmas; Blue Christmas; Santa, Bring My Baby Back (to Me)*
Side 2: *O Little Town of Bethlehem; Silent Night; (There'll Be) Peace in the Valley (for Me); I Believe; Take My Hand, Precious Lord; It Is No Secret (What God Can Do)*

5. LPM-1707   March 1958
   Elvis' Golden Records
Side 1: *Hound Dog; Loving You; All Shook Up;*
         Heartbreak Hotel; Jailhouse Rock; Love Me;
         Too Much
Side 2: *Don't Be Cruel; That's When Your*
         Heartaches Begin; Teddy Bear; Love Me
         Tender; Treat Me Nice; Any Way You Want
         Me; I Want You, I Need You, I Love You

6. LPM-1884   August 1958
   King Creole
Side 1: *King Creole; As Long As I Have You; Hard-*
         headed Woman; T-R-O-U-B-L-E; Dixieland
         Rock
Side 2: *Don't Ask Me Why; Lover Doll; Crawfish;*
         Young Dreams; Steadfast, Loyal and True;
         New Orleans

7. LPM-1951 (DELETED)   November 1958
   Elvis' Christmas Album
RCA reissued *Elvis' Christmas Album* with a new
cover and prefix.

8. LPM-1990   February 1959
   For LP Fans Only
Side 1: *That's All Right; Lawdy, Miss Clawdy;*
         Mystery Train; Playing for Keeps; Poor Boy
Side 2: *My Baby Left Me; I Was the One; Shake,*
         Rattle and Roll; I'm Left, You're Right,
         She's Gone; You're a Heartbreaker

9. LPM-2011   September 1959
   A Date with Elvis
Side 1: *Blue Moon of Kentucky; Young and*
         Beautiful; Baby, I Don't Care; Milkcow
         Blues Boogie; Baby, Let's Play House

Side 2: *Good Rockin' Tonight; Is It So Strange; We're Gonna Move; I Want to Be Free; I Forgot to Remember to Forget*

10. LPM-2075　　　　　　　December 1959
50,000,000 Elvis Fans Can't Be Wrong
Side 1: *I Need Your Love Tonight; Don't; Wear My Ring Around Your Neck; My Wish Came True; I Got Stung*
Side 2: *One Night; A Big Hunk o' Love; I Beg of You; A Fool Such as I; Doncha' Think It's Time*

11. LSP/LPM-2231　　　　　　　April 1960
Elvis Is Back!
Side 1: *Make Me Know It; Fever; The Girl of My Best Friend; I Will Be Home Again; Dirty, Dirty Feeling; Thrill of Your Love*
Side 2: *Soldier Boy; Such a Night; It Feels So Right; The Girl Next Door (Went Awalking); Like a Baby; Reconsider, Baby*

12. LSP/LPM-2256　　　　　　　October 1960
G.I. Blues
Side 1: *Tonight Is So Right for Love; What's She Really Like; Frankfort Special; Wooden Heart; G.I. Blues*
Side 2: *Pocketful of Rainbows; Shoppin' Around; Big Boots; Didja Ever; Blue Suede Shoes; Doin' the Best I Can*

13. LSP/LPM-2328 (DELETED)　　December 1960
His Hand in Mine
Side 1: *His Hand in Mine; I'm Gonna Walk Dem Golden Stairs; In My Father's House; Milky White Way; Known Only to Him; I Believe in the Man in the Sky*

Side 2: *Joshua Fit the Battle; Jesus Knows Just What I Need; Swing Down, Sweet Chariot; Mansion over the Hilltop; If We Never Meet Again; Working on the Building*

14. LSP/LPM-2370   June 1961
Something for Everybody
Side 1: *There's Always Me; Give Me the Right; It's a Sin; Sentimental Me; Starting Today; Gently*
Side 2: *I'm Comin' Home; In Your Arms; Put the Blame on Me; Judy; I Want You with Me; I Slipped, I Stumbled, I Fell*

15. LSP/LPM-2426   October 1961
Blue Hawaii
Side 1: *Blue Hawaii; Almost True; Aloha Oe; No More; Can't Help Falling in Love; Rock-a-hula Baby; Moonlight Swim*
Side 2: *Ku-u-i-po; Ito Eats; Slicin' Sand; Hawaiian Sunset; Beach Boy Blues; Island of Love; Hawaiian Wedding Song*

16. LSP/LPM-2523   June 1962
Pot Luck
Side 1: *Kiss Me Quick; Just for Old Time Sake; Gonna Get Back Home Somehow; (Such an) Easy Question; Steppin' Out of Line; I'm Yours*
Side 2: *Something Blue; Suspicion; I Feel That I've Known You Forever; Night Rider; Fountain of Love; That's Someone You Never Forget*

17. LSP/LPM-2621   November 1962
Girls! Girls! Girls!
Side 1: *Girls! Girls! Girls!; I Don't Wanna Be Tied; Where Do You Come From; I Don't Want To; We'll Be Together; A Boy Like Me, a Girl Like You; Earth Boy*

Side 2: *Return to Sender; Because of Love; Thanks to the Rolling Sea; Song of the Shrimp; The Walls Have Ears; We're Comin' In Loaded*

18. LSP/LPM-2697 (DELETED)　　　　April 1963
It Happened at the World's Fair
Side 1: *Beyond the Bend; Relax; Take Me to the Fair; They Remind Me Too Much of You; One Broken Heart for Sale*
Side 2: *I'm Falling in Love Tonight; Cotton Candy Land; A World of Our Own; How Would You Like to Be; Happy Ending*

19. LSP/LPM-2765　　　　September 1963
Elvis' Golden Records, Volume III
Side 1: *It's Now or Never; Stuck on You; Fame and Fortune; I Gotta Know; Surrender; I Feel So Bad*
Side 2: *Are You Lonesome Tonight?; His Latest Flame; Little Sister; Good Luck Charm; Anything That's Part of You; She's Not You*

20. LSP/LPM-2756　　　　December 1963
Fun in Acapulco
Side 1: *Fun in Acapulco; Vino, Dinero y Amor; Mexico; El Toro; Marguerita; The Bullfighter Was a Lady; No Room to Rhumba in a Sports Car*
Side 2: *I Think I'm Gonna Like It Here; Bossa Nova Baby; You Can't Say No in Acapulco; Guadalajara; Love Me Tonight; Slowly but Surely*

21. LSP/LPM-2894　　　　March 1964
Kissin' Cousins
Side 1: *Kissin' Cousins; Smokey Mountain Boy; There's Gold in the Mountains; One Boy,*

Two Little Girls; Catchin' On Fast; Tender
Feeling
Side 2: Anyone; Barefoot Ballad; Once Is Enough;
Kissin' Cousins/Echoes of Love; Long
Lonely Highway

22. **LSP/LPM-2999**   October 1964
Roustabout
Side 1: Roustabout; Little Egypt; Poison Ivy
League; Hard Knocks; It's a Wonderful
World; Big Love, Big Heartache
Side 2: One-track Heart; It's Carnival Time; Carny
Town; There's a Brand New Day on the
Horizon; Wheels on My Heels

23. **LSP/LPM-3338**   April 1965
Girl Happy
Side 1: Girl Happy; Spring Fever; Fort Lauderdale
Chamber of Commerce; Startin' Tonight;
Wolf Call; Do Not Disturb
Side 2: Cross My Heart and Hope to Die; The
Meanest Girl in Town; Do the Clam;
Puppet on a String; I've Got to Find My
Baby; You'll Be Gone

24. **LSP/LPM-3450**   July 1965
Elvis for Everyone
Side 1: Your Cheatin' Heart; Summer Kisses,
Winter Tears; Finders Keepers, Losers
Weepers; In My Way; Tomorrow Night;
Memphis, Tennessee
Side 2: For the Millionth and the Last Time; Forget
Me Never; Sound Advice; Santa Lucia; I
Met Her Today; When It Rains, It Really
Pours

25. **LSP/LPM-3468** (DELETED)   October 1965
Harum Scarum

Side 1: *Harum Holiday; My Desert Serenade; Go East, Young Man; Mirage; Kismet; Shake That Tambourine*

Side 2: *Hey, Little Girl; Golden Coins; So Close, Yet So Far; Animal Instinct; Wisdom of the Ages*

26. LSP/LPM-3553 (DELETED)   April 1966
Frankie and Johnny

Side 1: *Frankie and Johnny; Come Along; Petunia, the Gardener's Daughter; Chesay; What Every Woman Lives For; Look Out, Broadway*

Side 2: *Beginner's Luck; Down by the Riverside/ When the Saints Go Marching In; Shout It Out; Hard Luck; Please Don't Stop Loving Me; Everybody Come Aboard*

27. LSP/LPM-3643   June 1966
Paradise, Hawaiian Style

Side 1: *Paradise, Hawaiian Style; Queenie Wahine's Papaya; Scratch My Back; Drums of the Islands; Datin'*

Side 2: *A Dog's Life; House of Sand; Stop Where You Are; This Is My Heaven; Sand Castles*

28. LSP/LPM-3702 (DELETED)   October 1966
Spinout

Side 1: *Stop, Look and Listen; Adam and Evil; All That I Am; Never Say Yes; Am I Ready; Beach Shack*

Side 2: *Spinout; Smorgasbord; I'll Be Back; Tomorrow Is a Long Time; Down in the Alley; I'll Remember You*

29. LSP/LPM-3758   March 1967
How Great Thou Art

Side 1: *How Great Thou Art; In the Garden;*

Somebody Bigger Than You and I; Farther
Along; Stand by Me; Without Him

Side 2: So High; Where Could I Go But to the
Lord; By and By; If the Lord Wasn't
Walking by My Side; Run On; Where No
One Stands Alone; Crying in the Chapel

30. **LSP/LPM-3787** (DELETED)   June 1967
Double Trouble

Side 1: *Double Trouble; Baby, if You'll Give Me
All of Your Love; Could I Fall in Love;
Long-legged Girl; City by Night; Old
MacDonald*

Side 2: *I Love Only One Girl; There Is So Much
World to See; It Won't Be Long; Never
Ending; Blue River; What Now, What
Next, Where To*

31. **LSP/LPM-3893** (DELETED)   November 1967
Clambake

Side 1: *Guitar Man; Clambake; Who Needs Money;
A House That Has Everything; Confidence;
Hey, Hey, Hey*

Side 2: *You Don't Know Me; The Girl I Never
Loved; How Can You Lose What You Never
Had; Big Boss Man; Singing Tree; Just Call
Me Lonesome*

32. **LSP/LPM-3921**   February 1968
Elvis' Gold Records, Volume IV

Side 1: *Love Letters; Witchcraft; It Hurts Me;
What'd I Say; Please Don't Drag That
String Around; Indescribably Blue*

Side 2: *(You're the) Devil in Disguise; Lonely Man;
A Mess of Blues; Ask Me; Ain't That
Loving You, Baby; Just Tell Her Jim Said
Hello*

33. LSP-3989 June 1968
Speedway
Side 1: *Speedway; There Ain't Nothing Like a
Song; Your Time Hasn't Come Yet, Baby;
Who Are You?; He's Your Uncle, Not Your
Dad; Let Yourself Go*
Side 2: *Your Groovy Self; Five Sleepy Heads;
Western Union; Mine; Goin' Home; Suppose*

34. LPM-4088 December 1968
Elvis—TV Special
Side 1: *Trouble/Guitar Man; Lawdy, Miss Clawdy/
Baby, What You Want Me to Do;
Heartbreak Hotel; Hound Dog; All Shook
Up/Can't Help Falling in Love; Jailhouse
Rock/*(Dialogue); *Love Me Tender*
Side 2: (Dialogue); *Where Could I Go But to the
Lord; Up Above My Head/Saved; Blue
Christmas/One Night; Memories;* Medley:
*Nothingville/Big Boss Man/Guitar Man/
Little Egypt; T-R-O-U-B-L-E; Guitar Man;
If I Can Dream*

35. LSP-4155 June 1969
From Elvis in Memphis
Side 1: *Wearin' That Loved-on Look; Only the
Strong Survive; I'll Hold You in My Heart;
Long Black Limousine; It Keeps Right on
A-hurtin'; I'm Movin' On*
Side 2: *Power of My Love; Gentle on My Mind;
After Loving You; True Love Travels on a
Gravel Road; Any Day Now; In the Ghetto*

36. LSP-6020 November 1969
*From Memphis to Vegas/From Vegas to
Memphis*
Side 1: *Blue Suede Shoes; Johnny B. Goode; All*

Shook Up; Are You Lonesome Tonight?;
Hound Dog; I Can't Stop Loving You; My
Babe
Side 2: *Mystery Train/Tiger Man; Words; In the
Ghetto; Suspicious Minds; Can't Help
Falling in Love*
Side 3: *Inherit the Wind; This Is the Story;
Stranger in My Own Home Town; A Little
Bit of Green; And the Grass Won't Pay No
Mind*
Side 4: *Do You Know Who I Am; From a Jack to a
King; The Fair's Moving On; You'll Think
of Me; Without Love (There Is Nothing)*

37. LSP-4428   February 1970
  Elvis in Person
This LP featured the same tracks as the live
segments from LSP 6020 (sides 1 and 2).

38. LSP-4362   June 1970
  On Stage, February, 1970
Side 1: *See See Rider; Release Me; Sweet Caroline;
Runaway; The Wonder of You*
Side 2: *Polk Salad Annie; Yesterday; Proud Mary;
Walk a Mile in My Shoes; Let It Be Me*

39. LPM-6401   August 1970
  *Elvis: Worldwide 50 Gold Award Hits, Volume
1*
Side 1: *Heartbreak Hotel; I Was the One; I Want
You, I Need You, I Love You; Don't Be
Cruel; Hound Dog; Love Me Tender*
Side 2: *Any Way You Want Me; Too Much; Playing
for Keeps; (I'm) All Shook Up; That's When
Your Heartaches Begin; Loving You*
Side 3: *Teddy Bear; Jailhouse Rock; Treat Me Nice;*

I Beg of You; Don't; Wear My Ring Around Your Neck; Hard-headed Woman

Side 4: *I Got Stung; A Fool Such as I; A Big Hunk o' Love; Stuck on You; A Mess of Blues; It's Now or Never*

Side 5: *I Gotta Know; Are You Lonesome Tonight?; Surrender; I Feel So Bad; Little Sister; Can't Help Falling in Love*

Side 6: *Rock-a-hula Baby; Anything That's Part of You; Good Luck Charm; She's Not You; Return to Sender; Where Do You Come From; One Broken Heart for Sale*

Side 7: *(You're the) Devil in Disguise; Bossa Nova Baby; Kissin' Cousins; Viva Las Vegas; Ain't That Loving You, Baby; Wooden Heart*

Side 8: *Crying in the Chapel; If I Can Dream; In the Ghetto; Suspicious Minds; Don't Cry, Daddy; Kentucky Rain;* Excerpts from *Elvis Sails*

40. LSP-4429   November 1970
Back in Memphis
This LP featured the studio tracks from LSP 6020 (sides 3 and 4).

41. LSP-4445   December 1970
That's the Way It Is
Side 1: *I Just Can't Help Believin'; Twenty Days and Twenty Nights; How the Web Was Woven; Patch It Up; Mary in the Morning; You Don't Have to Say You Love Me*

Side 2: *You've Lost That Lovin' Feelin'; I've Lost You; Just Pretend; Stranger in the Crowd; The Next Step Is Love; Bridge over Troubled Water*

42. LSP-4460   January 1971
    Elvis Country
Side 1: *Snowbird; Tomorrow Never Comes; Little*
        Cabin on the Hill; Whole Lotta Shakin'
        Goin' On; Funny How Time Slips Away; I
        Really Don't Want to Know
Side 2: *There Goes My Everything; It's Your Baby,*
        You Rock It; The Fool; Faded Love; I
        Washed My Hands in Muddy Water; Make
        the World Go Away

43. LSP-4530   June 1971
    Love Letters from Elvis
Side 1: *Love Letters; When I'm over You; If I Were*
        You; Got My Mojo Working; Heart of Rome
Side 2: *Only Believe; This Is Our Dance; Cindy,*
        Cindy; I'll Never Know; It Ain't No Big
        Thing; Life

44. LPM-6402   August 1971
    Elvis: The Other Sides; Worldwide Gold Award
    Hits, Volume II
Side 1: *Puppet on a String; Witchcraft;*
        T-R-O-U-B-L-E; Poor Boy; I Want to Be
        Free; Doncha' Think It's Time; Young
        Dreams
Side 2: *The Next Step Is Love; You Don't Have to*
        Say You Love Me; Paralyzed; My Wish
        Came True; When My Blue Moon Turns to
        Gold Again; Lonesome Cowboy
Side 3: *My Baby Left Me; It Hurts Me; I Need*
        Your Love Tonight; Tell Me Why; Please
        Don't Drag That String Around; Young
        and Beautiful
Side 4: *Hot Dog; New Orleans; We're Gonna*

> Move; Crawfish; King Creole; I Believe in
> the Man in the Sky; Dixieland Rock

Side 5: *The Wonder of You; They Remind Me Too
Much of You; Mean Woman Blues; Lonely
Man; Any Day Now; Don't Ask Me Why*

Side 6: *His Latest Flame; I Really Don't Want to
Know; Baby, I Don't Care; I've Lost You;
Let Me; Love Me*

Side 7: *Got a Lot o' Livin' to Do; Fame and
Fortune; Rip It Up; There Goes My
Everything; Lover Doll; One Night*

Side 8: *Just Tell Her Jim Said Hello; Ask Me; Patch
It Up; As Long As I Have You; You'll Think
of Me; Wild in the Country*

45. LSP-4579 (DELETED)   October 1971
The Wonderful World of Christmas

Side 1: *O Come, All Ye Faithful; The First Noel;
On a Snowy Christmas Night; Winter
Wonderland; The Wonderful World of
Christmas; It Won't Seem Like Christmas
(Without You)*

Side 2: *I'll Be Home on Christmas Day; If I Get
Home on Christmas Day; Holly Leaves and
Christmas Trees; Merry Christmas, Baby;
Silver Bells*

46. LSP-4671   January 1972
Elvis Now

Side 1: *Help Me Make It Through the Night;
Miracle of the Rosary; Hey, Jude; Put Your
Hand in the Hand; Until It's Time for You
to Go*

Side 2: *We Can Make the Morning; Early Mornin'
Rain; Sylvia; Fools Rush In; I Was Born
About 10,000 Years Ago*

47. LSP-4690 April 1972
He Touched Me
Side 1: *He Touched Me; I've Got Confidence;*
Amazing Grace; Seeing Is Believing; He Is
My Everything; Bosom of Abraham
Side 2: *An Evening Prayer; Lead Me, Guide Me;*
There Is No God But God; A Thing Called
Love; I John; Reach Out to Jesus

48. LSP-4776 June 1972
Elvis As Recorded at Madison Square Garden
Side 1: *Also Sprach Zarathustra; That's All Right;*
Proud Mary; Never Been to Spain; You
Don't Have to Say You Love Me; You've
Lost That Lovin' Feelin'; Polk Salad Annie;
Love Me; All Shook Up; Heartbreak Hotel;
Medley: *Teddy Bear/Don't Be Cruel/Love*
Me Tender
Side 2: *The Impossible Dream;* Introductions by
Elvis; *Hound Dog; Suspicious Minds; For*
the Good Times; American Trilogy; Funny
How Time Slips Away; I Can't Stop Loving
You; Can't Help Falling in Love

49. VPX-6089 February 1973
Elvis: Aloha from Hawaii
Side 1: *Also Sprach Zarathustra; See See Rider;*
Burning Love; Something; Lord, This Time
You Gave Me a Mountain; Steamroller
Blues
Side 2: *My Way; Love Me; Johnny B. Goode; It's*
Over; Blue Suede Shoes; I'm So Lonesome I
Could Cry; I Can't Stop Loving You;
Hound Dog
Side 3: *What Now, My Love; Fever; Welcome to My*

World; Suspicious Minds; Introductions by
Elvis

Side 4: *I'll Remember You;* Medley: *Long Tall
Sally/Whole Lotta Shakin' Goin' On;
American Trilogy; A Big Hunk o' Love;
Can't Help Falling in Love*

50. APL-0283 (DELETED)   June 1973
Elvis

Side 1: *Fool; Where Do I Go from Here; Love Me,
Love the Life I Lead; It's Still Here; It's
Impossible*

Side 2: *For Lovin' Me; Padre; I'll Take You Home
Again, Kathleen; I Will Be True; Don't
Think Twice, It's All Right*

51. APL-0388 (DELETED)   October 1973
Raised on Rock

Side 1: *Raised on Rock; Are You Sincere; Find Out
What's Happening; I Miss You; Girl of
Mine*

Side 2: *For Ol' Times Sake; If You Don't Come
Back; Just a Little Bit; Sweet Angeline;
Three Corn Patches*

52. CPL-0341   January 1974
A Legendary Performer, Volume I

Side 1: *That's All Right; I Love You Because;
Heartbreak Hotel; Don't Be Cruel; Love Me;
Tryin' to Get to You*

Side 2: *Love Me Tender; Peace in the Valley; A
Fool Such as I; Tonight's All Right for
Love; Are You Lonesome Tonight?; Can't
Help Falling in Love*

53. CPL-0475 (DELETED)   March 1974
Good Times

Side 1: *Take Good Care of Her; Loving Arms; I*

Got a Feelin' in My Body; If That Isn't
Love; She Wears My Ring
Side 2: I've Got a Thing About You, Baby; My Boy;
Spanish Eyes; Talk About the Good Times;
Good-time Charlie's Got the Blues

54. CPL-0606 (DELETED)   June 1974
Elvis: Recorded Live on Stage in Memphis
Side 1: *See See Rider; I Got a Woman; Love Me;
Tryin' to Get to You;* Medley: *Long Tall
Sally/Whole Lotta Shakin' Goin'. On/Your
Mama Won't Dance/Flip, Flop and Fly/
Jailhouse Rock/Hound Dog; Why Me, Lord;
How Great Thou Art*
Side 2: Medley: *Blueberry Hill/I Can't Stop
Loving You; Help Me; An American Trilogy;
Let Me Be There; My Baby Left Me; Lawdy,
Miss Clawdy; Can't Help Falling in Love;*
Closing vamp

55. CPM-0818   October 1974
Having Fun with Elvis on Stage

56. APL-0873   January 1975
Promised Land
Side 1: *Promised Land; There's a Honky Tonk
Angel; Help Me; Mr. Songman; Love Song
of the Year*
Side 2: *It's Midnight; Your Love's Been a Long
Time Coming; If You Talk in Your Sleep;
Thinking About You; You Asked Me To*

57. ANL-0971   March 1975
Pure Gold
Side 1: *Kentucky Rain; Fever; It's Impossible;
Jailhouse Rock; Don't Be Cruel*
Side 2: *I Got a Woman; All Shook Up; Loving You;
In the Ghetto; Love Me Tender*

58. APL-1039 June 1975
Today
Side 1: *T-R-O-U-B-L-E; And I Love You So; Susan
When She Tried; Woman Without Love;
Shake a Hand*
Side 2: *Pieces of My Life; Fairytale; I Can Help;
Bringing It Back; Green, Green Grass of
Home*

59. CPL-1349 January 1976
A Legendary Performer, Volume II
Side 1: *Harbor Lights;* Interview with Elvis; *I
Want You, I Need You, I Love You; Blue
Suede Shoes; Blue Christmas; Jailhouse
Rock; It's Now or Never*
Side 2: *A Cane and a High Starched Collar;*
Presentation of Awards to Elvis; *Blue
Hawaii; Such a Night; Baby, What You
Want Me to Do; How Great Thou Art; If I
Can Dream*

60. ANL-1319 March 1976
His Hand in Mine
This LP is an RCA reissue on the Pure Gold series.
It has the same selections as LSP/LPM 2328.

61. APM-1675 March 1976
The Sun Sessions
Side 1: *That's All Right; Blue Moon of Kentucky; I
Don't Care if the Sun Don't Shine; Good
Rockin' Tonight; Milkcow Blues Boogie;
You're a Heartbreaker; I'm Left, You're
Right, She's Gone; Baby, Let's Play House*
Side 2: *Mystery Train; I Forgot to Remember to
Forget; I'll Never Let You Go; I Love You
Because; Tryin' to Get to You; Blue Moon;
Just Because; I Love You Because*

62. APL-1506   May 1976
   From Elvis Presley Boulevard, Memphis,
   Tennessee
Side 1: *Hurt; Never Again; Blue Eyes Crying in*
         the Rain; Danny Boy; The Last Farewell
Side 2: *For the Heart; Bitter They Are, Harder*
         They Fall; Solitaire; Love Coming Down;
         I'll Never Fall in Love Again

63. ANL-1936   November 1976
   The Wonderful World of Christmas
This LP is an RCA reissue on the Pure Gold Series.
It has the same selections as LSP-4579.

64. APL-2274   March 1977
   Welcome to My World
Side 1: *Welcome to My World* (live); *Help Me Make*
         It Through the Night; Release Me (and Let
         Me Love Again) (live); *I Really don't Want*
         to Know; For the Good Times (live)
Side 2: *Make the World Go Away* (live); *Gentle on*
         My Mind; I'm So Lonesome I Could Cry
         (live); *Your Cheatin' Heart; I Can't Stop*
         Loving You (live—unreleased)

65. AFL-2428   June 1977
   Moody Blue
Side 1: *Unchained Melody; If You Love Me (Let*
         Me Know); Little Darlin'; He'll Have to Go;
         Let Me Be There
Side 2: *Way Down; Pledging My Love; Moody*
         Blue; She Thinks I Still Care; It's Easy for
         You

Index